The One Year Book of Quiet Times with God

(taken from *Wings: A Daily Devotional*)

The ONE YEAR® BOOK OF QUIET TIMES *with* GOD

Tyndale House

Publishers, Inc.

Wheaton, Illinois

Visit Tyndale's exciting Web site at www.tyndale.com

Published in association with the literary agency of Alive Communications, Inc., 1465 Kelly Johnson Blvd., Suite 320, Colorado Springs, CO 80920.

Printed in the United States of America

02 01 00 99 98 97
6 5 4 3 2 1

To him whom my soul loveth;
who wakens me morning by morning
and helps me rise up with "wings as the eagle"

WINGS

Give my words wings, Lord.
May they alight gently on the branches of men's minds,
bending them to the winds of Your will.
May they fly high enough to touch the lofty,
low enough to breathe the breath
of sweet encouragement upon the downcast soul.

Give my words wings, Lord.
May they fly swift and far,
winning the race with the words of the worldly wise,
to the hearts of men.

Give my words wings, Lord.
See them now
nesting—
down at Thy feet.
Silenced into ecstasy,
home at last.

JILL BRISCOE

Winged Words

The Sovereign Lord has given me his words of wisdom, so that I know what to say to all these weary ones. Morning by morning he wakens me and opens my understanding to his will.

ISAIAH 50:4

Isaiah spoke of the Christ who would come to earth with the "know-how" to wing his words into the hearts of the weary. As his Father had taught him, so would he speak.

When Christ was about to leave this world, he promised to send the same Spirit of truth that indwelt him to indwell us. This way we, too, could have the "know-how" to speak a word to the weary at the right time and in the right way. Our part would be to waken morning by morning "to hear" what he has to say and to "be open" to understanding his will! Then we would be ready for anything and anybody.

You and I are promised the "know-how" to answer a hostile teenager, even if we haven't had time to read a book on child rearing or pick up the phone to ask a friend's advice! We will discover that we can cope with an unbeliever's questions, however young we may be as Christians. We will find that the Christ within us will make our tongue know what to say to the weary ones around us, seasoned words that will help to ease their sufferings. In Christ we are promised both the "know-how" and the "know-when" that we cannot possibly know without him!

Swift to Hear—Sure to Bless

> **You ride upon the wings of the wind.**
>
> PSALM 104:3

Wings occur frequently in the imagery of King David. If he wasn't speaking of the warm wings of God's comforting and immediate presence, he was writing of other sorts of wings. In Psalms 10 and 18, he sings of deliverance, praising God not only for protection in the midst of his internal troubles, but also for the intervention of God in his external problems. He has been delivered from the hand of King Saul. He speaks of the Lord God who flew "mounted on a mighty angel" (Psalm 18:10).

Again, in Psalm 104:3, he reminds himself of the God of creation who can "ride upon the wings of the wind." I love the image of the Lord God who made all things using the tempests as stepping stones. He strides across our world watching out for us or riding the storm to fly to our aid. Such poetry teaches me God's grand ability to be there wherever and whenever I need help. I do not really believe he rides an angel like a horse or that the winds truly have wings, but I *do* believe that he is swiftly able to control, not only my troubled heart, but also my troubled world whenever and however he wills. There are no winds that will blow upon me that are not the winds of his will.

Next time you hear the wind rustling the leaves or whirling around the eaves, listen awhile. God has come to remind you that he is present—slow to anger, swift to hear, and sure to bless!

Weird Birds

As a hen protects her chicks . . .

Matthew 23:37

David prayed, "Guard me as the apple of your eye. Hide me in the shadow of your wings. Protect me from wicked people who attack me, from murderous enemies who surround me" (Psalm 17:8-9).

David looked for a secret place of security and found a ready refuge in God. David cried, "I will hide beneath the shadow of your wings until this violent storm is past" (Psalm 57:1). The "violent storm" was the result of David's disastrous relationship with King Saul, who had forced David to run for his life and hide in the caves of the rock.

Do you know where to go in the midst of your storms? Is there a familiar saving shadow known to your spirit? When Jesus walked our earth, he described people as "baby chicks" running around in circles, scattering in every direction. He longed to gather men and women under his wonderful wings of love—but they wouldn't let him. It's a silly chicken who would rather be in the middle of the storm than be sheltered by the Christ. It is my sad conclusion that our world is populated with such weird birds! Are you "under his wings" or "out in the storm"? The choice is yours.

When I received news of my father's death, my first reaction was to call a friend, summon my children to comfort me—to enlist support. But I remembered his wings and ran to him. Then peace came!

We need to pray, "Lord Jesus, shelter me in your shadow, welcome me under your wings—till these storms have passed."

Weary Women

But those who wait on the Lord will find new strength. They will fly high on wings like eagles. They will run and not grow weary. They will walk and not faint.

ISAIAH 40:31

Weary women everywhere! I see them, I listen to them, I look into their tired eyes and wonder how they became so "wearied out" in the first place. Life has surely ground some of them right into the ground! To others life has apparently been good, but still a weariness invades their personalities. In the midst of luxury, even laziness becomes a wearisome thing clouding their waking moments. Their "get up and go" has "got up and gone." Their inner lethargy has nothing to do with a lack of sleep or increasing years.

In the Bible the unweary God speaks to the point, telling us that "even youths will become exhausted." Everyone seems to be looking for someone to blame for their lagging spirits. Yet there is nothing so wearying as a complaining spirit!

The Creator who is never weary invites the wearied ones to spend time in his presence; to bathe in the atmosphere of eternal strength; to drink in the air of his power-giving presence—to "wait" long enough to renew their lives. God would mend our raw nerve endings with the stitches of his peace. God's promise to those who look to him for such renewal is that they shall *not* be disappointed (see Isaiah 49:23). Are you weary with weariness? Wouldn't you like to rise above it? Have confidence in the Lord who can help you to soar on wings like the eagle!

The Discipline of Dropping Things

Those who wait on the Lord . . .

ISAIAH 40:31

When I begin to "wait" on the Lord, the difference will be felt deep down within me. He will do "a new thing" inside, while the old things outside remain the same. There *will* be a difference! But I shall need to learn the discipline of dropping things from my busy schedule. I will not get all accomplished in a day. Some *important* tasks will not get done, because the *all-important* must.

But I *will* meet with you, my God! You and I shall talk together. Then you will tell me not to dwell upon the past—to forget the former things. You will make a way in the desert and pour streams into the wasteland. You will give my thirsty soul a drink! As I learn to listen to the heartbeat of your soul, you will help me to rejoice. We will talk about our children, and I shall draw courage from your promises to Israel. I will hear you say, "I will pour out my Spirit and my blessings on your children" (Isaiah 44:3b).

Yes, there will be a difference when I wait—not a change of circumstance without, but certainly a change of attitude within. Dropping the lesser to pick up the greater must become a daily habit, a question of necessity, not choice. A life like the one awaiting us in heaven. If I will but wait upon the Lord, then other things will have to wait. My schedule will not be my master, but my slave. Time is for choosing to take time—to make time—for eternal things.

Catalogs

Not even a sparrow, worth only half a penny, can fall to the ground without your Father knowing it.

MATTHEW 10:29

I love ordering things from clothes catalogs. The order forms, with the specific facts required, are like hard crossword puzzles—but with all the answers provided. I feel really great, clever, and all that because I can fill them in!

The order is mailed and forgotten in the rush of more immediate things. Then *bang,* right in the middle of some activity totally unrelated to my catalog order, the parcel is delivered!

How like God. The specifics of my order are carefully tabulated and delivered in his time and with eternal efficiency. The answers are sent to prayers I prayed months, even years, ago—long after I have forgotten my requests. Sometimes it no longer really matters to me if the parcel even arrives! But my words are not allowed to fall to the ground. Angels catch them and register the demand. How good of God (see Revelation 8:3-4).

Sometimes, when the earthly clothes arrive, they don't quite fit. But there is a difference with our heavenly requests. Those goods that finally arrive are perfect! I think of the time I prayed for my children to find Christian friends at school when they were very small. They went right through grade school and junior high without that support. One day when we were hosting a barbecue for dozens of their lovely Christian high school friends—I remembered—and I thanked him!

Making the Team

I want your will, not mine.

MATTHEW 26:39

Our son Peter was trying out for the basketball team and asked me to pray that he would acquire one of the coveted positions.

I was going away but informed our younger son that I would pray about the selection of players. "I'll ask that the right thing will happen for you," I told him.

Pete shot me a somewhat apprehensive glance. "Don't do that, Mom," he pleaded. "Just pray that I make the team!"

Teenage sentiments? Amusing? Perhaps, but how like my praying! So often I don't want the *right* thing to happen; I just want to make the team. I can remember praying "Pete prayers" when I was very young. "O God," I would say, "I want a pretty day on Saturday," or "Please help me to pass the examination without having to do any studying!" Children make such elementary requests.

But when we become adults, we are supposed to put away childish things (see 1 Corinthians 13:11). God intends us to learn how to praise him for Saturday's rain and to ask him for help as we do our homework.

Peter grew up to play basketball for his college. The last time I talked to him about making the team, he was trying hard to qualify for a place. "Pray for me, Mom," he said.

"What for, Pete?" I asked.

"Pray I will make the team only if I'm the best man for the job," he said quietly. Pete has come a long way.

Have I? Have you? Prayer after all is the means by which we sense God's desires, and they become our own. We might even begin to care more about the team than we care about the team's caring for us!

Satisfaction

> **When he sees all that is accomplished by his anguish, he will be satisfied.**
>
> ISAIAH 53:11

The Scriptures tell us that Jesus found satisfaction *after* his sufferings. For some of us it will be the same. Death, which has been described as the last step of faith, will see us through the door to daylight's delight. Satisfaction, as the world understands it, may never come to some of us in this life. But one day *after* it is over, we will be met with the Savior's "Well done," and we will be satisfied.

What is satisfaction? Hollywood insists that it includes "beauty" and must be pursued by all means and to all ends. We are asked to believe that to be truly satisfied with ourselves we must be truly beautiful. Yet in Isaiah 53, we read about Jesus: "There was nothing beautiful or majestic about his appearance, nothing to attract us to him" (53:2). Apparently, in God's value system, appearance is not all that important! It's what people *do* because of who they *are* that matters in the highest place, not how they dress it up or paint it on. Jesus, contrary to popular opinion in his day, was a divine success and gained satisfaction from knowing that "the Lord's plan will prosper in his hands" (53:10).

The one who concentrates on pleasing him *before* death discovers that after the crushing and the cross there will be the crown! *So be it.*

JANUARY 8

Cause and Effect

> **And this righteousness will bring peace. Quietness and confidence will fill the land forever.**
>
> ISAIAH 32:17

"How can I ever gain peace of mind and some confidence?" inquired a timid youngster. A mother, signing into the psychiatric ward, despaired deeply over the same problem. Surprisingly, the same question was asked by a bright, glamorous starlet who had "arrived" overnight.

Isaiah gave the answer for all three: It's a matter of cause and effect. The cause is righteousness; the effect, quietness and confidence forever.

What then is righteousness? It's a right relationship with God based on his forgiveness and cleansing in Christ, and righteousness spills over into right relationships with others. If we want quietness and confidence *forever,* then we must stop expecting programs, pills, or people to produce them. These qualities are the effect of righteousness!

Do you need self-confidence? A quiet assurance that will keep you calm when the office erupts around you, or your husband calls to tell you your in-laws are coming for an unexpected visit? If we have made our peace with God, then the effect of our relationship with him will be a quiet manner where panic fears to tread and confidence is nurtured. But how does this relationship start? The Lord can't make it right for us unless we first admit we've been wrong with him. He can't forgive us unless we say we're sorry—not just sorry for ourselves, but sorry for our sin. That is our introduction to eternal security.

Mouth Traps

> **My God sent his angel to shut the lions' mouths so that they would not hurt me.**
>
> DANIEL 6:22

We were enjoying a prayer meeting. That's right, I said "enjoying," not "enduring"! Fifteen women had gathered to talk to God. To encourage our hearts, we were reading together from the Word, and we marveled at Daniel, noting that something wonderful happened every time he prayed.

"How brave and courageous he was," said one.

"How close he kept to the Father," exclaimed another.

"How special his gifts—and how faithful a servant!" added a third. There was silence. . . .

"What I like best about this story," said one of my friends, "is the bit about the lions. If God shut the lions' mouths, I know he can surely shut mine!"

We prayed about that—all of us.

Daniel himself had had to learn to keep his mouth shut. He had also learned when to open it. When he was a young man and a slave, he had asked his captors that he and his friends be allowed to eat vegetables, rather than the food and drink that had been ordered for them by the king (see Daniel 1:8-16). Because he had already earned the favor of the chief official, he was granted his request. As the years passed, Daniel relied on his God and learned when to open and when to close his mouth, so his wisdom was esteemed by Nebuchadnezzar, Belshazzar, and Cyrus. Even Belshazzar's mother recommended he listen to Daniel's words of wisdom: "There is a man in your kingdom who has within him the spirit of the holy gods. During Nebuchadnezzar's reign, this man was found to have insight, understanding, and wisdom as though he himself were a god" (Daniel 5:11).

When you can control your tongue, God gets the glory and people are amazed.

A New Song

Sing a new song to the Lord.

PSALM 98:1

Who needs a new song? Do you ever get tired of the old tune? I do! Listening to the radio, I tend to search for a variation on the old theme, a melody that brings notes of newness into my head and my heart.

A new song! Spiritually, many of us need a new song to sing. Some of us are sung out, tired of singing solo or of being lost in a big choir where no one notices our contribution! God can give us a new song to sing. It will start when we meet with God and tune in to the vibrations of heaven. Songs you've never sung before have a fresh, sweet, winsome sound that alerts those around you to the state of your soul. God gave me a new song when my children got married, when my husband had to be away a lot, and when I got sick and had to have a scary operation. They were new songs because I'd never been in those situations, and new situations require new songs. They were not always happy songs, but who says all songs are happy ones? A minor key can be just as pretty as a major one.

The important thing is to sing a song—a new song of faith and hope, of self-discovery or God-discovery, at every turn of the road, every station, every resting place. Just today I asked him to help me find something to sing about as I washed up a pile of dirty dishes. He helped me compose a new song over the kitchen sink. God is never stuck for a tune. New songs are the Spirit's business—ask him to give you one.

THE SONGWRITER

> **Yet they don't ask, "Where is God my Creator, the one who gives songs in the night?"**
>
> JOB 35:10

These were the words of Elihu who was reminding his troubled friend Job of an aspect of the character of God. God is a songwriter, he said.

The psalmist exhorts people to "sing for joy as they lie on their beds" (Psalm 149:5)—and for good reason. After all, "through each day the Lord pours his unfailing love upon me, and through each night I sing his songs, praying to God who gives me life" (Psalm 42:8).

But I have observed that it is comparatively easy to whistle a tune under a cloudless sky. In fact, I seldom suffer from insomnia when all is well. It is trouble that chases sleep away.

When I can't sleep, when I am afraid and find no comfort, when my thoughts run around in my head and refuse to let me rest, then I need to ask God to fill my nights with joyful songs (Psalm 77:6). I need to remember other nights and how the day dawned and the shadows flew away as he gave me a song to sing.

Not long ago I lay awake worrying about a relationship that was damaging our family. My mind raced round and round the situation, trying to find an answer to the dilemma.

Then I deliberately began to remember other nights. There was the dark hour of my mother's death, but oh, the song of triumph as the day dawned at last and she flew away. There was the lonely period of separation when my husband traveled continually, the frightening night of suspense at the bedside of a child.

Nights there have been, but never a night unmatched by a song! God writes the songs—it is up to us to thank him, to learn them, and then to sing them!

SURELY

Surely your goodness and unfailing love will pursue me all the days of my life.

PSALM 23:6

"Surely," not "maybe"! That's what the text says. But how can that be?

The same man who wrote those words, David, was a man who experienced God's goodness and mercy all his days and nights. Whether the sun was shining, or it was midnight in his soul, David was able to say, "Surely your goodness and unfailing love will pursue me."

It's so much easier for us to say "most of the days" or "some of the days." Yet the text promises his presence *all* of our days. This is not a promise that all our days will be good or merciful, but rather an assurance that the God of mercy will follow us through the good and the bad days, the rich and the poor days, the sick and the well days—*all* the days of our life.

When we believe this promise, we bring his "presence" into our problems. It is his presence in all of our nights that wrings from our lips the certain cry, "Surely!" and his sweet friendship lights up good days and makes them even better. So, we do not have a "maybe" or a "perhaps" or a "hopefully"—but a "surely" that is rooted in the proven promises of God!

On an airplane I was sitting next to a lady who lived in Florida. She kept looking out the window and moaning about the weather. I was able to tell her that you can't have a world without clouds, but you can have a heart full of sunshine!

Follow me, Father, into my night.
Give to my blindness excellent sight.
Spirit of cheer, stay with me here.
Be to my soul a delight.

New Clothes

To all who mourn in Israel, he will give beauty for ashes, joy instead of mourning, praise instead of despair. For the Lord has planted them like strong and graceful oaks for his own glory.

ISAIAH 61:3

A certain situation arose in my life that caused me to go to bed in "despair" and to awaken feeling as if I had not slept at all. I can only describe the experience as a "spirit of heaviness." I walked bowed down under the weight of my problem.

Then I came upon Isaiah 61:3. What a promise! He would give me "joy instead of mourning" and "praise instead of despair"! But how? A change of attitude was surely necessary, but the heaviness I felt had seemingly robbed me of the strength to even try!

Examining the burden I was carrying, I recognized that *I* had picked it up and put it on myself. The burden was weighing me down, binding up my movements, making me unable to function, keeping me from reaching out and touching people.

The problem had to do with a fellow Christian—someone I had loved but now had almost come to hate! Victory gained on my knees would dissipate immediately upon sight of this person! The enemy would come in like a flood and almost drop the burden back on me, weighing me down once again. Praise to God for coming along and trading the burden for a load of joy.

If we will allow God to place on us a load of joy and praise, we will begin to sing again; and others, who are also carrying burdens, will listen to our song!

THE SECOND TIME

Then the Lord spoke to Jonah a second time: "Get up and go to the great city of Nineveh, and deliver the message of judgment I have given you."

JONAH 3:1-2

I can't help feeling encouraged when I read that the Lord came to Jonah *a second time.*

Like Jonah, I have often run away from my God-given responsibilities, trying to hide from God and his demands on my life. But the Lord has given me many a second chance, forgiving my ineptitude, picking me up, dusting me off, and setting me out in the right direction again.

I have observed, however, that when the second message comes it is usually the same as the first! God had nothing new to say to Jonah until the rebellious prophet heeded what had been said already. We should not expect some new word from the Lord if we have journeyed to Tarshish in disobedience and are sleeping our way through the resultant storm!

Have you ever told a child to do something and then discovered he or she had disobeyed? How hard it is to give the child a second chance and to patiently repeat the instructions, as God did with Jonah. Have you ever trusted your husband to remember something that is really important to you, only to have it slip his mind? Have you ever expected a word of appreciation, only to be ignored? Are we good at giving others a second chance? Do we come to show our love "a second time," trust them twice, and risk yet another disappointment? God risked all of that with Jonah. Should we, his followers, do less?

Doing Things That Have Been Done Before

I have decided to write . . .

LUKE 1:3

The fact that others had written the story of Jesus and the Good News did not hinder Luke from taking up the pen. He acknowledged the fact that "many people have written accounts about the events that took place among us" (1:1), but Luke also decided to write.

Sometimes we become stagnant because others seem to be doing all the work. Why offer to teach Sunday school if there are plenty of teachers? Why join the choir when it has a full contingent of sopranos? Why write a book when others have written before us? Why visit the sick when there's a committee appointed to do all of that?

The answer to the *why* is found here. Luke knew others had written, but he decided to also do so. What others do is their business; what I do is mine. We need to find the good will of God for our life and to do it cheerfully. Jesus said to God, "I brought glory to you here on earth by doing everything you told me to do" (John 17:4), and then he went home to heaven. We must do the same; whether others have taught, sung, written, or visited the sick before us is really quite irrelevant. We must seek God's face, discover our gifts, and do his will with all our might. When it seems good to me, and I sense his direction, I go ahead and leave the rest to him.

On Being "Too Spiritual" with Your Husband

If I could speak in any language in heaven or on earth but didn't love others, I would only be making meaningless noise like a loud gong or a clanging cymbal.

1 CORINTHIANS 13:1

My waking thought was of my husband Stuart's fine sermon on Noah and his ark. Earnestly looking into what I could see of Stuart's 6:00 A.M. eyes, I said intensely: "Darling, I want to be like Mrs. Noah today! You are my Noah, and I think of you as providing and building an ark so you can invite people to come in out of the judgment of God! I want to be your helpmeet in this wonderful work."

There was silence, then he said, "Good! Why don't you get up and clean the ark?"

We can be far too spiritual, especially at six o'clock in the morning! I am an extremely intense sort of person, while my husband is practical and relaxed. I had to learn to show him my love in concrete ways, instead of just talking about it all in spiritual terms. I came to realize that after teaching and preaching all day long, Stuart did not need to come home to some more sermons! What he needed was to be the recipient of some "love in action" by way of a good meal ready on the stove, a warm tidy house, and a wife ready to enjoy her husband. And so I put away my Bible dictionaries well before supper time and began to practice love "God-style" as explained to me by the apostle Paul.

The animals need feeding, Mrs. Noah—let's be up and at 'em!

Success

Oh, the joys of those who do not follow the advice of the wicked, or stand around with sinners, or join in with scoffers. But they delight in doing everything the Lord wants; day and night they think about his law. They are like trees planted along the riverbank, bearing fruit each season without fail. Their leaves never wither, and in all they do, they prosper.

PSALM 1:1-3

All things being equal, those who follow the Lord shall succeed. Perhaps you reply: "But I fail so often—I fail to avert a fight between my children, I fail to show my husband how much I love him, I fail to do for God the things he wants done." The promise from our unfailing God, however, is that our efforts *will* prosper.

God assures us that we can be like trees standing by a riverbank bearing luscious fruit. Even in our deepest despondency, his Word restores us to green, springy vegetation, offering shade to those we shelter, joy to those who watch us flower! All we do can be "green" with verdant visibility; we can have a fresh face, a happy heart, a willing will. We can even know that our actions will evoke divine delight as God sees us in a prayerful posture!

The secret lies in "thinking about" God's law—his Word. To *think about* means to chew it, digest it, enjoy it! His nourishing Scriptures are ours for the digesting, and they will prosper our days.

Our dear Lord, our Friend, who day and night provides the river to refresh our failing moments, will water us always and without fail, if we fulfill the conditions. And what are they? To keep the right company, to ask the right questions of the right people, and to avoid becoming as cynical as the world around us!

The Sound of Silence

Dear friends, be quick to listen, slow to speak.

JAMES 1:19

Listening works wonders! Loving silence has no sound, but tells the one sitting next to you that you care. It can say to the hurting heart, "I want to free you to think about yourself, your failures, and your goals. Because I love you and am interested in you I am willing to sit in silence with you."

Can you sit with a friend without talking? Ecclesiastes 3:7 tells us there is "a time to be quiet and a time to speak up"! Can you sit with your husband in silence? Or do you, as I tend to, complete all his sentences for him? That particular habit irritates him to distraction, but I find myself doing it anyway. It's such fun to guess the ending of his story and race him there! I have to confess, though, that both God and Stuart have been working on me lately to exert more self-control. I am learning to use a short reply because it invites more response! I have thanked God that he has graced me with a companion, and I have reminded myself that he is indeed a companion and not a competitor in a word game!

I have learned to listen and discover with joy the unusual and unique facets of the one I love. I pray hard to fight down my impulsive, emotional response and let him talk.

For this I need to rely on Jesus, of course. I love to gab. I have discovered that God is delighted to tame my tongue and tune my ear; and whenever he has been allowed to do so, he has filled my heart with the knowledge that listening with love brings love in return!

In Step

Let us follow the Holy Spirit's leading.

GALATIANS 5:25

Another Bible translation renders this verse, "Let us *keep in step* with the Spirit" (NIV). How do we do that?

When we first come to faith in Christ we feel we can conquer the world—with God's help, of course! We wonder if the Spirit will be able to keep up with us. After a little going, a little knowing, and a little growing, we begin to realize this "walk" of faith requires training, stamina, and expertise. We cannot help asking ourselves the question, "How long will I be able to stay caught up with the Spirit?" Farther down the hard course of life, tripped up by sin, or distracted, like Martha, by much serving, or just plain jaded with the constant fight of faith, we find ourselves fervently echoing Paul's exhortation to simply "follow" the Holy Spirit.

God delights to hear and answer that request. He wants us to *follow*. He doesn't wish to see us galloping ahead or dragging behind, but following, going where he goes, marching as one person toward the finish line.

The Holy Spirit is described in Scripture as the Helper. He will not walk *for* us—he will walk *with* us and *lead* us; and make no mistake about it—he won't stop going even if we do. There is grace to help in time of need: strength for the day, confidence for tomorrow, direction in the dark, company in the light—even power to plod—and it's all within our reach. It is his to supply, and it is ours to use.

Home Is the Will of God

On that day I will gather you together and bring you home again. I will give you a good name, a name of distinction among all the nations of the earth.

ZEPHANIAH 3:20

Stuart and I were halfway through a two-month tour of ministry in Africa. Every four days or so we set off for the next conference, traveling by small plane, car, truck, or even bush taxi, arriving at new compounds and having every meal with a new family. We slept in different beds, met different bugs, ate different food, and drank different water. All of this did not make for a particularly settled feeling!

The "listening" was hard. Being an outside ear meant that we were there to do a lot of loving listening. The new missionaries were struggling with culture shock, relational problems, the absence of mail for eight weeks at a time, or the unsafe feeling of living miles away from a hospital (one country didn't even have an ambulance!). They needed someone to talk to.

There were desperate needs on every hand—lepers, crippled children, ignorance, and apathy. Add to this the militant march of Islam and you get the picture. This was certainly not the sort of environment to make anyone feel at home.

But watching and listening to those missionaries, I learned that *home* isn't a little box in a safe subdivision. Being settled isn't a car in the garage, membership in a club, or even model children making model grades. Being fulfilled does not consist of a husband's climb up the corporate ladder or paid vacations to Hawaii!

Home is the will of God, and if you are settled into his will, you will be settled into whatever way-out situation you find yourself. The God of Peace will see to that!

Little Foxes

Catch all the little foxes before they ruin the vineyard of your love, for the grapevines are all in blossom.

SONG OF SONGS 2:15

Our lives are like vineyards. God is the caretaker, and it is he who plants us with "the choicest vine." Jesus said that he is God's true and chosen vine, planted deep within the heart of repentant men and women.

The devil is God's enemy. He sends his "little foxes" into the vineyard to spoil the fruit of the vine. In my experience, it has usually been the little foxes that have caused the most damage to my Christian testimony. Big adversaries like the big old bear are easy to see, but "little foxes" are harder to find! There are the little foxes of lying, slander, laziness, and selfishness. I've seen the little fox of fear or anger spoil an entire testimony.

But take courage: In the midst of the vineyard there is a tower where the Owner lives. He keeps a holy watch for the little foxes so that the fruit of his choice vines may be preserved.

Once God desired to grow the fruit of maturity in my vineyard. My husband was away a lot, and I had to attend to such housekeeping matters as catching the field mice that had found their way into our kitchen. The vermin were everywhere! As a child I had been afraid of such creatures, but now I was an adult and needed to behave like one! God reminded me that I had not been "blessed to be beaten" and helped me to deal with the problem. When the fruit of the vine is preserved, the Owner of the vineyard is glorified!

Knowing

I am the Alpha and the Omega—the beginning and the end.

REVELATION 1:8

You know—he knows something we don't know. How good of God to shield the future from us! How could we live well or sleep easily if we knew the death we'd die, the child who would go wrong, the house that would burn to the ground, or the poverty we might be brought to? Our language is full of words like *maybe, perhaps,* and *someday*. But he knows something we don't know; his language consists of "shall be" and "will be," because he knows ahead, while we but "know behind."

To know him who knows the "something we don't know" is comfort indeed. Knowing *the beginning and the end,* he waits ahead for us, surprising us with steady provisions of his love. I am so glad that when I married I did not know my husband would travel so much, my daughter would have a bad accident, and I would have a serious car crash. If I had known, I would have worried for months before my husband began his itinerant ministry, would have been an overprotective mother, and would never have bothered to get my driver's license! It is enough that God knows. He does not send me into my future alone but waits for me to meet him there.

I praise him for being there at the *beginning* and for the situations where he is waiting at the *end,* and I will try to remember—he knows something I don't know.

Trust Me

The Lord is my strength, my shield from every danger. I trust in him with all my heart. He helps me, and my heart is filled with joy. I burst out in songs of thanksgiving.

PSALM 28:7

I had a burden; I had a beautiful daughter who was really excited about taking on life with all it had to offer! The dating had begun, and I was frightened. She told me not to be afraid. "I'm not afraid, Mom," she said cheerfully. "That's why *I* am," I replied grimly. What do you do when your daughter refuses to allow you to go along on her dates? I discovered one thing I could do was to pray. Another thing I could do was to trust. I asked Jesus to tell the Father, "Someone I love needs shielding." He did, of course. The Father told Jesus to tell me he'd look after it for me; Jesus told me.

The next day I was driving along the highway in my car, and I asked Jesus to remind the Father about my burden. He told me: "The Father would like to remind you that he doesn't need reminding!" *I* was the one who needed that!

The following day, when I knelt in prayer, I told Jesus to tell the Father I loved him. The Father, through Jesus, thanked me and told me he would like to hear me say something else. He would like to hear me say, "And I trust you, too!" Trust comes with knowing God and leaning hard when hard things come. Trust comes with experiencing his presence, taking the risk, and meeting him in the dark.

WITHOUT DISTRACTION

> **I want you to do whatever will help you serve the Lord best, with as few distractions as possible.**
>
> 1 CORINTHIANS 7:35

Paul says that the state of being single is a privilege, not a punishment. He encourages us to look upon singleness as a gift. What do you do with a gift? You say thank you, unwrap it, and discover its charm or usefulness. Some of us have tended to be rudely resentful, or even have been known to refuse God's gift of singleness, pouting and complaining petulantly that we would much rather have been graced with the gift of marriage.

Paul says the advantage of being single is that we might serve the Lord "with as few distractions as possible." There is no doubt in my mind that husbands can be distractions! Dear distractions they may be, but certainly they can cause inner conflict. "How can I please my husband?" those of us who have a mate wonder, as we worry away our days in this delightful pursuit. On the other hand, the single person is free to ask, "How can I please my Lord?"

The advantage of the solitary life is obvious. Without the distraction of an earthly husband the needs of the heavenly husband can be met. Married women must juggle divided loyalties and seek to pay attention to two partners at once.

So what joy, what unbounded freedom, what purpose is ours if we are privileged to live a single life.

If you have been blessed with this gift, can you pray this prayer? "O Lord, forgive my resentment. Here are my open hands. I receive the gift of singleness you offer me. Help me discover the sweet surprises of the single life. Make me content."

You That Are Men

Elijah was as human as we are, and yet when he prayed earnestly that no rain would fall, none fell for the next three and a half years!

JAMES 5:17

I had arranged a large women's seminar. (Let me rephrase that: I had arranged a large seminar for women!) Many women would be traveling many miles to attend. Our church facilities would be overflowing with guests, and we needed a pretty day! So we asked the Lord of the skies to arrange suitable weather for us.

I told my son Peter about our prayer, but he didn't seem particularly impressed. "Well, Peter," I went on, "Elijah prayed and it didn't rain; we've got three thousand women praying, so that should do something!" There was a long, quiet pause, as the information sank in. "You mean," said Peter at last, "that it's going to take three thousand women to do what one mere man did?" I threw a cushion at him, as he quickly disappeared.

Then I thought about the fact that so many more women were involved in church work or had offered to serve God on the mission fields of the world than had men, and I prayed for the movement of God's Spirit in the hearts of men everywhere. I asked that they would not think that Christianity was a woman's religion but would realize that Jesus Christ was the manliest man of all! If one righteous man's prayers could keep the rain from falling, think what many righteous men can do!

JESUS CHRIST IN YOU IS ADEQUATE

Don't we have the right to bring a Christian wife along with us as the other disciples and the Lord's brothers and Peter do?

1 CORINTHIANS 9:5

Stuart and I had been invited to visit nine African nations so that we might minister to the missionaries as well as to national leaders. As I contemplated the tour, I wondered if the wives of the apostles and evangelists of the early church had ever felt as I was feeling. I was glad that God had given the apostles the right to bring along their wives and reflected that Stuart had been given the same happy privilege. I rejoiced that I was the wife he would "bring along."

Never having been very good at geography, and having already confused Liberia and Libya, I was thankful to not be leading, but going along! Even so, a great sense of inadequacy gripped me. Would I be able to have a useful part in the ministry? Could I be an encouragement to the missionaries? What would happen if I got sick? And what about the bugs? Seeing a tiny ant, I tried to envisage what it would look like six inches larger! Had the wives of the early disciples faced similar challenges as they ministered alongside their traveling husbands?

Somehow I knew they would not have been the sort of women that "just went along for the ride." I remembered my husband encouraging a timid friend: "Jesus Christ in you is adequate; get on with it!"

"All right, Lord," I whispered, "I will! Let's go!"

A Special Attitude

Well done, my good and faithful servant.

MATTHEW 25:21

Someone has said, "Missionaries are ordinary people in extraordinary circumstances expected to do numerous things with nothing much!"

I was reminded of this while in Africa visiting the head office of a mission station. A young girl sat typing diligently. Behind her a pink-and-green poster displayed the words:

We the unwilling
led by the unknowing
are doing the impossible
for the ungrateful.
We have done so much
for so long with so little,
we are now qualified
to do anything
with nothing!

I liked it! I used to think that the people whom missionaries went to serve would be so thankful that they would roll out the red carpet, fly the flags, and get the bands to play. I learned differently. The doctors bringing healing are given little thanks, the development team proposing change is met with suspicion, and the radio station that broadcasts, among other things, "Do not steal," is plundered constantly, despite the hired guards.

In such situations, to be able to give without counting the cost takes a special attitude. Notice I didn't say a special person! It takes a servant spirit—to go, to stay, and to be faithful to the loving God who has called you to his work.

When you pray for missionaries—and I hope you do—pray that the unwilling will be made willing, the unknowing will be given light, and the servants of the Lord will be satisfied with his "well done" at the end of their day!

"WHAT TO DO?"

> **Work hard and cheerfully at whatever you do, as though you were working for the Lord rather than for people. Remember that the Lord will give you an inheritance as your reward, and the Master you are serving is Christ.**
>
> COLOSSIANS 3:23-24

The people in Liberia have many problems. But when they come to an impasse, they simply smile a marvelous Liberian smile, shrug their shoulders, and say, "What to do?"

Coming from a culture that tends to believe that people can do anything they want to do if they try hard enough, we may think that this sounds like a weak excuse. However, simple acceptance of the situation may be the first step to the realism required to live amidst trying circumstances without falling apart.

Christians are instructed to "wait upon the Lord" until we are told "what to do," and herein lies our rest. In acceptance we find peace. Once instructed, however, we must "work hard and cheerfully." Enthusiastic "doing" delights the heart of God! Our daily "doing" must not be for our earthly honor or success either. We must not "do" for people so that people will "do" for us! Instead, we must "do" for people as though we are "doing" for God.

My mother-in-law was a great example of this text. Whenever she cleaned a pair of shoes, they shined as if Christ were going to wear them; whenever she cooked a meal, she cooked it as if Christ were joining us for dinner. And she was satisfied to receive her "reward" from him!

Dear Lord—when I know not "what to do,"
still me.
When you've shown me "what to do,"
fill me,
That I may "do" your will with all my might!

And Peace Came

My God, my God, why have you forsaken me?

MATTHEW 27:46

I was worried because my mother, who lived in England, was very ill. "Heavenly Father," I prayed, "she whom I love is sick. I know you know the time and manner that you will take her to be with yourself, but I'm three thousand miles away, so I'd like to know, too." I was feeling panicky, imagining her voice calling for me; I couldn't bear the thought of not making it over the Atlantic in time to be at her side when the end came.

"My child," the Father said to me, "I wasn't there when my Son died! He cried out to me, 'My God, my God, why have you forsaken me?' and I heard his voice but could not be at his side! I understand what that feels like!"

"I'm glad you understand, Father," I said, "but the problem is, will my mother understand?"

"My child," he replied, "it is because I could not be there when my Son died that I can promise to be there when your mother dies! So trust me with the details and let my peace garrison your heart and mind about the matter!"

I trusted him, and peace came.

Much later I made the long journey to see my mother. I wanted to be able to share some precious moments while she was still able to enjoy my company. During my visit, she died suddenly and unexpectedly. She did not go to be with the Lord before I had witnessed his very present help in her time of trouble. God took me across the ocean in time to watch him be all he had promised me. On the cross, Jesus was forsaken that we may never be! I saw him at my mother's side, and I praise him for his presence there!

ALWAYS!

Always be full of joy in the Lord. I say it again—rejoice!

PHILIPPIANS 4:4

Always, Lord? Always? The day my mother died I read in the Word of God that Jesus said to his disciples, "If you really love me, you will be very happy for me, because now I can go to the Father" (John 14:28).

"Can't you be happy for your mother?" the minister asked me.

"I could if I were not grappling with guilt," I replied.

How was I to cope with the guilt that said:

I had the chance, and I didn't take it;
I had the prayers, and I didn't pray them;
I had the love, and I didn't give it;
I had the words, and I didn't say them!

My friend reminded me that I needed to think of Mother instead of myself!

That day my mother was in heaven, where

God had the chance, and he was taking it;
He had the prayers, and he was praying them;
He had the love, and he was giving it;
He had the words, and he was saying them!

Sometimes I'm overwhelmed with a great hunger for a sight of her, a touch of her. Then I remember where she is, and I seem to imagine her saying, "You shouldn't feel my loss so much. You know where I am and who I'm with. Sooner than you know, you will be here, too!" I know one thing. She doesn't want me to carry the guilt of "all I didn't do," so I leave it at the empty tomb and rejoice!

There He Isn't

Away from these bodies . . . home with the Lord.

2 CORINTHIANS 5:8

The angels asked the women in the Garden of Gethsemane, "Why are you looking in a tomb for someone who is alive?" (Luke 24:5).

Why, indeed! The women who loved the Lord Jesus had come to his tomb to do what they could for him. But what can you do for the dead? Nothing much! You can wash the body and lay it out. You can wrap it tenderly in clean white cloths and gently place spices within the folds of fabric. You can try to frighten away the smell of death. You can weep until you can weep no more. You can gaze upon the beloved face that is almost unrecognizable in its immobility and search for a gleam of glory there. You can grieve that the good times are gone, and blame yourself for the bad times.

But why seek the living among the dead?

"He is not here but is risen!" said the angels.

One day I stood by an open casket with an elderly widow. A friend came by and, glancing inside the coffin, murmured, "There he is."

"On the contrary," the widow replied, "there he isn't! If I didn't believe that, I couldn't stand here beside a part of him that I loved and stay sane!"

In other words, the little lady was saying, "Why are you looking for the living inside a casket? He isn't here—he is risen!"

I had cause to remember these words years later as I stood beside my mother's coffin, seeking the living among the dead. "There she isn't," I whispered to the angels.

"That's right," they seemed to reply cheerfully. "She's with us!"

The Victory Is Ours, Thank God

How we thank God, who gives us victory over . . . death.

1 CORINTHIANS 15:57

Death, and with it the termination of human possibilities, comes to all of us, small and great, rich and poor, young and old. What place does the word *victory* have in the same sentence as the word *death*?

When Christ rose from the dead, he demonstrated immortality of the soul. He killed death through the Resurrection and blew hell wide open (see Hosea 13:14).

This truth, mixed with faith and the comfort of the Spirit, is intended to give us relief as we face the passing of someone close to us. Clark Pinnock says, "God is God not only of the sweet by and by, but of the bitter here and now!" As we believe the promise of victory over death, God will turn "the beating time" into "the blessed time."

If the last enemy is death, and Christ has defeated him, we can know that death is already retreating, wounded and bleeding to his own end. But a mortally wounded animal is the most dangerous animal of all. He will do as much damage as he can to anyone that dares to venture near. Watch him warily and with respect, remembering that in a little while he will be gone forever—and in that rejoice. As we stand helplessly by, watching dark death snatch our dear treasures away from us, let us remember that death cannot but loose our beloved ones into God's loving arms.

Shutting Us into the Family

"Go into the boat with all your family." . . . Then the Lord shut them in.

GENESIS 7:1, 16

Noah was building something he'd never built before, something that would shield his family. So must we build. We should always be listening for God's instructions so we can be creating something new to bless our relationships with our loved ones, something fresh that we've never tried before.

"But," you say, "I've tried everything I know, and there is still hostility, misunderstanding, and estrangement." Just as God instructed Noah with the specifics of his boat, so he can tell you the dimensions of a new structure for the blessing of your family. He forced Noah to spend more time in close contact with his loved ones. God will give you ideas of how to create those kinds of opportunities.

We mustn't shut out the people who should be close to us, but let God shut them in to us. We need to be like Noah and spend time asking God for the dimensions of the structure we must build for the blessing of our family. Relationships take a long time to construct, but then it took Noah a long time to build the boat. What projects can we plan that will lock our family into each other? One day, if we allow God to lock us up together, we may find the door open to new heights. The boat came to rest on Mount Ararat, which means "heavenly places." It turned out to be a whole new world of discovery for Noah's family.

Winning over Weariness

Never get tired of doing good.

2 THESSALONIANS 3:13

Jesus was never too faint to fight for a soul, never too tired to talk with those who sought him, never too weary to listen in love, never too exhausted to walk the extra mile with a group of despised Samaritans. But because he experienced our human infirmities, he knows how tiredness can weaken our bodies and understands what it is like to be on the edge of tears. Aren't you glad about that? Jesus, having been weary himself, is able to care when we are strung out from our daily struggles, wearied out with kingdom work. Now Jesus rejoices in heaven over the sheep on earth returning to the fold, and he prays for strength for us to continue his work for him.

Many a time as I tumble into bed, my preacher husband, weary himself, reaches over to welcome me with a kiss of comfort. "Welcome home, little girl," he says. "I know you are weary in well doing, but doesn't that feel sort of good?" And you know, it really does! A journey with Jesus is not an easy thing. You won't get to your destination without sand in your sandals and dirt in your hair, but you will have the incalculable joy of his company. His abundant sympathy and his "well done" at the end of the day will be worth it all.

Weary me, Lord,
with work for the kingdom.
Use me to do your marvelous will.
Keep me productive and make me a blessing,
your precious will to fulfill!

Prayer Is a Place

As was the custom of the priests, he was chosen by lot to enter the sanctuary and burn incense in the Lord's presence.

LUKE 1:9

Prayer has been described in many ways—intercession, praise, the debating chamber of the soul. Prayer is all these things and more. But prayer, first and foremost, is a place to meet. In the Old Testament, God invited his people to meet him at the altar of incense in the tabernacle: "This is to be a daily burnt offering given from generation to generation. Offer it in the Lord's presence at the Tabernacle entrance, where I will meet you and speak with you" (Exodus 29:42).

In the New Testament, Jesus spoke of finding a private place where you can shut the door behind you and pray (Matthew 6:6)—and he served as an example for us by going frequently to a solitary place. "But," wails a young mother, "what can I do? I have forty kids under three years of age!"

Now, I know *that* is not really true! You only have four—it just feels like forty! I managed to find a place once when I was in a similar predicament. I climbed into the children's playpen and put the toddlers out! Five minutes with God by my "altar of incense" made all the difference in the world—my world!

Yes, prayer is a place to meet; this is God's design. We need to pray about finding that personal place of prayer.

"Lord, help me to find my solitary place; and whether it be in church, in a closet, or even in a playpen, meet me there—even as you promised. Amen."

Prayer Is a Time

While the incense was being burned, a great crowd stood outside, praying.

LUKE 1:10

For Aaron, his sons, and, indeed, for all people, God designed a specific time for prayer. Every morning and evening the priest burned holy incense upon the altar in the tabernacle. This was to be done not only when the people were faced with trials, fears, or death; it was to be offered perpetually—"from generation to generation" (Exodus 30:8). Often, however, we rush to that altar only in times of extremity, anxiety, or perplexity. We don't practice perpetual praise, and therefore we are not in the habit of giving thanks in all things when trouble comes (see Ephesians 5:20). But our text from Luke reminds us that the people were praying regularly "while the incense was being burned"—not just in the hour of need!

Jesus told us that his people should pray constantly and never give up (Luke 18:1). "Keep on praying," echoed the apostle Paul (1 Thessalonians 5:17).

God designed the altar of incense so that it could be carried by the children of Israel in their desert pilgrimage—a perpetual reminder of their perpetual privilege (see Exodus 30:1-10). However, it is worth noting that such prayer was to be a privilege of obedience. God's rules are rules. He didn't say, "I'll meet you there if you like, if you remember, or if you're desperate!" God told Aaron that "he *must* burn fragrant incense on the altar" (Exodus 30:7, italics mine). Such perpetual praise is not merely an option for the child of God. It is a simple, sweet necessity, for it glorifies the Lord.

Holy Habits:
I will pray,
Lord, I'll meet you come what may.
Though dark my days, or weather fair,
I'll be obedient . . .
I'll be there!

The Things That Happen to Me!

Everything that has happened to me here has helped to spread the Good News.

PHILIPPIANS 1:12

Pressed for time, I boarded a plane and settled down to study. The man next to me began to read my notes over my shoulder, and that irritated me! "O Lord," I prayed, "I don't have time to talk; I need to get ready for the challenge of the day!"

"He *is* the challenge of the day," the Lord seemed to say!

The man began to question me, and I put my books away to give him my full attention. Later, as we began to land, a light aircraft spun across our path, and our pilot dived sharply, narrowly avoiding a collision. Everyone screamed—me, too!

"I bet you just said a prayer or two," my companion gasped, ashen-faced.

"You bet I did," I replied, "but I'm ready to go! That doesn't mean it won't be scary getting there, but God has my life in his hands!"

"I'm not ready to go," the man said quietly, "and I'm scared to death!"

"Maybe you've been scared to life," I suggested.

I felt guilty about my earlier irritation with the man. I had forgotten that the things that happen to me happen in order to advance the gospel, and that I cannot afford to shut myself off behind my Bible from the people who live in the world. If I had not been plowing the ground before that frightening incident occurred, I could not have planted some seeds when trouble came.

That Calvary Be Worthwhile

Jesus soon saw a great crowd of people climbing the hill, looking for him.

JOHN 6:5

Watching the huge crowd at a Billy Graham crusade, I seemed to catch God's compassion for the multitude as we prayed silently together:

"Lord, where can we go but to you? We have no one in heaven besides you. No one on earth with your ability to touch our spirits, to lift our mood, to bless our kids, to stick us back together again when we fall apart, to sew a torn relationship into place. We come to ask for the consciousness of your immediate and dynamic presence.

"We wonder what you see that we cannot: A crowd of cowards? A sea of sin? A morass of people picking and clawing at each other? Hurt husbands or rejected wives who find it difficult to look their neighbors in the face? Or do you, perhaps, see those of us who are celebrating our independence—the 'I have need of nothing' individuals, the 'keep your religion, I have mine' group, the cynic or the scoffer, or even little children capable of huge injustice on their own sweet level?

"Find us, tonight, God, find us. Nudge us into your will and away from our wants; reduce us to size; show us your mighty arm; carry away our sin.

"Move us into action, help us make a walking statement that will tell our world that Jesus is our public choice.

"We request that you fasten our mind with the nail of urgency to the wall of decision; and we ask it all, Jesus, that Calvary be worthwhile. Amen."

Keeping House

> **If you are the Son of God, change this stone into a loaf of bread.**
>
> LUKE 4:3

For years I had many conversations with the Lord, having discovered I needed help with my weight. I tried all the fad diets and fasting regimes that people told me about, but in the end my help came from the Lord.

On one occasion I had been alone in the house for a long time. I opened the refrigerator door and started to pig out.

Later, as I was reading my Bible, I read about some people whose "god is their appetite" (Philippians 3:19).

"O Lord, why did you have to say *that?*" I complained. "That's hard to hear! I struggle with my weight. You know I try to be a good 'temple keeper,' but it's so difficult, and the older I get, the harder it seems to be! The problem is worse when no one is around to see me snitch! The only way I can stop is to keep an empty refrigerator, and then my kids come home from college and complain that they're not on war rations, even if I am!"

"Once my Son was hungry," said God. "The devil tempted him to satisfy his appetite by turning stones into bread. But he chose to do my will—not the will of Satan nor the will of his stomach—and so he stayed hungry."

"You mean you didn't take away the hunger pains?" I asked.

"His meat was always to do my will," replied the Father, "and in that instance it meant having an empty stomach."

"Be the God of my appetites, Father," I prayed.

"I will," responded the Father cheerfully. "So let's start by putting that big piece of pumpkin pie right back in the pan, where it belongs!"

THE BIRTHING WING

I was to speak to a hospital auxiliary. The evening began with a tour of the nursery and a visit to the new hospice where, my host explained, dying was made a matter of dignity. The facilities were beautiful and had been made as much like "Home sweet home" as possible. *But these people aren't "home" yet,* I thought. *This is the start, not the finish; the beginning, not the end.*

They are natural human bodies now, but when they are raised, they will be spiritual bodies. . . . For our perishable earthly bodies must be transformed into heavenly bodies that will never die.

1 CORINTHIANS 15:44, 53

Turning to the doctor at my side, I said, "I see that this is your birthing wing!"

"No, no," he said somewhat despairingly, "we have just toured the birthing wing. That was the place where the babies were laid out neatly in rows, you remember!"

There was a titter of laughter from the group. "You are mistaken," I said softly. "This is indeed the birthing wing! I believe that these people are soon to be born into a new dimension that God calls eternity."

There was an awkward silence, and then careless chatter drowned out our conversation. The opportunity had come and gone to remind my friends of the reality of the life waiting on the other side of the doorway of death!

Watering my words with prayer and trusting God to bring forth fruit in his own time, I followed the group into the auditorium to begin our meeting.

Born again to die but once
In the birthing wing;
Born a second time in heaven
To hear the angels sing!

JOY—WHATEVER, WHENEVER, WHEREVER!

Always be full of joy in the Lord. I say it again—rejoice!
PHILIPPIANS 4:4

We are to "be full of joy in the Lord." If we know how to do that, we won't be depressed by our circumstances. When we can't praise him for what he has allowed, we can thank him for "who he is" in the midst of what he has allowed!

The Lord Jesus reacted angrily to oppression, was deeply moved by cruelty, and wept at death. He was tenderly touched by human infirmities. We are not told to rejoice about the tragedies of life, but we are encouraged to rejoice in the Lord when hard times come. He promises to comfort us when we are mistreated and to help us to bravely endure when we suffer. We will be able to survive our circumstances with his help, because he has already survived his circumstances as the God-man, Jesus of Nazareth. In Christ, we have available to us all the heavenly support that was available to him here on earth.

We are to rejoice in our relationship with him *always*. That doesn't mean just when the sun is shining; it means when it rains, hails, snows, and even if a tornado hits our life! "Always" means "always." I have a friend who worked with people who had multiple sclerosis. One day she became a victim of the disease herself. "All my life I have dreaded this happening," she told me. "I have had nowhere to go with this but to God, and he is being a source of great joy to me in my trouble!"

Joy is the badge of the believer. Paul, writing from his prison cell, emphasized the inability of circumstances to stifle his enjoyment of the Lord. "Rejoice," he exhorted his beloved Philippians. "I say it again—rejoice!"

Rewinding the Unraveled

Keep on praying.

1 THESSALONIANS 5:17

The young mother asked me how she could keep "sane" when she lacked adult company all week long. "Does anyone else feel the way I do?" she wondered. She felt guilty even asking the question, lest I think she didn't enjoy her young children.

I told her about the time we lived in a very tiny house in England, and I, too, was shut in with our three preschoolers. As most people know, there are only two seasons in England—winter and the second week of August! By the end of each rainy day, I felt like an unraveled ball of wool! Once I took a guest to the train station, and he kindly suggested that I try to meet regularly with other adults. "Why?" I asked, startled. "Because on the way here," he replied, "you pointed out the window and told me to look at the nice little baa-lambs playing in the fields!"

Prayer winds up the unraveled ball of wool. We have to find a place and time for that to happen. I looked around my tiny house and found the place—then I had to find the time.

My packed calendar showed me a regular time for prayer was impossible since each day's schedule was so different. But I found twenty minutes here and ten minutes there, and blocked them off. Writing on my calendar that way helped me to keep the divine appointment. God and I needed to be alone long enough for him to wind the ball of wool back together again. It was good advice to seek more "adult time," but what I needed above all else was to find more "God time," and that, in the end, was the thing that kept me sane!

Help These Women

And now I want to plead with those two women, Euodia and Syntyche. Please, because you belong to the Lord, settle your disagreement.

PHILIPPIANS 4:2

Once I heard a Bible teacher name these two ladies "Odious" and "Soon Touchy." I had to admit there could be women with such traits in my church just as there were in the Philippian church. Here were two strong women who couldn't agree in the Lord. They began to form factions and spread dissension. Paul appeals to some hapless man he calls a "true teammate" to intervene—a rather hazardous request, to say the least! What man in his right mind would want to settle a fight between two stubborn Christian women? This was no yellow fellow! Why not just let the women pick each other to pieces?

Paul's appeal to his friends is based on his argument that mature Christian behavior is harmonious behavior. He wants them to be "united in the Holy Spirit" (Ephesians 4:3), and he reminds his friends that Christ had promised to be a very present help working with them in the power of his resurrection to "conquer everything" (Philippians 3:21). Paul's plea is couched in such terms as "I plead" and "I ask," and it paints a portrait of his heart's desire for these Christians.

I believe Paul is also praying for us, and I can imagine him echoing Jesus' prayer in John 17:20: "I am praying not only for these disciples but also for all who will ever believe in me because of their testimony."

And so, true teammates, whoever you are, "help these women"! All of us are instructed to endeavor to be "united in the Holy Spirit" and bound together "with peace" (Ephesians 4:3), lest we give occasion to the enemies of Christ to accuse us.

THE OTHER SIDE OF GIVING

You know how full of love and kindness our Lord Jesus Christ was. Though he was very rich, yet for your sakes he became poor, so that by his poverty he could make you rich.

2 CORINTHIANS 8:9

Have you ever been on the *other* side of giving? It's hard to receive from others. It can be humiliating, frustrating, or demeaning. Missionaries know what that is like—receiving, as they often do, cast-off clothing, once-used tea bags, and broken appliances that *perhaps* they can fix up and use! Having to borrow things that belong to others because we have no things that belong to ourselves is another touchy assignment.

Jesus understands both of these things. Aren't you glad?

He borrowed a bed to lay His head,
When Christ the Lord came down;
He borrowed an ass in the mountain pass
On which to ride to town.
But the crown that He wore and the cross that He bore
Were His own—the cross was His own!

He borrowed a room on the way to His tomb
The Passover lamb to eat;
He borrowed a cave—
For Him a grave—
He borrowed a winding sheet.
But the crown that He wore and the cross that He bore
Were His own—the cross was His own!

The thorns on His head were worn in my stead;
For me the Saviour died.
For the guilt of my sin
Those nails drove in,
When Him they crucified—
Though the crown that He wore and the cross that He bore
Were His own—they were justly mine.

ANONYMOUS

Privilege or Punishment

Children are a gift from the Lord; they are a reward from him.

PSALM 127:3

Do you believe children are a privilege or a punishment? I expect it depends on where you are in the child-rearing process! The image in Psalm 127 is that of children being like arrows in a quiver. "How happy is the man whose quiver is full of them," exults the writer of the psalm (127:5). But even one child is enough to make some parents "quiver"! Perhaps you are wishing you had never had your children. Many parents feel that way. When Esau met Jacob, his brother, after years of separation, he saw Jacob's wives and children and asked, "Who are these people with you?" Jacob answered, "These are the children God has graciously given to me" (Genesis 33:5). If children are gifts from a gracious God, a precious heavenly inheritance, then it follows that parents will not be able to do justice to this responsibility unless they maintain a personal and responsible relationship with him.

Psalm 128:3 promises happiness to those who walk in the Lord's ways. "Your wife will be like a fruitful vine, flourishing within your home. And look at all those children! There they sit around your table as vigorous and healthy as young olive trees." This does not mean that mother will be climbing the walls, but that many sons and daughters brought up in the nurture and admonition of the Lord will bring many blessings. The woman who loves and obeys the Lord and teaches her children to do the same will at the end of the day have joy and reward; they will "stand and bless her" (Proverbs 31:28).

Family Foundations

Unless the Lord builds a house, the work of the builders is useless.

PSALM 127:1

So much writing in the epistles has to do with the Christian walk and work in the power of the living Christ. The discovery that God "is able to accomplish infinitely more than we would ever dare to ask or hope" has been thrilling to me (Ephesians 3:20). The building of our family relationships, for example, has been based upon the ability of God to do what he has promised. That fact has been the foundation of our marriage, and while the building has sometimes shaken, the foundation has never moved.

When Stuart and I became engaged, we chose a three-stoned ring to represent Christ in the center and Stuart and me on either side of him. Knowing our selfish natures, we were well aware that it would take his preeminence to bind us together in a life of commitment to each other and a ministry partnership for the kingdom of God.

Looking back after twenty-five years of marriage, we can both say that God has done "infinitely more" than we asked or even thought. The Lord has been the foundation of our building and has lent us the power to complete that which we promised to each other and to him!

Jesus was invited to a wedding in Cana of Galilee as a guest, not a master of ceremonies. When the wine ran out, he was asked to take charge, and he turned water into wine that was better than any they had had before (see John 2:10). When Christ takes charge of our marriage, he turns a flat relationship into a sparkling, joyful experience—better than any we have had before!

Dinner Plates

To God's holy people in Ephesus, who are faithful followers of Christ Jesus.

EPHESIANS 1:1

Paul wrote many letters to the groups of believers scattered around Asia Minor, and in many versions of the Bible, he addressed these "holy people" as "saints." A "saint" in this sense was not a sinless person or someone in a medieval painting with a gold dinner plate behind his or her head. A "saint" in the New Testament sense was a saved sinner. It is through faith in the Lord Jesus Christ that a sinner becomes a saint.

But what does the word *saint* mean? The Greek words *hagios* for "saint" and *hagiazo* for "sanctify" are related. The vessels in the temple were sanctified—set apart for God and for his service—and so are ordinary people who come in faith to Jesus Christ. All New Testament believers are holy people—saints—regardless of their progress or growth.

Paul addresses his letters to ordinary believers who were called by God to be saints, just as surely as Paul was called by God to be an apostle (Romans 1:1).

Some people protest the word *holy* or *saint,* saying they don't want to be called by such a high and holy title. It means they have to live up to it! Too many Christians want to be saved by the Lord yet live like the devil. When once you realize that being a true Christian means being "Christianly" true in character, and when you decide to live in obedience to your calling, then God will set you aside for his very special service, just as he did the vessels in his temple.

Whether we like it or not, we are holy people, saints. We bear the responsibility of his name and should live accordingly!

Much More

Paul says God has blessed us in the realm of spiritual experience with a special benediction. The Lord thinks so highly of the people he created that he commanded certain things be done for them—thus blessing them.

How we praise God, the Father of our Lord Jesus Christ, who has blessed us with every spiritual blessing in the heavenly realms because we belong to Christ.

EPHESIANS 1:3

The Old Testament tells us about Noah and his family, who were sheltered in a huge boat from God's judgment. Then after forty days and nights, the waters receded and their boat rested on Mount Ararat, whose name means "heavenly places." What a lovely picture of the things God wants to do for us! We deserve the judgment of God for our wrongdoing; but Christ is our lifesaving boat, and sheltered in him we escape the retribution due to us.

But Christianity is not escapism. Christianity is opening the door to a whole new world—a spiritual Mount Ararat. As Romans 5:10 puts it, "For since we were restored to friendship with God by the death of his Son while we were still his enemies, we will certainly be delivered from eternal punishment by his life." Major Ian Thomas explained it this way in a sermon: "Christ's death makes us fit for heaven—Christ's life makes us fit for earth!"

Becoming a Christian means understanding God's judgment and sheltering in Christ; being a Christian means exploring Mount Ararat—the heavenly slopes of spiritual experience. It's hard to take in anything more once we have grasped the meaning of the Cross, but the "much more" of the gospel leads us into spiritual blessings and heavenly experiences that will bring a song of praise and love from our heart.

Election

Long ago, even before he made the world, God loved us and chose us in Christ to be holy and without fault in his eyes.

EPHESIANS 1:4

The book of Ephesians records some mountain-top blessings from God. The first one is election. The word literally means "to call out" or "to mark out beforehand." The loving God Almighty, knowing all things, wrote down, as it were, our names for that happy future.

Some people have problems trying to reconcile the free will of man and the sovereignty of God. But Richard C. Halverson, former chaplain of the U.S. Senate, says, "Nothing God planned interferes with human freedom; nothing humans do frustrates God's sovereign plan." If we are tempted to think that God is unfair, we need to remember that the choosing and the blessing of us unworthy sinners in Christ are in the hands of a loving and infinitely trustworthy Sovereign's love! One thing we can be sure about: God will do the right thing!

To those of us who struggle with a negative self-image, the doctrine of election gives a great sense of worth! Watch a shy teenage girl chosen by a handsome boy to attend the senior prom, realizing she's been marked out beforehand! See what that does for her confidence. See a "plain Jane" blossom into vibrant womanhood when she gets engaged. Her fiancé had all the world to choose from, and he chose *her*.

Experience the love of God in your own heart and mind and realize he wanted *you* to be his very own—as if there were no other in the whole wide world—and you are well on the way to believing you are a valuable, eternal person.

Redemption

He is so rich in kindness that he purchased our freedom through the blood of his Son, and our sins are forgiven.

EPHESIANS 1:7

Another blessing recorded in Ephesians is the purchase of our freedom—redemption. The word *redemption* means "to buy back with a ransom." The slave market is in Paul's mind as he tries to find images to convey the state of our spirits as slaves to sin and the love of our Redeemer, paying with his own precious blood the ultimate price for our freedom. Some think that because Christ died, all receive redemption automatically. Not so! We have to say thank you and take advantage of that freedom by walking away from our old master and serving the one who has bought us with such a price—whose service is perfect freedom!

An African chief raided a village and took captive a young boy. The child became his favorite servant. Years later the boy's aged parents, having spent years sacrificing, took their very lives in their hands and journeyed afar to lay the redemption money at the chief's feet and claim their now-grown son. Free to go, the son declined, choosing to stay and serve his master. His sorrowing parents returned to die alone in their old age. A few years later the chief died, and according to custom, the favorite servant was buried alive with him to keep him company in the afterlife. The young man had refused to be redeemed.

Have you refused to be redeemed? That is a very dangerous thing to do!

Adoption

But when the right time came, God sent his Son, born of a woman, subject to the law. God sent him to buy freedom for us who were slaves to the law, so that he could adopt us as his very own children.

GALATIANS 4:4-5

Galatians 4:7 tells us we are no longer slaves, but adopted children; we have full status as heirs of God through Christ. It's through Jesus that we come to be related to the Father. When we receive the Holy Spirit, we are adopted into God's family forever.

A friend of mine had three boys and then adopted a little girl. One day as I was taking the adopted child home, I was quite surprised to hear her tell the other little girl who was in my car, "I'm adopted, you know."

"Oh, I wouldn't like that," responded her friend with tactless candor.

"Why not?" asked my friend's child. "After all, your parents had no choice about you—mine picked me out!"

That little girl had a great sense of her election and therefore a great pride in her adoption. She knew that all that belonged to the natural sons of the family also belonged to her, for she was not a stranger, a visitor, or a servant in her parents' house—but a chosen child and therefore an heir!

Similarly, God has chosen us (Ephesians 1:4). It is God's will that we give him credit for this heavenly blessing. Praise, after all, is the act of giving credit where it is due—and in this case, it is due to grace! My adoption into Christ and my spiritual inheritance in him are because of GRACE—once defined as:

God's
Riches
At
Christ's
Expense.

A Celestial Agatha Christie

God's secret plan has now been revealed to us; it is a plan centered on Christ, designed long ago according to his good pleasure.

EPHESIANS 1:9

Is God's will a mystery to you? Have you ever been able to fathom what he is doing? This verse tells us that God has made known to us his "secret plan." Such are our spiritual blessings in heavenly places!

Do you think of God as a sort of celestial Agatha Christie who delights in fooling you? Do you believe that when you finally get to heaven the last chapter will tell all? Well, this is not what is meant by the word *secret*. God is speaking here of previously hidden truths that are now divinely revealed. He wants us to know them. Paul may have had the secret, mysterious religions of his day in mind when he used this word. These religions were secret societies whose mysteries were revealed only to initiated members. If we have been initiated into the kingdom of God by receiving God's Spirit, the secrets of that kingdom are ours. The same thought is found in 1 Corinthians 2:9-10:

> "No eye has seen, no ear has heard, and no mind has imagined what God has prepared for those who love him."

But God has revealed them to us through his Spirit. For the Spirit searches all things—yes, the deep, secret things of God.

Spiritual truths are not found in human wisdom but rather are revealed by God. The promise of Scripture is that we have received "his Spirit (not the world's spirit) so we can know the wonderful things God has freely given us" (1 Corinthians 2:12). Furthermore, it is God's *good pleasure* that we should know them!

People Who Don't Need Praying For

Ever since I first heard of your strong faith in the Lord Jesus and your love for Christians everywhere, I have never stopped thanking God for you. I pray for you constantly.

EPHESIANS 1:15-16

What motivates you to pray? Bad news? That seems to be a pretty common motivation. There's nothing like a good crisis to drive us to our knees! When trouble confronts us, we tend to pick up God like a crutch, only to discard him when trouble is past! But good news, not bad news, is Paul's motivation. He teaches us a much-needed lesson, showing us how to pray for people who don't need praying for! Paul describes these Christians at Ephesus as having lots of faith in God and lots of love for each other. These Christians were living a life full of joy and making their mark in society. "Why waste valuable prayer time on them?" you may ask.

There are so many needy Christians, sick people, and marriages in trouble. First of all, Paul tells us to undergird and protect the strong ones in prayer. That's important. The devil keeps his sharpest arrows for his most effective enemies. The apostle prays that these Christians might know the Lord Jesus even better than they do already. He prays that they will have hearts flooded with light so that they can see something of the future God has called them to share. He prays they will experience strength of will through God's power.

This is a fine passage of Scripture to use in praying for those who don't need praying for. Use it—believers will thank you for making mention of them in your prayers.

Adequate

I pray that you will begin to understand the incredible greatness of his power for us who believe him. This is the same mighty power that raised Christ from the dead and seated him in the place of honor at God's right hand in the heavenly realms.

EPHESIANS 1:19-20

Paul talks of the working of God's "mighty power" on our behalf. "I pray that you will begin to understand the incredible greatness of his power for us who believe him," that same mighty power that raised Christ from the dead and seated him in the place of honor at God's right hand in heaven. If you've ever seen a dead body, then you will be able to understand a little of the power it must take to restore it to life! It will take more power than sending an astronaut to the moon and bringing him back again! After all, *people* have the power to do all that! But people do not have the power to raise the dead. God did that when he raised Christ, and now he tells us that the same power works in each believer! That means his mighty power in me is adequate for any situation.

A man from Australia bought a Rolls Royce in England and took it home with him. However, he neglected to find out the horsepower. He wrote to the manufacturer but received only the terse British reply, "Adequate!" The British firm believed that that was all the owner of the car needed to know.

We don't need to know how God's power works; we only need to know that his power in us is available and wholly "adequate." Use it to its full advantage for God's kingdom!

Over My Head But under His Feet

And God has put all things under the authority of Christ, and he gave him this authority for the benefit of the church.

EPHESIANS 1:22

A dear friend was journeying with me to a conference and began to share the story of her thirty-year marriage. "If you had told me two years ago that my husband would walk out and leave his three lovely children and his wife after thirty years, I would have said you were crazy," she said soberly. "But here I am. I still think of my oldest boy on the day my husband left, saying, 'But, Dad, you've always said Mom is one in a million.' 'Well, now I've found one in a billion,' he coolly replied, and walked out of our lives. For a few months I was swamped," she continued, "but then I found Christ, and the Scriptures told me that anything 'over my head' was under his feet! I learned that his mighty strength would work for me. I read that Jesus Christ my King was triumphant, and that in him, I could be triumphant, too!"

I told my friend—my brave and beautiful friend—that kings of ancient times put their feet on the neck of their enemies in a symbolic gesture, and that God our King had put his foot on the neck of his enemies, too.

What's over your head? Has your husband left you to face life alone? Do you have to cope with aging parents or rebellious teenagers by yourself? Remember, whatever is over your head is under his feet—and therefore, under yours, too. Ephesians 2:6 says that God has "raised us from the dead along with Christ, and we are seated with him in the heavenly realms—all because we are one with Christ Jesus."

The Living Dead

But the widow who lives only for pleasure is spiritually dead.

1 TIMOTHY 5:6

How can you live and be dead? What does Paul mean? He means that you can be physically alive but spiritually dead.

Jesus talked to Nicodemus about this, saying that every person has been given physical life but needs to be given spiritual life (see John 3). How do you know if someone is physically dead? Well, to begin with, he has no appetite. Offer a dead man a big, juicy steak, and he will show no interest whatsoever! How do you know if someone is spiritually dead? Offer a spiritually dead person a sermon, devotional book, or a Bible conference, and he will show similar disinterest.

Second, a physically dead person will have no liveliness. Everything about a corpse is still, and what a dreadful stillness it is! A spiritually dead person will be "still," too. There will be no spiritual activity in his life, no swift feet taking the gospel to those who have never heard, no busy hands alleviating other's needs. If a person lives only for pleasure, he is spiritually dead.

Then how do you start to live when you are dead? You stop living for pleasure and start living for God! And how do you do that? Recognize that just as a dead body needs life, so does a dead soul! Jesus Christ said, "I am the way, the truth, *and the life*" (John 14:6, italics mine). Ask Jesus Christ for his eternal life, and he will give it to you. The apostle John assures us, "And this is what God has testified: He has given us eternal life, and this life is in his Son. So whoever has God's Son has life; whoever does not have his Son does not have life" (1 John 5:11-12).

A Woman of Action

For we are God's masterpiece. He has created us anew in Christ Jesus, so that we can do the good things he planned for us long ago.

EPHESIANS 2:10

Other translations of this verse say that we are to "do good works, which God prepared in advance for us to do" (NIV), and "Long ages ago he planned that we should spend these lives helping others" (TLB).

These "good things" are not actions that get us into heaven, but are rather the tasks awaiting us once we enter there! And that doesn't mean we have to die first. We enter heaven the day heaven enters us! "Heaven came down and glory filled my soul," says the song. When Jesus Christ comes into my life, I enter heaven on earth—I *am* seated with him in heavenly places. Once that union with Christ is established, what a relief to discover that God has something for me to do!

I'm a woman of action, and the idea of sitting around on a misty pink cloud playing a harp is not my idea of heaven!

What a joy it was for me to discover that God has prepared some people that needed helping and that he had prepared me to help them! That brought a real sense of worth and purpose to my life.

Some people don't know how to find others who need help. One practical lesson I have learned is this: If possible, never say no to opportunities. If you become known as a willing servant, you will soon be given someone to serve. That's one way to find the "good things" that God has prepared in advance for you to do!

Start There

But when the Holy Spirit has come upon you, you will receive power and will tell people about me everywhere—in Jerusalem, throughout Judea, in Samaria, and to the ends of the earth.

ACTS 1:8

The book of Ephesians talks about our heavenly position; yet we must never be so heavenly minded that we are of no earthly use. Neither should we be so earthly minded we are of no heavenly use! There is a sweet balance running through Paul's teaching. The secret of that balance lies in our understanding of our heavenly position: It is the balance between grace and works. We are saved by grace through faith, not as a reward for the good things we have done "so none of us can boast," and yet we are saved "so that we can do the good things he planned for us long ago" (see Ephesians 2:9-10).

God never asks us to "do" in order to "be." He puts us into a relationship and tells us to be true to it. However, once inside that relationship, we have work to do.

"But where do I start?" you ask. Start where you are, and with what you've got! Start in "Jerusalem," that is, in your own hometown. I remember looking out my kitchen window wondering what I'd got! As far as I could tell, my Jerusalem contained a few older ladies who were my neighbors, and that was it. Could they possibly be these marvelous good works I had been saved to do? They were, indeed, I discovered. They didn't look as though God had prepared them for any such divine intent, but as I reached out and touched them, I found hungry, lonely hearts prepared to listen to the gospel.

Try looking outside your kitchen window: "Jerusalem" is full of lonely old ladies, unhappy teenagers, damaged people! Start there.

Second Fiddle

> **Don't be selfish; don't live to make a good impression on others. Be humble, thinking of others as better than yourself.**
>
> PHILIPPIANS 2:3

One way to discover the works of service God wants you to do is to offer to play second fiddle. "It matters more than tongue can tell to play the second fiddle well," quips the couplet. Playing second fiddle, particularly when you have first-fiddle gifts, is a marvelous way to start serving others. There are so many second-fiddle positions to fill. Very few people want them, as most people are heading for the top and working at being visible. If we would only roll up our sleeves and "have a go," as we say in England; if we would but get involved wherever there is a need, then God could maneuver us into the right niche.

You can't guide a stationary car, you know—just as God can't guide a stationary Christian. We need to start going somewhere, doing something, soon! You may complain, "But it isn't my thing to teach Sunday school, help with the food collection, mow yards, pick up old folks, count money, wash dishes, give my testimony." Maybe not, but have you ever considered it might be *his* thing for you? The Lord taught me years ago that if I would stop worrying about playing first fiddle, and would start with second and do it well and to the glory of God, I would stumble over those prepared works along the way!

Have you taken your place in God's orchestra yet? What are you waiting for? Why not start by playing second fiddle?

Becoming

In those days you were living apart from Christ. You were excluded from God's people, Israel, and you did not know the promises God had made to them. You lived in this world without God and without hope.

EPHESIANS 2:12

Paul talks to the Ephesians about citizenship. He reminds them that at one time they were strangers from the things of God, "living apart from Christ . . . excluded." He may have been using a reference to the greatly coveted and privileged Roman citizenship (see Acts 22:28). The Greeks called those who lived outside their cities "pagans." The Jews also spoke disparagingly of the *ethne* or Gentiles, meaning those outside the knowledge of the God of Israel. Instead of thinking of them as those with whom they should have shared their knowledge of Jehovah, the Jews created a sense of alienation. But now these Ephesian Gentiles, these outsiders, had stepped inside the promises of God and had become true citizens of the heavenly kingdom. "But now you belong to Christ Jesus," Paul says. "Though you once were far away from God, now you have been brought near to him because of the blood of Christ. For Christ himself has made peace between us Jews and you Gentiles by making us all one people. He has broken down the wall of hostility that used to separate us" (Ephesians 2:13-14). Paul was doubtless referring to the wall of partition in the temple that separated Jews from Gentiles. This partition was truly a "wall of hostility."

Stuart lived for seven years in America as a registered alien. The day he became a United States citizen, I watched the brotherly hugs and handclasps and knew that the unseen wall had been broken down! Becoming a citizen of a great nation is a good thing, but becoming a citizen of heaven is even better!

Belonging

Together as one body, Christ reconciled both groups to God by means of his death, and our hostility toward each other was put to death.

EPHESIANS 2:16

If the wall of hostility has indeed been broken down by the death of Christ (see Ephesians 2:13-14), why then do so many people inside the kingdom still meet a stone wall where true fellowship is concerned? Why does the wall still divide black and white, rich and poor, those with social status and those without? I believe it is because Christians have not been taught that the basis of their unity is "belonging."

Unity begins when we get our theology straight. If the wall has been broken down and yet the wall is still there, it is because someone has been building it up again! What is a wall? It's a barrier—something that includes others and excludes you. We sense it, though it be unseen, between people inside the church. We see different factions with religious and personal differences. Yet our unity is in belonging. For through him we *all* have access by one Spirit to the Father. He sees all of us kneeling down at our bedsides at the end of the day!

I must tell Jesus, "The wall will not be built by my hands!" I must not be a builder of walls. I must lay down my trowel and use my hands rather to reach out to my brother and sister in love. I need to keep acting as if the barrier isn't there; I need to walk through it and speak into years of silence. I must write another letter and extend another dinner invitation. I must do what I can to make sure others know I believe in belonging!

WHOSE PRISONER?

I, Paul, am a prisoner of Christ Jesus because of my preaching to you Gentiles.

EPHESIANS 3:1

Was Paul the prisoner of Nero? Not in Paul's thinking. Paul believed that "everything that has happened to me here has helped to spread the Good News" (Philippians 1:12). He firmly believed nothing could happen to him without divine permission. Paul knew God had a plan for his life, and that it was no accident that he was in jail. He was able to say, and did quite regularly, "I don't know what the future holds, but I know the One who holds the future." No, Paul did not believe he was a prisoner of the Gentiles, but rather a prisoner of Jesus Christ for the sake of the Gentiles.

When I was a young mother with three children under school age, I came to a similar conclusion about my situation! I lived in a small house kept prisoner by my responsibilities to my family. But because of those confining duties, I began to know the older ladies who lived around me. I was able to say, "I am not a prisoner of my circumstances, but rather a prisoner of Jesus Christ for these dear ladies!"

Paul was more attuned to his calling than to his circumstances and cared more about the people whom he served than about the personal consequences of his service.

What circumstances imprison you? Are you a prisoner of Christ for the sake of someone else? Once you recognize this, your attitude will change and so will your actions. Just whose prisoner are you?

Body Language

> **When I think of the wisdom and scope of God's plan, I fall to my knees and pray to the Father, the Creator of everything in heaven and on earth.**
>
> EPHESIANS 3:14-15

Paul was kneeling before the Father. No matter that a Roman guard was in the room, perhaps even chained to him; no matter whether the guard was scoffer or brother. Paul was on his knees.

You know, seeing someone pray has great impact! I will never forget one instance when I was a student and had been sent with a message to the president of the student body. Knocking briefly, I rudely burst into the girl's room and found her at prayer. The sight of this beautiful girl, unashamedly bowing her knees to the Lord Jesus Christ, had a profound effect on me. I was somehow angry with her because she made me feel awkward, and yet her very body language preached an eloquent sermon of commitment that I badly needed to hear! I would not have listened to her words, but I could not ignore her message.

We do not always have a quiet room to run to. Sometimes the most important praying must be done in the midst of turmoil, people, and problems! I don't think any one of us will be forced to have our quiet time as Paul did, accompanied by the clanking of chains! It's so easy for us—but we don't do it! People like Paul, prisoners for Christ, pray for *us!* It's time that free people prayed, too!

Do you ever say grace in a restaurant? Do you say, "Lord, we bow our heads in this public place in acknowledgement of whose we are and whom we serve"? That's body language that tells a powerful story!

Who Is My Family?

The Father, the Creator of everything in heaven and on earth.

EPHESIANS 3:14-15

In this prayer, Paul had the spiritual and universal community of believers very much on his mind. He said that this forever family had the Father's name, and that some of the family are "in heaven" and that some are "on earth." The rabbis of Paul's day called angels the upper family and Israel the lower family. This idea may have molded Paul's language. What a family we belong to—it is made up of angels and loved ones! Heaven becomes dearer to me the older I get, as more and more of the people I love go there! Not long ago I visited a Christian at the point of death. "Say hi to my mother for me," I whispered. She smiled and nodded.

Today the family structure is disintegrating. Divorce is rampant. This very week I got a letter from a teenager who had seen her parents split up; she was now being required to show allegiance to her "new" family. "But just who is my family?" she inquired. "I'm so confused. Is it my father and the woman he is living with or my mother and her boyfriend? Or is it my grandmother with whom my little sister and I are living at the moment?"

I couldn't help her sort the mess out, but I could remind her that she belonged to a more secure family structure whose Head she could call Father and whose family members were her new sisters and brothers in Christ.

If you are a Christian, you need never ask, "Who is my family?" You'll know!

GROUNDED IN LOVE

And I pray that Christ will be more and more at home in your hearts as you trust in him. May your roots go down deep into the soil of God's marvelous love.

EPHESIANS 3:17

Paul prayed that the Ephesian Christians would be strengthened internally. He prayed for power in their inner spirit. He asked God that Christ would so settle down in their hearts and lives that their hearts and lives would be settled down. He begged God that the young believers would put their roots downward and bear fruit upwards. He wanted the church to be grounded in love, for to be established in love *is* the Christian life.

Jesus said that there is not much merit in merely loving those who love you—even sinners do that (see Luke 6:32)! But when you begin to love people who don't love you and even get around to loving your enemies, then you are becoming established in love.

This love requires renewal in the inner spirit. If the inner spirit is starved, the outer person will show it. If we ourselves are malnourished, we will be lethargic, self-absorbed, and disinterested in anyone else's misfortunes. But as we make Christ at home in our heart, he will constantly shed abroad his love, supplying us with the ability to love the "whole family" in heaven and on earth (Ephesians 3:15).

If only Paul hadn't said that! If he had said that we were *part* of a family, or that there were a couple of family members he would like us to try to get along with . . . but he didn't. He reminds us that we are part of the "whole family," a family that needs loving and that is going to take a whole lot more love than just mine. It's going to take Christ in the inner spirit—in all of us!

Bent Knees, Wet Eyes, and a Broken Heart

May you experience the love of Christ, though it is so great you will never fully understand it. Then you will be filled with the fullness of life and power that comes from God.

EPHESIANS 3:19

"What equipment do I need if I am going to serve the Lord, sir?" a young missionary recruit asked a veteran Christian. The old saint quickly replied, "Bent knees, wet eyes, and a broken heart!"

The bent knees were mentioned first. The hardest thing for a missionary to do is to remember to bend them, because there are so many holy and good substitutes! There is the sweet fellowship with other great missionaries. There is the edification of fellow national believers. There is the corporate time of prayer that the staff enjoys each day. There are family devotions around the breakfast table with the children. But the bent knees that lead to the wet eyes that result from a broken heart come from the isolation of the soul.

The most important transactions take place alone—absolutely alone! That is the time when you are able to comprehend, to really grasp what is the breadth and length and depth and height of the love of Christ.

One day Jesus looked out on a needy multitude and was moved with compassion (see Matthew 14:14, KJV). The word *moved* could well be translated "convulsed." That deep, deep love came from Christ's time spent alone with his Father—with bent knees, wet eyes, and a broken heart!

Missionaries, of course, are not the only ones who need to practice bent knees! If a missionary is "an ordinary person called to do extraordinary things with very little help," then that includes all of us!

Our Vocations

Therefore I . . . beg you to lead a life worthy of your calling, for you have been called by God.

EPHESIANS 4:1

When it was time for me to leave high school and go to college, the "vocational" teacher interviewed me to see if I had any idea of what I wanted to do with my life. "What vocation do you have in mind?" she asked me sternly. I went to a school that expected its graduates to pursue a vocation—no, not vacation—vocation! The idea of simply leaving to "get a job" was unthinkable. Since the vocational opportunities for girls in my day were somewhat limited to the teaching and nursing fields, I hastily said "teaching," though, to be honest, the thought had never occurred to me till then! I had been taught that those privileged with higher knowledge are called to higher vocations! Certain behavior was expected of us—a worthy walk anticipated. I was left with no doubt that I had an obligation to live in a manner that would not besmirch the name of my school.

It is even more important for Christians who have "learned" Christ to live in a manner that does not besmirch the name of their Savior. This manner of living is described as a "walk." It's not a leap of faith, not one giant stride, but, to quote my husband, "one simple, practical step after another. Certainly, as in ordinary walks, some steps will be greater than others, a few will be harder than others, and some will lead to higher ground than others, but the spiritual life is a walk."

Are we living a life worthy of our calling in Christ?

Making Allowances

> **Be humble and gentle. Be patient with each other, making allowance for each other's faults because of your love.**
>
> EPHESIANS 4:2

Are you good at making allowances for people? Or do you have ridiculously high expectations?

Our lives should say, "I make allowances for people," for this is the language of love. Forbearance is a divine quality. Romans 2:4 talks of the kindness, tolerance, and patience of God. His followers should do no less. We ought to willingly make allowances for one another *because* we love one another. This means I should hold back my quick judgment and should not evaluate or dissect people's motives.

What a challenge to walk through life like this! Are we making allowances for our teenagers, for example? I remember Pete, our youngest, growing daily right out of his socks—at fourteen years of age he was six feet four inches tall. Quite an achievement over such a small amount of time! But I didn't make allowances for his grand accomplishments! His schoolwork zeroed; around the house he was lazy and undisciplined; he couldn't be bothered even to pretend he wanted to go to church anymore! "No wonder," laughed the wise counselor I resorted to in deep distress. "He's put everything he's got into blood and bones and height!" I got the point and made allowances.

Bishop H. C. G. Moule has said that forbearance is "allowing for each other's frailties and mistakes; aye, when they turn and wound you 'in love,' finding it easy to see with their eyes and if need be to take sides with them against yourselves!" That's making allowances!

True Humility

> **Be humble and gentle. Be patient with each other, making allowance for each other's faults because of your love.**
>
> EPHESIANS 4:2

Do you have a humble estimation of yourself? Do you conduct yourself with perfect "modesty and gentleness" (Moffatt)? Do you accept life with "humility and patience" (Phillips)? To the Greeks, humility was not a virtue. The Greek word for *humble* denotes "slavish, mean, ignoble." It was only when Christ came that lowliness became a virtue. Christ's life and death were service and sacrifice without thought of reputation (see Philippians 2:6-11).

Saul was chosen to be king of Israel partly because of his humble attitude. "But I'm only from Benjamin, the *smallest* tribe in Israel, and my family is the *least important* of all the families of that tribe! Why are you talking like this to me?" (1 Samuel 9:21, italics mine), Saul said to Samuel the prophet. It was pride that later caused his downfall. Samuel rebuked him with these words: "Although you may think little of yourself, are you not the leader of the tribes of Israel? The Lord has anointed you king of Israel" (1 Samuel 15:17). Paul, also of the tribe of Benjamin (Romans 11:1), had many natural reasons to be proud, but said, "I am what I am because of the grace of God!"

Humility is an unreserved, simple-hearted submission under trial. It denotes "the enduring, unwearable spirit which knows how to outlast pain or provocation, a strength learned only at the Redeemer's feet. It is the noble opposite to the short temper which soon gives way and whose outbursts are only sinful weakness under the thinnest mask" (Moule). Paul tells us to be humble, gentle, and patient with one another. How do you treat your fellow believers—even those who disagree or frustrate you? Do you gently and patiently correct them? How humble are you?

Before It Falls Apart

Always keep yourselves united in the Holy Spirit, and bind yourselves together with peace.

EPHESIANS 4:3

Do you make every effort to maintain the unity that already exists between Christians? We are exhorted to make that our goal.

My sister, who has been a valuable model to me in maintaining excellent personal relationships, said one day, "I refuse to have a row with that girl—life's too short to fall out with anyone." We can refuse to have a row if we want to. That is making an effort to keep what we already have—unity. The problem is that if we have unity among ourselves, we sometimes ignore or neglect it. We start to work on it only when a relationship falls apart! But we must get to work *before* it falls apart. We must endeavor to maintain it. We do that by building an already good relationship into something even better. That takes time and effort.

We have good relationships with our church staff, but they can always be better. We schedule regular times to eat, to have fun, and to pray together. It's such a comfort and delight to meet with people on the same spiritual level as ourselves and enjoy a time of maintaining our unity!

I have a friend who often spends time with me—playing tennis, talking, shopping, or just relaxing—and she never fails to say before she leaves, "Let's pray together." It's just a brief glance heavenward, but what a bond of peace it adds to our relationship!

What practical things are you doing to maintain the unity of the Spirit?

Majoring on Majors

There is only one Lord, one faith, one baptism.

EPHESIANS 4:5

The basis for the unity that we have with other believers is set out for us in Ephesians 4:4-6. The little word *one* appears often. There is *one* body, and Christ is the head. A body is an earthly vehicle whereby a spiritual being gets around in a physical environment. We are to be vehicles for his actions. We are *one* in the Spirit, for we have access by one Spirit to the Father. All who have the Spirit have one common hope—that one day we shall be like him.

A friend was complaining about a fellow church member. I told her to imagine what the lady would be like without Jesus—and "one day in heaven she *will* be like him!" I added. That helped!

We have *one* Lord, too. When David gathered his band of distressed and discontented men around him in the cave of Adullam, he became captain over them. Those men saw each other, not so much as potential threats, competitors, or enemies, but as comrades in arms united by their leader (see 1 Samuel 22:2).

We have *one* faith, sharing the same vital truths concerning the Lord, his work, and purpose. We share *one* baptism, for we are all baptized into the body of Christ (see Galatians 3:27). All believers see baptism as a rite of identification with the Lord Jesus. It should be a unifying factor, for in every baptism there is a statement of relationship to the risen Lord.

Lastly, we have *one* God and Father of all. If we can keep in mind the many things we agree upon, we will maintain the unity of the Spirit through the bond of peace.

The Loveliest Symphony of All

However, he has given each one of us a special gift according to the generosity of Christ. That is why the Scriptures say, "When he ascended to the heights, he led a crowd of captives and gave gifts to his people."

EPHESIANS 4:7-8

Did you know you have a spiritual gift that was given to you for the church's benefit? My husband was asked to visit a family who was thinking of joining our church. "Pastor Briscoe," began the father, "what does your church have to offer my family?"

"What does your family have to offer to my church?" replied my husband. He explained that the policy of our fellowship is to help people discover their spiritual abilities and exercise them for the good of the whole.

Paul explains that persons are gifts (see Ephesians 4:11). There have been apostles who had a distinctive position, prophets with inspired utterance, evangelists with the ability to spread the Good News, pastors and teachers to shepherd the flock under Christ. All these people are there to teach the believers to do the work of ministry (see Ephesians 4:12). The greatest mistake people can make is to think of church as a spectator sport.

Paul also writes that gifts are given to *all* Christians. Each one of us has a special gift (see Ephesians 4:7). Each gift is different, and there is a diversity as subtle and beautiful as the spots on a leopard, snowflakes on the grass, grains of sand on the seashore. Each personality with its matching gifts is unique, but, like a note in a chord of music, or an instrument in an orchestra, it is intended to blend with others so that the message of salvation becomes the loveliest symphony of all.

Easy Prey

> **With the Lord's authority let me say this: Live no longer as the ungodly do, for they are hopelessly confused.**
>
> EPHESIANS 4:17

A warning is necessary if you are a new Christian living among old pagans. Your lifestyle has to be different! How do the pagan nations live? People wander in a world of illusion and futility (see Ephesians 4:18). Love has become lust, and their darkened understanding says that what is temporal is eternal, and what is eternal is irrelevant. Spiritual experience is not for people living in the real world, they say!

This worldly thinking is the result of calloused hearts (see Ephesians 4:18). People sin and get away with it, then stick out their chins and say, "See, the sky didn't fall on my head!" They are greedy, wanting more of everything even though they have most everything. They indulge in outrageous conduct, living without care for high personal standards or social sanctions, and they have a passion for sexual indulgence at the expense of others. This is how the nations without Christ walk about this earth. They become so indifferent, even to the sanctity of human life, that they reduce everything to the mighty dollar.

The story is told of a man's watching another man drown in Hong Kong harbor. The drowning man begged the observer to jump in and save him, but the man refused until a passerby offered him some money! Not every unbeliever behaves in such a callous way, but every unbeliever, with no mighty checking power within, has the potential for all of the above. Alone against the foe, the Christless one is easy prey.

IMITATORS

Follow God's example in everything you do, because you are his dear children.

EPHESIANS 5:1

Our son Pete wanted a bird! His sister had left for college, and he was feeling lonely. Without giving the matter much thought, I bought him a cockatiel. When Pete emerged bleeding from the bathroom after the first and last training session with his new-found friend, "Cornbread" (we found out later he should have been called "Cornelia") was relegated to a life within the walls of the cage in Pete's room. "Talk to him, Pete," I urged my son over the next few weeks; but the novelty of the pet wore off and my urging was to no avail. We donated Cornbread to a friend (now an enemy!) and told her, "Don't worry when you hear deep breathing in the middle of the night!" The poor bird had heard nothing more than Pete's deep, slumbering sighs, and so had imitated them! Have you ever heard a cockatiel deep-breathe? It's eerie.

But all of us learn by imitation, by following others' examples. Paul said, "Follow my example, just as I follow Christ's" (1 Corinthians 11:1). We are to watch carefully, listen acutely, and pick up every inflection of our Master's voice!

Would we want people following our example? The very fact that we are being watched should force us to deal with our erratic behavior and not cause others to stumble. Jesus had some hard words about people who cause others to fall. He said it would be better if stones were tied around their necks and they were cast to the bottom of the sea (see Luke 17:2)!

Buying Time

Make the most of every opportunity for doing good in these evil days.

EPHESIANS 5:16

We must buy up the opportunities we have before the night comes.

This is the day of opportunity. Our church took a survey of two thousand women in our community to find out what they were thinking and how our women's ministry could best meet their needs. Out of all of those interviewed, only a handful of women were hostile or refused to talk with us. We need to buy up these opportunities.

Colossians 4:5 tells us to "live wisely among those who are not Christians, and make the most of every opportunity." Paul goes on to explain that in this wise walk, our speech must be salty (there will be a tang to it) so that we may know how to answer every person. Making the most of every opportunity means cultivating the "know-how" of argument and debate. Making the most of every opportunity means that by our very lifestyle, we will engender some questions from others.

Once in a train full of rowdy, drunken football fans, a young Christian was sitting quietly, reading. An old gentleman, observing first the drunks and then the young man, said to him, "You seem to have found the secret to life—do you want to share it?" Our young friend lost no time "making the most of the opportunity"!

We must ask God for a great sense of urgency so that we can make the most of every opportunity to serve and share him.

MISCONCEPTIONS

And I will ask the Father, and he will give you another Counselor, who will never leave you.

JOHN 14:16

Before I came to the United States, I thought sidewalks were pavements, cookies were biscuits. Hoods and trunks of cars were bonnets and boots, and "showers" belonged in the bathroom—all misconceptions!

Before I came to Christ, I thought God lived in a church-shaped box and was very old with a very bad memory. Misconceptions!

Before I read my Bible, I thought the Holy Ghost was a sheet-shrouded spook that haunted old English houses, a theme for conferences, or a subject for argument. Misconceptions!

I learned from the Scriptures that the Holy Spirit is not an ecstatic feeling, an "it," a happening, or a packet of dynamite that I decide what to do with. I discovered he is a divine Person, and he will decide what to do with me! The Trinity is a revealed doctrine, and the fact that God is three persons is not a fact that people discovered, but that God revealed. We need to accept this truth by faith, even though we cannot fully understand it.

Jesus taught that there was a distinction between the three persons in the Godhead: There was the Father, the Son, and a person called "the Counselor"—the Holy Spirit. When the disciples were sad because the Lord had just told them he was going to leave them, he promised he would send "the Counselor" so that they would never be alone again.

I used to think I could be a Christian without the indwelling Holy Spirit. I discovered that that was the greatest misconception of all!

Cheeky Charlie

He is the Holy Spirit, who leads into all truth. The world at large cannot receive him, because it isn't looking for him and doesn't recognize him. But you do, because he lives with you now and later will be in you.

JOHN 14:17

Did you know the Holy Spirit can live in you? When Jesus told the disciples this, they couldn't grasp what Jesus meant; and sometimes it's hard for us to understand, too.

I remember listening to a street preacher trying to explain how Jesus could come and live inside the heart through the Holy Spirit. A man in the crowd, called Cheeky Charlie, a professional heckler of open-air speakers, shouted out, "Nonsense! How can Jesus come and live in your heart? Why, I've just passed a butcher's shop and seen a heart hanging in the window—it's nothing but a blood pump!" The preacher, well used to Cheeky Charlie's interruptions, asked him if he ever went "courting," and if he ever looked deep into his sweetheart's eyes and said, "Darling, I love you with all my blood pump"? Charlie got the point.

The word *heart* is used as a figurative expression for the seat of the mind, will, and emotions—the deepest part of our being. God, through the Holy Spirit, wants to invade that region and live there! This is what makes a person a true Christian.

Jesus described the experience of the infilling of the Holy Spirit both as a well and as rivers of water. The Holy Spirit will be in you a perpetual spring, he said (see John 4:14), and out of your innermost being will "flow rivers of living water" (see John 7:38, KJV). Doesn't that sound like a refreshing experience? Do you want to know how the Holy Spirit comes to live in you? You simply have to ask him. Invite him to come into your life. He will. Jesus promised he would.

Grieving God

You weren't lying to us but to God.

ACTS 5:4

"What can God do for me?" inquired a divorced woman. "I am a Christian, but I'm lonely and bitter and all my friends have turned away from me." I began to work with her on studying the Bible and learning about the Holy Spirit who had come to be her Companion and Helper. At the end of our time together she said, "I started off asking what he could do for me—but I've found out what I've been doing to him!" She had learned that we can grieve, quench, and resist the Holy Spirit. We can even lie to him!

There was a married couple in the early church who tried to do that. Their names were Ananias and Sapphira. They sold a piece of property for the church and, keeping back part of the price for themselves, brought the rest of the money and laid it at the apostles' feet, saying they had brought it all! Both died as a result of their deception (see Acts 5:1-10).

Did you know you can grieve, quench, and resist the Holy Spirit? Have you ever told him a lie? Have you ever said, "Lord, I give you my life"—and then kept back part of it; or "Lord, I give you my money"—and kept back part; or "Lord, I give you my heart"—and again kept back part to love a person you knew he would not have you involved with?

When people say they would like to go back to the days of the early church, I wonder if they take into account God's drastic dealings with his people. Grieving God is a grievous thing!

Like a Cup under a Faucet

Don't be drunk with wine, because that will ruin your life. Instead, let the Holy Spirit fill and control you.

EPHESIANS 5:18

"Have you ever been drunk?" a man asked me. I confessed I had not. "I have," he said. "Everything was affected. My eyesight, my balance, and my judgment!"

Interestingly, Paul uses drunkenness to teach us about the fullness of the Spirit. Don't be controlled by drink, but be controlled by the Spirit, he says. Let the Holy Spirit affect the way you look at things and the way you walk. Being filled with the Spirit will be a happy experience. God will not make us miserable if we let him rule us. Our hearts will be singing all day long, and in fact, we will be able to thank God always for all things! (See Ephesians 5:19-20.)

Paul doesn't say to have *some* of the Spirit for *some* things. Christianity is a religion of "alls." It's an "all or nothing" faith in an all-sufficient God. The Holy Spirit is to "fill and control" us. Once the Holy Spirit fills us and gains control, he can enable us to do what he tells us to do!

Like a cup under a faucet, our lives must be held under God's Spirit. If we grieve or pull back or lie to him, confession will be necessary or we shall lose the fullness. Notice I didn't say lose the *Spirit*—but the fullness. Once the Holy Spirit comes into our heart as resident and not as renter, he comes to stay! (See Matthew 28:20.) It is up to us to make him as comfortable as possible in our life.

I Think of It As Loving

You wives will submit to your husbands as you do to the Lord.

EPHESIANS 5:22

If I want to know how and why I should submit to my husband, I need to ask myself how and why I submit to the Lord. How do I submit to the Lord? Joyfully! I love Jesus. He walked into my young life, looked around, and knew he was welcome to stay. He comforted me when I was sick, kidded me when I took myself too seriously, encouraged me when I was depressed, provoked me when I was lazy. We ran together through my twenties, and when I had my babies, he laughed his eternal laugh of joy. He knew how I felt as no one else could, for he knows the mystery of creation.

Why do I submit to the Lord? Because he is my life, my breath, my castle, my rock, the foundation of all I believe, the source of all meaning. He keeps me sane; he's grown me up to middle life, and he tells me I'm just the right age! He doesn't let me baby myself, although he's a good friend, an ally, a teacher, a counselor—he's wonderful!

Do you think I have to be beaten into submission to respond to Jesus? Not me! So when I come across a verse like, "You wives will submit to your husbands as you do to the Lord," it's easy to obey! What joy to respond to Stuart even as I do to my Lord! I can hardly think of doing anything else. It's as natural as breathing. You see, I love him—almost as much as I love Jesus. I don't think of it as submission because it's all joy! I think of it as loving!

"Not I!" Said I!

> **No one hates his own body but lovingly cares for it, just as Christ cares for his body, which is the church.**
>
> EPHESIANS 5:29

What should your husband do for you? Nourish and cherish you—just as the Lord does his church. What does that mean? It means your husband will help you not to lose your identity. He'll want you to be the unique person that God made you to be, and he'll want you to discover and develop your talents and gifts. That's what the Lord does for his bride, the church. As your mate is helping you grow to your full potential, he'll be cherishing you, too. That word means "to protect," as a hen does her chicks. I thank God for a husband who does these two important things for me.

Stuart has insisted I be myself. He saw abilities in me I never dreamed existed and made it possible for me to hone and use them. "You can speak," he said. "Not I!" said I! "Yes, you can—take ten minutes at my meeting tonight," he insisted. I found out he was right. "You can write," he said. "Not I!" said I! "Try doing what the publisher believes you can do," he said. Again, he was right! Now time has come for Stuart to cherish me—to help me not to overload. "Enough's enough," he says when book contracts pile up. "I need my shirts washed," he teases. Then he helps me to determine my priorities.

Do you feel frustrated and think your husband doesn't understand you? Talk to him about it. The Lord loves for his bride to talk to him about her gifts. According to Ephesians 5:29, your husband should be delighted, too!

Pleasant Places

The land you have given me is a pleasant land. What a wonderful inheritance!

PSALM 16:6

The Bible tells us that when the children of Israel entered the Promised Land, Joshua, Eleazar, the priest, and the heads of the tribes divided the land for inheritance by their borders (see Joshua 19:49). The "land" in our text had definite boundaries so that each tribe knew its own property. David, thinking about this, was able to look at his life and say, "The land you have given me is a pleasant land."

I once found myself raising my voice in praise to God for exactly the same reason. I thanked God for the "pleasant land" of our home, our marriage, and our relationship with our grown children. I praised him for our ministry and for our friendships. I thought about the pleasant place around our dining table and our bank balance with enough money to buy clothes and necessities. Like King David, I could truly say, "Yes, the land you have given me is a pleasant land!" (Psalm 16:6).

Then another thought came to mind, engendering petition. This time it was a warning.

> For the Lord your God is bringing you into a good land. . . . When you have eaten your fill . . . beware that in your plenty you do not forget the Lord your God. . . . That is the time to be careful. Do not become proud at that time and forget the Lord your God. . . . He did it so you would never think that it was your own strength and energy that made you wealthy. (Deuteronomy 8:7-18)

It was quite simple, really; I had been reminded, not to make my pleasant land my god, but to worship the God who graciously gave me my pleasant land!

The Helper

But when the Father sends the Counselor as my representative—and by the Counselor I mean the Holy Spirit—he will teach you everything and will remind you of everything I myself have told you.

JOHN 14:26

Is your memory a thing you forget with? Are you good at remembering birthdays, wedding anniversaries, the names of your in-laws' family? How about Scripture? Are you good at memorizing verses from the Bible? We are told to hide God's Word in our heart, and it will "check" us when we think of sinning (see Psalm 119:11). Jesus promised his disciples that he would send the Holy Spirit into their hearts to help them remember his words. That promise was for all disciples in all ages—people like you and me!

But even the Holy Spirit can't help us remember what we've never taken the trouble to learn! Some people seem to think the Holy Spirit is a magic wand standing in the corner of our mind. When we are too lazy to learn something, we somehow expect him to cheat for us by whispering the right answer in our ear. But he won't do that. He never said he would. Our Lord said the Holy Spirit would be sent to teach us all things and would then help us to remember what had been taught.

Now I don't know about you, but my memory needs help. It stands to reason that I might need heavenly help when it comes to heavenly things. But I must learn the spiritual concepts, do the studying, and work at the memorizing. Only then will my heavenly Helper aid in the recall of all that hidden treasure of wisdom in the vault of my heart.

No One Ever Gets Lost

"No, we don't know, Lord," Thomas said. "We haven't any idea where you are going, so how can we know the way?" Jesus told him, "I am the way, the truth, and the life. No one can come to the Father except through me."

JOHN 14:5-6

"Nobody ever gets lost," Stuart assured me. I was about to set off on a complicated journey and was trying to figure out the airplane schedule. How would I know which plane to get on when I arrived at the large airport? I'd been to that particular terminal once before and remembered the disembodied voices talking to me through the loudspeaker! No people, just voices—it was eerie! I had found myself asking the unseen airport voice a question—but received nothing but the taped staccato warning to step away from the doors!

"Have you ever heard of anyone who didn't eventually arrive at his destination?" Stuart continued patiently. "Well, no." I had to admit I hadn't. Delayed, perhaps, bumped a time or two, even hijacked—but apart from crashing, people always got there in the end!

Jesus said that he was "the way." I can hear his voice, just like the voices in the airport, saying, "This is the way; walk you in it."

But the difference between airports and the Christian life is considerable. The unseen voice of Jesus will talk back to me if I am confused, and even though he may allow me to be delayed or rerouted a time or two, he promises to get me to my final destination. Even if I crash, I will just get where I am going a whole lot sooner—that's all.

Nobody who knows Christ ever gets lost—he *is* the way!

YES, HE DID—NO, HE DIDN'T

As a result, I can really know Christ.

PHILIPPIANS 3:10

Didn't Paul already know Christ? Well, as Campbell Morgan puts it, "Yes, he did—no, he didn't!" Didn't Columbus discover America? Yes, he did—no, he didn't! We are still discovering America! That's how it is when we meet Christ. We are introduced to him, and then the lifelong relationship begins. Just as the full discovery of America was left to people who would press on to explore the land, so the full realization of God will take investigation on our part.

But just how do we get to know him? We first discover him in the Old Testament. Jesus said, "The Scriptures point to me" (John 5:39). Then we develop close fellowship with Jesus through the Gospels. We see the pen portrait of him in Matthew, Mark, Luke, and John and look hard till the Lord Jesus lives in those portraits and can step out of the book into our conscience.

Campbell Morgan wanted to get to know his Lord and Savior Jesus Christ better, and so he spent three years following him through the Gospels. "After that time," he said, "I got such a vision of the splendor of my Master that I've never been the same since."

When we've read of him in the Old Testament, followed him through the Gospels, and seen him as he is in the book of Revelation, then we will know the Lord! How long has it been since you were introduced to Jesus Christ? Do you really know him? Would you have to answer: "Yes, I do—no, I don't"?

Double-Dyed

"Come now, let us argue this out," says the Lord. "No matter how deep the stain of your sins, I can remove it. I can make you as clean as freshly fallen snow."

ISAIAH 1:18

Isaiah was a great prophet. His messages brought comfort to the few among God's people who were true believers. He constantly reminded them of the "covenant of grace." At the same time, he brought a message of severe warning to those who refused to listen to the doctrine of life. When the Lord called his rebellious people to "argue this out," he did not call them to debate, but rather to agree with his verdict. He wanted them to acknowledge that their actions had not been in accordance with reason.

All sin is unreasonable. The people's sin is described as a deep stain (other versions say "scarlet," a red stain that we know is difficult to remove). This contrasts to the stark whiteness of snow. When yarns were dyed scarlet (or crimson) in biblical times, the process required two baths or double-dyeing. When Christ forgave my sin, I was very conscious that grace invited not a dialogue but a reasonable confession of the "double-dyed" mess I had made of my life. God wanted me to agree with his verdict and submit to his decision concerning my sin. I felt like a small sheep whose wool had been dyed crimson by wrongdoing, and I was pretty red-faced about it all.

What joy to enter the "covenant of grace" and experience the whiteness of the soul that coming to God brings! Have you come to the point of accepting God's verdict of your life, or are you still arguing your case?

Wild Grapes

> **Why did my vineyard give me wild grapes when I expected sweet ones?**
>
> ISAIAH 5:4

In Israel, great events were usually described in poetic form that they might be more easily remembered and repeated by everyone, and so that a lasting record of them might thus be preserved. Isaiah composed a poem about a vineyard on behalf of God. It is a love song, a lament of unrequited love. The nation of Israel is likened to a vineyard—a metaphor frequently used by the prophets. Few possessions were dearer to a man in that culture than his vineyard. None demanded more care and persevering toil. The song reminded God's people of the love and benefits bestowed upon them. There was the favorable situation of the "rich and fertile hill" (Isaiah 5:1). There was the watchtower for protection. The tower had a place in the base for the gardener to live at harvesttime, and the top served as a lookout for enemies who would spoil the fruit. Yet in spite of all this, the vineyard produced wild grapes. "What more could I have done?" God asked.

Our lives are like a vineyard. Those of us who live in the Western world have been hedged about; we live in the most fruitful of hills. What is more, we have a place within our personalities that is like the tower in the vineyard. God can come within that place and abide. He rightly expects sweet fruit from our lives, so why do we produce wild grapes?

Do you have an acid spirit? Why do you imagine the Gardener came into your life? To attend to your whims and caprices, or to prune your life for spiritual fruitfulness? When God asks, "Why the wild grapes?" he expects an answer. Let's be certain it's a good one!

FRESH FRUIT

And planted it with choice vines.

ISAIAH 5:2

After fencing his vineyard, God did everything necessary to ensure good fruit, including planting the fertile soil with "choice vines." The word *sorek,* used to describe the plant, is the name of an especially fruitful species. The rest of the world had not been cultivated by divine revelation. Only Israel received the pure religion, the excellent law. Ordinances that would help the Israelites keep up their acquaintance with God had been carefully and prayerfully instituted. But God's chosen ones became a wild vine, and because Israel would not listen to reason, the Lord tore down the fences, rained no rain upon them, and let the land be destroyed. But God also promised that he would preserve the few who believed and that from the stock would come the very choicest of vines—Jesus Christ. Our Savior used this vineyard metaphor in the Gospels, saying, "I am the true vine, and my Father is the gardener" (John 15:1).

Did you realize you have been planted with the choicest vine? His Father is your Father and mine—the gardener. The fruits of his Spirit—"love, joy, peace, patience, kindness, goodness, faithfulness, gentleness, and self-control" (Galatians 5:22-23)—will grow within us. When the branch abides quietly in the vine, it is pruned into usefulness and nourished by faith. Fruit hangs on the outside of the tree—displaying the tree's nature, enhancing the tree's beauty, and refreshing those who partake of it.

When we are inwardly submissive, we are outwardly obedient—and a hungry world is glad!

Worship

In a great chorus they sang, "Holy, holy, holy is the Lord Almighty! The whole earth is filled with his glory!" The glorious singing shook the Temple to its foundations, and the entire sanctuary was filled with smoke.

ISAIAH 6:3-4

The temple shook at the voice of him who cried. I used to think that this verse referred to God, but then I realized the text reveals it is the voice of the angel that shakes heaven. If such a tumult occurs at the voice of an angel, whatever will happen when God himself speaks?

We take the privilege of worship far too lightly. We get too chummy with God, or try to bring him down to our level. A friend he is—but an almighty friend, a holy friend. As we come to understand his ineffable nature, we shall be saved from irreverent attitudes in prayer. And yet he encourages us to "come boldly to the throne of our gracious God. There we will receive his mercy, and we will find grace to help us when we need it" (Hebrews 4:16). It is because Jesus our advocate is at the right hand of God that we dare to come boldly before his throne.

When God's angels acknowledged God's person and attributed worth to him, "the entire sanctuary was filled with smoke." This undoubtedly refers to the *shekinah* glory—the presence of God made manifest. So when you and I attribute worth to God in worship, heaven is moved and God will show himself—if not to the world, certainly to the worshiper. The awesome reality of God may cause us fear, as it did Isaiah, but it hopefully will lead us to submission and a deep desire to serve our lost world.

Lips of Truth

Then one of the seraphim flew over to the altar, and he picked up a burning coal with a pair of tongs. He touched my lips with it and said, "See, this coal has touched your lips. Now your guilt is removed, and your sins are forgiven."

ISAIAH 6:6-7

When we have a vision of him, we get a true look at ourselves. "My destruction is sealed!" we say. Seeing him looking at me makes me aware of the blemishes in my character. When I see the Lord, I see the world, too. I stop saying, "Here am I, send somebody else," and I start saying, "Lord, I'll go! Send me." He then equips me by cleansing me for service and giving me "hot lips." What I say will burn its way into people's thoughts and bring them to the point of deciding for or against God.

"But whom do I talk to?" you may ask. "How am I expected to know who needs God's message?" God told Isaiah what to tell "these people." "These people" were the same people Isaiah had been preaching to for a long, long time. He had been getting discouraged because they hadn't responded, but God sent his prophet right back to tell them all over again. What was more, the Lord told Isaiah that they still wouldn't listen! But that was not to be his concern.

How do you keep going when all your effort seems futile? You'll need time to get a fresh vision of God—which will give you a fresh vision of yourself, a new look at your world, and a new concern in your heart. Then you'll be able to go back to rebellious people and see a difference—not in them, perhaps, but certainly in you! You'll find you have the capacity to be faithful without having to see the results.

A Remnant

And he said, "Yes, go. But tell my people . . ."

ISAIAH 6:9

Can't you just hear Isaiah groaning, "O Lord, not *those* people?" Have you ever had a similar experience? I have. I can remember telling God just where to send me. I wanted to work with teenagers. They had caught my attention and captured my heart, and I kept saying to the Lord, "I'll go! Send me!"

"Go and tell *these* people," the Lord replied, drawing my attention to some very old ladies who were my neighbors. They were all over seventy years of age, one was crippled, one blind, and one deaf! I obediently, though grudgingly, complied, inviting them to a Bible study. Only the deaf one responded. Sitting in my little living room and screaming into her ear was a far cry from youth evangelism. I comforted myself with the thought that God promised Isaiah there would be a remnant that would respond! Even as I had that thought, the remnant was sitting looking at me! This deaf lady accepted Jesus and went to be with him shortly afterward!

I suddenly realized the necessity of reaching the aged; they don't have as much time as the young! It is hard going, as older people tend to be adamant where change is concerned, and accepting Christ means change. When they have always done something one way, another way seems impossible. But he who said he was "the way" showed these ladies "the truth" and gave them his "life," and "these people" became *my* people! What joy!

When God says go and tell "these people," don't argue—go! You'll find that a remnant will respond.

Light at the End of the Tunnel

The people who walk in darkness will see a great light.

ISAIAH 9:2

Are you in need of a glimmer of light at the end of the tunnel? Isaiah promises that even in darkness, even in death itself, there is good ground for hope, for the power of God is able to restore life to his people even when they appear to be already dead!

Have you given up seeing light brought to bear in a "dark" church situation? Are there factions splitting people apart from each other into dark debates and despondency? There's a great light shining! There's a great light because a great Savior came. "The people who walk in darkness will see a great light." What people? This prediction was fulfilled when Christ preached along the Galilean seacoast (see Matthew 4:16); the light brought promise of deliverance for Israel. A new day had come!

The Savior is a great source of comfort to us, too. Many live in the darkness of divorce or in the shadow of death. Some watch a loved one slowly disintegrate before their eyes. Others, in seemingly "perfect" circumstances, live in the deepest darkness of all—depression that nothing seems to penetrate! Listen to the Good News! There's a light at the end of the tunnel—look up and see Jesus standing there! Hear what he says: "I am the light of the world. If you follow me, you won't be stumbling through the darkness, because you will have the light that leads to life" (John 8:12).

The Key to Blessing

And the government will rest on his shoulders.

ISAIAH 9:6

The image in this verse reflects the custom of carrying long, heavy, frequently used keys over the shoulder. The symbolism is extensive. The very act says "authority"! The priest who exercised such authority had command of the royal chambers and a right to admit or refuse people to the royal presence. Referring to Eliakim, high priest of Israel, Isaiah says, "I will give him the key to the house of David—the highest position in the royal court. He will open doors, and no one will be able to shut them; he will close doors, and no one will be able to open them" (Isaiah 22:22). John, in Revelation 3:7, describes the risen, ascended, glorified Lord Jesus as our High Priest: "He is the one who has the key of David. He opens doors, and no one can shut them; he shuts doors, and no one can open them."

God invested all priestly authority in Jesus Christ, his Son. It is Jesus who has the keys! The government is upon his shoulders!

And what does all this mean to you and me? It means Jesus Christ has command of God's royal chambers—and the right to admit us into God's presence. That is why Hebrews 4:16 says, "So let us come boldly to the throne of our gracious God. There we will receive his mercy, and we will find grace to help us when we need it."

The Scriptures say we have a high priest (see Hebrews 4:14). You can know you have such a high priest if he "has" you! Has he forgiven your sin? If not, he has the right to refuse your entrance to the King's chambers; but if so, then you can be assured that when you draw near to the throne, there will be grace to help.

Go to God

> **These will be his royal titles: Wonderful Counselor . . .**
>
> ISAIAH 9:6

Our Lord Jesus Christ is called a Wonderful Counselor. In Christ are hidden invaluable treasures (see Colossians 2:3). Christ is called Wonderful because he has inconceivable methods of assisting us! He is a wonder of a counselor! The counsel he gives will be above the counsel of ordinary people. It will be the counsel of Yahweh, because he is Yahweh. Isaiah 28:29 tells us "the Lord Almighty is a wonderful teacher." The child who shall be called such wonderful names will give exceptional counsel to a confused world, said Isaiah. "We have never heard anyone talk like this!" echoed an astonished multitude in the Messiah's day (John 7:46).

We have to learn to get our counsel from God. "Oh, the joys of those who do not follow the advice of the wicked," says the psalmist (Psalm 1:1). Before we telephone in despair to a friend, spill our physical and emotional pain in the doctor's office, or shout our problem from the housetops in the frantic hope that help will appear, we need to go to God! Are you worried? Go to God! Depressed, sick, frightened? Go to God. Are you dejected? Go to God. My friend who helped me to find my faith did the best thing for me; she taught me to look to God for counsel. She herself was so knowledgeable that it was hard for me to look elsewhere. But she was wise enough to teach me that she was not as wise as my wonderful counselor.

A young pastor's wife wrote a troubled letter to her mother, who was also a pastor's wife. Her mother withheld her reply. "She knows where to go," she said. "Jesus is a wise counselor—he will be able to help her far better than I." Wise words!

The Mighty Model

These will be his royal titles: . . . Mighty God . . .

ISAIAH 9:6

All of us need a hero. The modern term for hero is *model*. Isaiah told us that the child to be born would be called the Mighty God—a hero of a God, strong and powerful. This tells us we have a God we can rely upon with assurance. He is so mighty that he has defeated both the devil and death. We know that the last enemy is death; it would catch us all, but God has been pleased to battle on our behalf and has swallowed up death in victory. When Jesus died, death swallowed him up for a while, but when he rose again, he swallowed up death once and for all (see 1 Corinthians 15:54)!

He is my hero and my mighty model, and I must learn to draw my strength from him!

He giveth more grace when the burdens grow greater,
He sendeth more strength when the labors increase.
To added affliction He addeth His mercies,
To multiplied trials He's multiplied peace.
When we have exhausted our store of endurance,
When our strength has failed ere the day is half done,

When we've come to the end of our hoarded resources,
Our Father's full giving has only begun.
His love has no limit, His grace has no measure,
His power no boundary known unto men,
For out of His infinite riches in Jesus
He giveth and giveth and giveth again.

A World without Fathers

These will be his royal titles: . . . Everlasting Father . . .

ISAIAH 9:6

Christ—the Everlasting Father! This is what Jesus of Nazareth was talking about when he claimed deity. In the unity of the Godhead, he claimed equality with the Father. I had never thought of Christ as an "Everlasting Father" until I read this verse! I do not comprehend how the Son can be the Father, but neither do I need to. The thought, however, brings me wondrous comfort. I understand that Christ will do for his children in eternity what a perfect earthly father will do for his own as long as he lives. The father image is used figuratively as both a protector and benefactor.

One of the problems we are wrestling with today is the breakup of the family structure. We live in a "world without fathers." Many children lack a father who provides care, concern, and a protective, nurturing relationship that draws an appreciative "Abba Father"—"my own dear daddy"—from them. We need to preach biblical fatherhood, using the model of our heavenly Father.

One day as I was speaking at a single parents' gathering, three women, all in their thirties, came up to me. All were alcoholics, and one had a daughter who was involved with drugs. All were in tears. "Do you give hugs?" one asked wistfully. I put my arms around her in response! Then I sat down and told them about their Everlasting Father and assured them that "his everlasting arms" were under them (Deuteronomy 33:27)!

If You Go Deep Enough

> **These will be his royal titles: . . . Prince of Peace.**
> ISAIAH 9:6

When Jesus Christ has authority over us and when the government of our lives is upon his shoulder, then the Rule of Peace ensues.

Once Stuart and I were invited to go snorkeling in the Cayman Islands. We ventured out beyond the reef, accompanied by some young experts who swam as well as the fish they chased to the depths with their spearguns. "Don't worry, Mrs. Briscoe," they said, seeing my frightened face. "We'll be your guardian angels!" So saying, they threw the anchor overboard and followed it! Hastily abandoning ship to keep up, Stuart and I followed suit. Never having snorkeled, I drank lots of ocean water and met lots of fish I never knew existed. Every so often I came up for air. It was rough being on top of the waves, but on the other hand, it was peaceful in the depths! Our "guardian angels" had disappeared, chasing their prey and leaving their prey chasing us! As soon as I panicked and tried to stay on top of the water, I nearly drowned. When I obeyed the scanty instructions I had received and dived deep, I had peace—even among my new "friends."

That's how it is when you follow Jesus. If you go deep enough, it will be still enough. We need to do what we are told! "Here on earth," Jesus said, "you will have many trials and sorrows" (that's like being battered to bits on the top of the ocean), "but take heart, because I have overcome the world" (that's like obeying instructions and diving deep!) (John 16:33).

Chosen and Precious

Look at my servant, whom I strengthen. He is my chosen one, and I am pleased with him. I have put my Spirit upon him. He will reveal justice to the nations.

ISAIAH 42:1

Most commentators point to the Lord and the Lord's *servant* as the two heroes of the drama described for us. Who is this "servant"? Some say Isaiah speaks of the Jewish people in exile; others, the prophets. Still others say the servant is King Cyrus, whom the Scriptures acknowledge as an elect instrument.

The role of the servant of the Lord is fulfilled only in Jesus Christ. The servant is described as upheld by God even while he lays a charge upon him, as masters do with faithful servants. He is elected for the service to which he came, and he dwells deeply in God's love. Peter describes Christ Jesus as a precious cornerstone of God's building (see 1 Peter 2:6-7). "This is my beloved Son" (Matthew 3:17), God announced at Christ's baptism. "He is very precious to you who believe" (1 Peter 2:7), Peter says.

Is God's servant, Jesus Christ, precious, beloved, to you? Or is he merely a name in a book, a founder of a church, a historical character, or a nice idea? If Jesus is chosen and precious to God, then it follows that he should be chosen and precious to us.

Does our soul delight in God's Servant? I have heard people say, "I love God, but I have no time for Christ." But how can you love God and yet have no feeling for him in whom his soul delights? Jesus said, "My prayer for all of them is that they will be one, just as you and I are one, Father" (John 17:21). He also said, "The Father and I are one" (John 10:30). To love God is to love Christ. They are one and the same person!

What the World Is Waiting For

Look at my servant, whom I strengthen. He is my chosen one, and I am pleased with him. I have put my Spirit upon him. He will reveal justice to the nations.

ISAIAH 42:1

What is God's elected servant sent to accomplish? The work God intends has to do with judging the behavior of the people of the earth. He is going to "reveal justice" on the earth.

Now, none of us can argue against the fact that justice is the principal need of mankind! "Justice for all," preach the political candidates. "Attend to the poor," plead the social workers. "Deal with corruption," cry oppressed minorities. If only people would do what is just, good, and right, instead of that which is popular, profitable, and easy, then our old world would be a better place! The world has almost given up hope for a kingdom where rightness reigns.

The servant undertook to meet this great need of the world, coming to earth and explaining quietly and confidently—"He will be gentle—he will not shout or raise his voice in public" (Isaiah 42:2)—that he had come to bring a word of rightness and salvation to the hearts of all people by a gentle inward and spiritual method. Christ's ministry was unhysterical, humble, and quiet. John Calvin said, "He did not boast or forbid people to publish his message."

God dressed his servant in his own Spirit and sent him forth. "I have put my Spirit upon him," he said. God's sweet spirit of rule and judgment, with all his efficiency and authority, belongs to Christ. The spiritual endowment for the work required is his, and God's immediate assistance is promised.

No wonder the "distant lands beyond the sea will wait for his instruction" (Isaiah 42:4).

The Death of Discouragement

I, the Lord, have called you to demonstrate my righteousness. I will guard and support you, for I have given you to my people as the personal confirmation of my covenant with them. And you will be a light to guide all nations to me.

ISAIAH 42:6

The Lord promises to direct his servant, to be his protector and keeper, sharing his presence in all things. "I will guard and support you," God promises.

There must have been many wearisome days when Jesus of Nazareth, the servant of the Lord, thought of those words. Did he recite: "He will not stop until truth and righteousness prevail throughout the earth" (Isaiah 42:4), as he wrestled with ornery disciples, rebuked pious Pharisees, or dealt with the rank unbelief of the people? When the process was slow and the days were long, Jesus Christ experienced the immediate assistance of God. And so may we!

We, too, are his servants. If we have been born from above, we are dressed in his Spirit. We, too, must bring a right answer to a wrong world, and we, too, can know he will guard and support us, and give us his immediate assistance in the face of frustration and persecution.

If Christ is not discouraged, knowing his kingdom has come in the hearts of people and will one day come universally, then we need not be discouraged either. God gave Jesus his "personal confirmation of [his] covenant with them. And you will be a light to guide all nations to me" (Isaiah 42:6). The word *covenant* means "promise." God promised us light in place of darkness. He promised that prisoners would be set free (Isaiah 42:7). The death of discouragement and true spiritual freedom begin here and now for the Lord's servants!

Bruised but Never Broken

> **He will not crush those who are weak or quench the smallest hope.**
>
> ISAIAH 42:3

You would think that the bruises that the Savior endured on earth would have crushed the spirit right out of him. But God helped him. "Look at my servant, whom I strengthen" (Isaiah 42:1), he said. The Lord will not allow the weak to be crushed or the smallest hope to be quenched.

There is no question about it. On the cross, our Savior was bruised and battered beyond measure, and his light was almost extinguished by the deluge of our sin, but he was never broken beyond mending. What a tender word this is!

One version translates this verse, "A bruised reed he will not break" (NIV). The reed or dalamus plant has a hollow stem and grows by the sides of lakes and rivers. It was used for making music or fashioned into pens for writing. It is weak, fragile, and brittle. It is easily snapped by the foot of a wild beast, by the wind, or even by a bird that lights upon it. Once it is broken it is of no use whatsoever. Other stems can be mended, but not the reed. Jesus was bruised but never broken. God looked at his precious, bruised one and said, "I must mend this reed. It was meant for music!"

Other versions translate the rest of this verse, "A smoldering wick he will not snuff out" (NIV). God saw his Son as a smoldering wick upon the cross. He placed his hands around his flickering life and gently blew the flame of the resurrection light alive again.

Are you bruised? Do you feel like a flickering wick, about to go out? Listen to the promise of God: "Never crushed or quenched"! Dare to believe it!

YOUR SERVANT

Look at my servant, whom I strengthen.

ISAIAH 42:1

Some aromatic plants, when bruised, give forth the sweetest fragrance! Some reeds were used to write the Scriptures! These thoughts and others from Isaiah 42 inspired a prayer poem.

Touch my stem, Lord—
Low I bend with bruisings—
Gently now, for I'm Thy damaged reed.
Break me not, my Promiser of Power,
Raise not Your voice; yet rather meet my need.

Speak tenderly that therapy of caring
May cool the angry swellings down—
softly.
Relieve the heat of hurts so deep and crushing,
I in the sea of them am likely to drown.

So mend and mold me into stern believing
That shaped and sharpened, healed and held,
A pen I'll be,
To write Your words of healed relieving
Within the hearts and lives of broken men.

BEAUTY

From Mount Zion, the perfection of beauty, God shines in glorious radiance.

PSALM 50:2

What is *beauty?* There is a beauty of form and figure that catches the breath by its sheer symmetry. Then there is the beautiful supple strength of the athlete. But we are thinking "outward." What about the "inward," the beauty of a bright mind, for instance? The writer of Proverbs 31 warned, "Charm is deceptive, and beauty does not last; but a woman who fears the Lord will be greatly praised" (31:30).

The most radiant beauty of all is spiritual beauty, that inner tranquility that comes from a meek and submissive spirit resting at the Savior's feet. Moses prayed that the beauty of the Lord would be upon his people. When David had placed the ark of God inside the tent that he had pitched for it, he offered burnt offerings and told the people to worship their Lord in the splendor and beauty of his holiness.

Romans 10:15 tells us that the feet that take the gospel to the lost are beautiful. But how perfectly beautiful is our Savior Jesus! Beautiful in love, holiness, forgiveness, and grace! If we will only pray the prayer of Moses as we worship Christ, the Lord will think us beautiful, too. We will hear our Savior whisper, "How beautiful you are, my beloved, how beautiful!" (Song of Songs 4:1).

When Your Hands Are Tied

> **"Woman, he is your son." And he said to this disciple, "She is your mother."**
>
> JOHN 19:26-27

Take courage! Jesus did more with his hands tied than anyone else on earth! When Pilate sent Jesus to Herod, Herod's soldiers tied his hands behind his back so they could better buffet him. Then they sent him back to Pilate. "Herod and Pilate, who had been enemies before, became friends that day" (Luke 23:12). Jesus had an amazing effect on people, even when they hated him. He even helped people get over their quarrels when his hands were tied!

The soldier untied Jesus' hands, only to nail them firmly in place upon the cross! But think what Jesus did when his hands were nailed into place—the soldier recognized who Jesus truly was! When Jesus' hands were tied, he never stopped helping people! Seeing his mother standing at the foot of the cross watching him die, and seeing his best earthly friend supporting her, he gave his mother into John's hands. He could no longer take care of Mary; his hands were tied. But he still had a mind alert enough to plan for those he loved, and even through his desperate thirst, he could still speak words of encouragement. Jesus, choosing to die, could not do much for Mary and John, but he did what he could—and it was enough.

Are your hands tied? Are you imagining yourself helplessly restricted? Think about Jesus. Ask him for a way around the dilemma. He'll show you! He'll tell you, "It's amazing what you can do when your hands are tied!"

Mission Accomplished

It is finished!

JOHN 19:30

"Tetelestai!" cried Jesus. "It is finished!" Notice that he did not say, "*I* am finished!" He was shouting in triumph, witnessing to heaven and earth and sea that the work of redemption was accomplished. These were not the whimpering words of a defeated man, but the victory salute of a Conqueror. "I brought glory to you here on earth by doing everything you told me to do," he said to his Father in the upper room. Will we be able to say, "It is finished," when our time comes? Not about the work of redemption, for only one could accomplish that—but about the work of telling the world about him. Will we cry, "*I* am finished" or "*It* is finished" when God calls us home?

Recently I heard of a young Christian man who died in an accident. He had lived his short life for his Lord, making every happy moment count. His life had not been "cut off" as some suggested, but completed. If we have sought to finish the work he has given us to do (notice it does not say that we are to finish the work he has given someone *else* to do!), then like our Savior we will be able to commit our spirit into the Father's keeping—in peace (see Matthew 27:50). Jesus, because he was Jesus, could say, "Spirit, go home." We are not God and do not have the capacity to make our spirits obey us. But when God says to us, "Spirit, come home," we shall go. May our missions be accomplished and a glad cry of "*Tetelestai*" be on our lips!

Lonely Loads

Share each other's troubles and problems.

GALATIANS 6:2

There is a time for everything, a season for this and a season for that. There is a time to bear a care in solitude, and a time to share a prayer with a friend. We need the wisdom to know when to shoulder responsibility, when to delegate, and when to cast it all upon Jesus—our incomparable burden bearer.

Sometimes I have to have a cry, then wash my face and get on with it! I know I must bear the thing alone. Another day, when I was burdened beyond belief after watching a loved one suffer, a friend came to me and touched my hurt with tenderness, mending the raw edges of my helplessness. Such love brought a blessed buoyancy that helped more than I could tell. Someone cared enough to help make my burden bearable. Yes, there is a season for sorrow, a time to bear another's burdens.

But there comes a time when only God's shoulders are broad enough to carry the weight of my worry. Then crushing burdens become carried burdens. Yoked to him, I can plow my lonely furrow, walk a straight path, cope with the intolerable, and figure out the impossible. Then, having been carried, I am sent on my way strengthened to help carry another. I need to pray:

> Show me when to share, Lord—
> Commission me to carry, Lord.

And teach me not to burden one of your special children, if I must bear my burden alone!

GULLIBLE GIVING

> **For they gave a tiny part of their surplus, but she, poor as she is, has given everything she has.**
>
> MARK 12:44

"Americans are so gullible," a rescue mission supervisor told me. "Did you hear about the man who went out and raised two hundred dollars in half an hour from people on the street by telling them he was collecting for 'The Unknown Soldier's Widow'?" I confessed I hadn't heard about it, but I wondered if it were true.

I thought about the money that I gave away to charity. Gullible giving is not God's way. Guidelines have been given to us: tithes first—10 percent of all our income. This is his. We touch it not, lest we be guilty of thievery—robbing divinity is a heinous crime! Offerings next. "I cannot present burnt offerings to the Lord my God that have cost me nothing" (2 Samuel 24:24), said David. What say you? Think of the widow. She only had two pennies. She could have thought that two pennies were too little to give. But Jesus didn't think so. He knew that casting in all your livelihood makes you rich with much more valuable coinage than can come from any earthly mint.

Spastic generosity, triggered by nerves, touched off by impassioned pleas of poverty, or doled out to starving unfortunates pictured in scraggy photographs, is not the best help we can give. Careful accounting of our budget—as if we were handling someone else's funds—is the way to go. After all, we are merely stewards, and as the Bible reminds us, "A person who is put in charge as a manager must be faithful" (1 Corinthians 4:2).

A Beautiful Bunch of Flowers

What makes you better than anyone else? What do you have that God hasn't given you? And if all you have is from God, why boast as though you have accomplished something on your own?

1 CORINTHIANS 4:7

I watched Corrie ten Boom receive people's heartfelt thanks for her ministry. She had saved Jews during World War II, endured the horrors of a Nazi prison camp, and lived to share the joy of Jesus with many people. "How do you stay humble, Corrie?" I asked her. "It must be hard not to get bigheaded when everyone keeps saying thank you all of the time."

Corrie smiled and replied, "I used to struggle with it, but not anymore. All through the day I collect people's appreciation as if I'm collecting a beautiful bunch of flowers. Then at the end of the day, I kneel by my bedside and offer my bouquet to Jesus. 'Here you are, Lord,' I say. 'They are all yours, for what have I that I did not receive?'"

Prayer keeps the glory where it is due. Shortly after I was converted to Christ at the age of eighteen, I found out I had been a help to a friend. To be a help and not a hindrance was such a new experience for me that I didn't quite know what to do with the pride and happiness that flooded my heart! I could have put Corrie's words to use then. "Collect the flowers and make sure they are offered to him at the end of the day." We are saved to serve, blessed to be a blessing; but we need to watch our attitude when someone thanks us for the help that we have been.

Do you struggle with pride when God uses you? Pray, and he will remind you that he is the source of your help, the giver of your gifts, and the enabler of your ministry. Therefore—to God be the glory!

A Thorny Problem

But to keep me from getting puffed up, I was given a thorn in my flesh, a messenger from Satan to torment me and keep me from getting proud.

2 CORINTHIANS 12:7

My friend and I had been talking about the way adversity forces us to trust God. "I've lived twenty years with a thorn in the flesh," my friend remarked. "How do I learn dependence now that the thorn is out?" We agreed that pride and fleshly energy take over so easily when the need to depend is removed. If we feel strong and confident *apart* from God—watch out!

Yet all of life will not necessarily be one long chapter of accidents. What about the times "the thorn" is removed or we find ourselves between thorns? To depend even when the sun shines is a real test of maturity. It helps to pray a lot. Prayer gives us a sense of our inadequacy at all times and this helps us lean on the Lord.

To be reminded of his person reminds me of my person, and that will surely help me to depend! Isaiah, seeing God high and lifted up, saw himself low and cast down (see Isaiah 6)! A season of prayer will help us to stop saying "Wow is me" and make sure we say "Woe is me"! Physical thorns can be in our fleshly nature until the day we die and should keep us in constant dependence on the Spirit of God to make good his strength in our weakness. This way we will *glory in his power* and not in our own strength.

Diabolical Footsteps

Now the serpent was the shrewdest of all the creatures the LORD God had made.

GENESIS 3:1

Satan is called the "serpent" both in Genesis and in Revelation (Revelation 12:9). In one frightening chapter of Genesis, we catch a glimpse of his powers. He is seen to be cunning, articulate, a liar, a deceiver and destroyer, and an enemy of the Lord Jesus Christ.

Eve's mistake was to take him on! She was no match for the serpent; neither are you and I. The second Adam, Jesus Christ, met Satan and withstood his temptations (see Matthew 4:1-11). Jesus overcame and destroyed Satan at the Cross. Because of Christ's victory, true Christians have the same power to overcome.

We are promised discernment to match Satan's cunning, truth to counter his lies, and weapons to fight the unseen battles of the spirit (see Ephesians 6:12-18). If we take on the old serpent in our own strength as Eve did, there is no contest. But that is more easily said than done! I like the story of the little boy who told his Sunday school teacher that when Satan knocked on the door of his heart, he sent Jesus to answer it! Very wise! The serpent is stronger than all our best intentions, but God is stronger than all the serpent's worst designs!

Do you not believe in Satan? Then you really have been deceived! The Bible plots his diabolical footsteps from Genesis 3 to Revelation 20. Jesus believed in him and showed us how to counter his subtlety with triumphant truth. The serpent may have been more cunning than the beasts of the field and the man who was set over them, but he is not more cunning than God and his Christ who caught and cursed him with eternal doom (see Revelation 20:10).

First Chair Clarinet!

As for me, I will certainly not sin against the Lord by ending my prayers for you. And I will continue to teach you what is good and right.

1 SAMUEL 12:23

"I've figured out why my attitude toward school has changed—it's because I'm praying about it," our daughter informed us at supper. "School's the same, but I'm different," she added. Prayer changes things, and prayer changes people!

Our youngest said he needed praying for, too. "What for?" we inquired, pleased that he would ask. "Pray I get first chair clarinet," Pete requested earnestly. "But you never practice," I protested. "I wouldn't need to pray if I practiced!" he retorted. We needed to explain a few prayer rules to Pete, and to encourage Judy in her growing experience of intercession. Through the years, Stuart and I have counted it a priority not only to pray for our children but to make sure they knew we were praying for them.

Samuel made sure the children of Israel knew he was praying for them, and that was important to them. But by far the most important thing we can do for our children is to help them develop a real prayer life for themselves. Somehow we have to help them catch the importance of praying for themselves, rather than leaving it all up to Mom and Dad.

My kids consider Mom to be the pray-er in the family, and I'm honored they should think that way; but I know I have failed them if I have not taught them how to become pray-ers in their own right. After all, I will not be around forever!

What Was Jesus Saying?

And Jesus replied, "I assure you, today you will be with me in paradise."

LUKE 23:43

Jesus talked to the repentant thief on the cross and promised him paradise. When you are by the side of a dying person, paradise is a great topic of conversation. Even if you, too, are suffering, thinking of paradise can help. Jesus cared about thieves, robbers, and scoundrels. He borrowed a cross from a murderer and chose to die among thieves! He forgave torturers and blessed the disciples that had abandoned him to his fate. He met treachery with the promises of God.

Are you sitting by the bedside of a dying friend? Think on paradise. Are you parting with a loved one? Listen to what Jesus is saying! "Today you will be with me in paradise." He will keep them safely for you, and he will keep you safely for them! He will reunite you in heaven—till then, abide in his love and care.

In heavenly love abiding, / No change my heart shall fear;
And safe is such confiding, / For nothing changes here.
The storm may roar without me, / My heart may low be laid;
But God is round about me, / And can I be dismayed?

Wherever He may guide me, / No want shall turn me back;
My Shepherd is beside me, / And nothing can I lack.
His wisdom ever waketh, / His sight is never dim;
He knows the way He taketh, / And I will walk with Him.

Green pastures are before me, / Which yet I have not seen;
Bright skies will soon be o'er me, / Where darkest clouds have been.
My hope I cannot measure, / My path to life is free;
My Saviour has my treasure, / And He will walk with me.

ANNA L. WARING, 1850

WHAT WAS JESUS DOING?

He asked Jesus question after question, but Jesus refused to answer.

LUKE 23:9

Perhaps you would never play such cruel word games with Jesus as Herod did, but there are other games just as hurtful to the Savior. Human beings can play the games of indifference, of rejection, or of willful ignorance. Modern people have grown "tolerant"—they simply walk over their Savior's sorrows and go on their way untouched, unreached, and unregenerate.

"Here is the man!" cried Pilate, displaying the tortured Christ, sure his sufferings would engender pity. Instead, like beasts smelling the blood of a kill, the chief priests and officers cried out, "Crucify! Crucify!" (John 19:6). And what was Jesus doing while all this was going on? Nothing! He who had the power to summon ten thousand angels to his help chose to stand helplessly, resigned to die because there was no other way to reconcile the world to God! He who had the power to consume his enemies with the breath of his mouth refused to answer, though every effort was employed to make him talk. Jesus didn't play games with his enemies; he was tall and straight and true. He told us he was the truth, the way, and eternal life—and then rested his case. He neither teased us with the unattainable nor taunted us with the irresistible, but simply offered us salvation. Here is the man! The man of men—God himself in human form!

Then dare to play your games if you will! As for me, I am sold—devastated by the story of the God-man subjected to humiliation that defies description. I am captured, reduced to tears—I worship!

What Was Jesus Thinking?

Finally, they came to a place called The Skull. All three were crucified there. . . . Jesus said, "Father, forgive these people, because they don't know what they are doing."

LUKE 23:33-34

What does a person think about when he is being crucified? When you are the Son of God dying for a lost world, you think of forgiveness. Jesus showed us how to react to the ones responsible for our agony! We are to pardon them for it! But how on earth do we do that? We pray about it! What a part prayer played in the life of our Lord—Jesus, hanging on the cross, was in prayer! He was in prayer for his tormentors. Whom did Jesus need to pardon? The disciples who forsook him and fled, the soldiers who played dice for his clothes, the Pharisees who railed at him, and the people who simply stood watching!

Who is causing your suffering? Have friends seen your misfortune and forsaken you? Are relatives trying to do you out of your property, a legacy, or something that they owe you? Have people railed at you in the heat of an argument? Have others simply stood seeing your pain and doing nothing to help? Whom do you need to forgive?

We are commanded to forgive by the one who forgave us. "Pray for those who despitefully use you, and forgive as you have been forgiven," Jesus said. When we understand the breadth of Christ's forgiveness, perhaps we will not find it impossible to pardon our own persecutors! Then we will need to tell those who have hurt us that we have forgiven them. Jesus prayed aloud, so everyone could hear:

> "Father, forgive these people, because they don't know what they are doing."

A Well of Water

Hagar, what's wrong?
GENESIS 21:17

Abraham had sent Hagar and her son Ishmael into the wilderness. It was very hot, and the water they had been given was gone. Hagar left her boy under a bush and, going a little distance away, waited for him to die. She couldn't watch him suffer. Then the Bible says, "God heard the boy's cries." It doesn't say that God heard Hagar's cry! "Hagar, what's wrong?" God asked her. "Do not be afraid! God has heard the boy's cries from the place where you laid him."

Ishmael didn't let tears stop him from praying. Hagar did, as we often do! Women, especially, are prone to have a good cry, and sometimes there is relief in being able to do that. But when God has to lean out of heaven and ask, What's wrong? it's time to stop! He will remind us that he is a God who answers prayer. God opened Hagar's eyes, and she saw a well. Then she filled the bottle with water and saved the boy's life.

Have you ever been so busy crying that you couldn't pray? Maybe you need to dry your tears and to hush your voice to listen in expectancy. Our cries can block out the voice of God, and our tears can blind us to the well of water that is right under our nose. God is waiting to show us the solution to our problem. There will always be a well of living water available to help us cope with our distress. We just need to stop crying long enough to see it. Sometimes it takes the simple prayers of a little child to teach us these things!

Faith Is the Best Handkerchief

Mary was standing outside the tomb crying.

JOHN 20:11

The angels in white, "sitting at the head and foot of the place where the body of Jesus had been lying," asked Mary, "Why are you crying?" Mary answered, "Because they have taken away my Lord . . . and I don't know where they have put him" (John 20:13). Tears, even necessary ones, can distort our vision. The distraught woman "glanced over her shoulder and saw someone standing behind her. It was Jesus, but she didn't recognize him." Again the question came: "Why are you crying? . . . Who are you looking for?" (John 20:14-15). Just see what tears can do! She, supposing him to be the gardener, said to him, "If you have taken him away, tell me where you have put him, and I will go and get him" (John 20:15).

How can you mistake the risen Son of God for a gardener? Quite easily—if tears do not turn into triumphant faith. Belief in the Resurrection is the best handkerchief I know! Mary was mourning her Christ, her Savior, the one who had cast out the demons that had tormented her. Beside herself with grief, she shed her necessary tears. But there came a moment when a question needed to be asked: "*Why* are you crying? Who are you looking for?"

Faith realizes that Christ is alive! Then *who* can cry? Are you in shock? in mourning? Can you not see the Christ presenting himself to you as the answer, even to death? Can you hear his voice calling your name? Mary's tears prevented her from seeing her Savior. Let faith dry your eyes, look up, look around—then look ahead!

Mary Magdalene

"Mary!" Jesus said. She turned toward him and exclaimed, "Teacher!"

JOHN 20:16

Mary's day was night, her world a world of tears. She watched him on the cross; she missed not one tortured movement, nor word, nor forgiving prayer. She watched him die, tormented by the demons he had cast out of her. Her Jesus! And now she sought his body and found it not—as if he never lived. As if it were a dream. As if he never touched her, healed her, loved her, and compelled her to lay down her sin.

Poor Mary! She knew He was dead; she'd watched Him die,
Hanging between the earth and sky.
She knew He was dead; she'd heard Him scream
As the filth of our sin had come in between
Himself and His God, as the punishment rod
Fell to chastise His choicest prize.
She knew He was dead, so pardon her
For thinking Him only the gardener!
He called her name; He was just the same,
Save the holes in His hands and His spear-pierced frame.
The love and the fire in His eyes were too much,
The strength and the thrill of His risen-life touch.
Dear Lord! Dear Lord! Oh, pardon her
For thinking You only the gardener!
Many folks that I know have a Jesus of gloom,
Alive, yet confined to His garden tomb.
Yes, He came alive, but was never the same,
He never called them by their very own name!
He lives in His tomb and He tends His grave,
Confined and helpless to seek and to save.
Look into His face, let go of His feet,
Stop trying to wrap Him in that winding sheet!
He isn't the gardener, a ghost, or a fake,
He's Rabboni, your Master, and He rose for your sake.

Tear Talk

In the ancient East, mourners would cry over a wineskin bottle and leave their tears at the door of the tomb. Perhaps the psalmist had this in mind when he wrote Psalm 56. Doesn't it help you to know that God sees your tears and writes them in his book?

You have collected all my tears in your bottle. You have recorded each one in your book.

PSALM 56:8

Tears talking,
pattering petition on the door of heaven,
Let me in.

Wet misery,
fountains of fury,
rivers of recrimination,
tears tearing down the riverbed of doubt—
stopping at the throng . . .
bottled bereavement
arranged by angels,
given to the King!

God tilts the bottle carefully over His book of remembrance,
letting the drops fall onto a clean page.
Transported in a teardrop,
translated into eloquence,
my washing woe writes its words of wounded worry down.

The Father reads my tears
then passes the book to the Son,
Who shares it with the Spirit—
The angels gather round—
some small celestial cherubs
are lifted to the Father's knees.
THE STORY IS TOLD.

They listen—they all listen—
I AM HEARD!

My Part

> **Do your part to live in peace with everyone, as much as possible.**
>
> ROMANS 12:18

I'm glad the Bible says "as much as possible"! Sometimes it is not! But I can't use that as an excuse. Have I really done my part to make it possible? The Scripture does say, "Do your part" or as another translation puts it, "As much as lieth in you." God depends on me to do my part! Did I confront the person? Did I write a letter, call her on the phone, ask a wise friend to intervene? Once I have done the things that only I can do and honestly can think of nothing else that can be tried, then I can rest, and pray, and wait for God to intervene.

The hardest part is the part that depends on the other person! Sometimes an offended or hostile adversary will reject my overtures and throw my best efforts back in my face. But I must remember that I am responsible only for my attitude—not for his or hers. I must seek to live peaceably with "everyone." If only Paul had said "most everyone," or "some people," or "your friends and other people you like," or "the people who like you"—but he didn't. Peace will require all my effort at all times to put it all right with *everyone*. But don't forget, Paul does say "as much as possible"! If it is, then God will bring reconciliation. If it is not, he knows—so I can stop blaming myself and rest in the knowledge that I have done my part!

Never, Ever Useless

So, my dear brothers and sisters, be strong and steady, always enthusiastic about the Lord's work, for you know that nothing you do for the Lord is ever useless.

1 CORINTHIANS 15:58

Many people have a dread of living in vain. I read about a man who left a request in his will that his ashes be used in egg timers so that his life would not be a total write off! The Bible tells me that my labor in the Lord is never useless. That's why I need to be steadfast and immovable in my determination to seek out the work that is his will for my life; and once I find it, I must do it with all my strength, all my days, keeping all eternity in mind.

Working for Jesus Christ and his kingdom has eternal repercussions. Are you ever so despondent that you feel you may as well end up in an egg timer? Come to God through Christ—ask him to help you spend your time wisely, and you will not feel that your life is empty and frustrating. However, if you begin to serve him, you may run into another problem. You will probably discover there is never enough time to accomplish everything that needs accomplishing!

"What do people get for all their hard work?" Solomon asks (Ecclesiastes 1:3). Solomon was the wisest of men, yet he still had his egg-timer moments! Paul, knowing believers get discouraged, told us that the secret of a meaningful life is to be enthusiastic in the work of the Lord.

The Uttermost Parts

He is the one who gave these gifts to the church: the apostles, the prophets, the evangelists, and the pastors and teachers.

EPHESIANS 4:11

Someone has to go to the uttermost parts of the earth with the Good News. God gives to a few the tools for the job and sends them out, even as the Father sent the Son. Jesus was the first missionary, and he left his home, his loved ones, and his comforts to bring us not only the message of redemption but himself! Self-sacrifice is part of the job. There is no way around the cost that some must pay to take the Christian gospel to those who have never heard the name of Jesus.

But what of those who are left behind—those who stay at home while the others go forth to battle? My heart goes out to mothers, wives, and children who "make do" without their men—because I've been there! For twelve years my husband was on the road for long periods of time. *How can a man fulfill his biblical role as a father when he's never around?* I would ask myself. Back would come God's answer: "How can a man fulfill the biblical role of an evangelist if he's always at home?" For those who are called, there is no choice about the matter—for when Jesus Christ is Lord, you follow him, even to the uttermost parts of the earth!

We need to ask God to help us remember to pray for traveling evangelists and to show us practical ways to encourage and support their families.

Reaping the Grain of Grace

Vast fields are ripening all around us and are ready now for the harvest.
JOHN 4:35

"Look around you," said Jesus to his disciples. "Vast fields . . . are ready now for the harvest," he exhorted them. Squinting against the midday sun, the disciples followed Jesus' gaze. Coming up the hill toward the village well were the men of Samaria, led by the woman to whom Jesus had been talking. Of course it was the men that the woman went to first. Men were her weakness, but men she knew, men she loved, and men she would tell about "a man who told me everything I ever did!" (John 4:29). Coming to Jesus, the men entreated him to stay with them, and he graciously accepted their invitation.

I am sure the disciples weren't sure about it all, but Jesus, who "had to go through Samaria" (John 4:4), knew he "had to" stay two days with the woman and her friends (John 4:40). And the inevitable miracle happened—many believed that Jesus "is indeed the Savior of the world" (John 4:42).

This, then, was the harvest Jesus spoke about to his disciples. To see similar possibilities, we will need to "look around." The disciples, assigned the mundane task of procuring bread from the village mill, had forgotten the Bread of Life, who walked by their side. We must raise up our eyes to him daily and then follow his gaze to the harvest fields that are white already!

Hard I look—
I see Thee,

I follow Thine eye—
I see them—

Running—Ready—Ripe
Send me forth, a harvester.

Valuable Virtues

He had to go through Samaria on the way.

JOHN 4:4

We were getting ready to do a "value survey" in our community. Being charged with the responsibility of women's ministries at our church, I needed to know what women thought in order to better serve and minister to them. We decided to collect data from five thousand ladies concerning their sexual, social, and spiritual values. Coming across the biblical record of Jesus' conversation with the woman of Samaria in John 4, I realized he was using the "survey method"! This gave me great encouragement, and I avidly researched his methods and noted the good results!

First of all, I noticed that he talked with the woman *when* he was wearied with his journey (John 4:6). Though faint with hunger and waiting for his disciples to bring meat, he knew that his "meat" was to do the will of the one that sent him. Jesus watched for every opportunity to interview people on the most personal levels concerning their values, without thought of the cost to himself.

Then I noted *where* he questioned the woman. He chose a center of ordinary daily activity—the village well. He did not go to the synagogue when seeking to answer the cry of lost sheep. He knew he would find such hungry souls outside church boundaries. We have to ask the right people the right questions in the right places if we are to have the glorious chance to give them the right answers.

And *why* did Jesus choose to challenge people to a personal faith in himself? He told the woman of Samaria, "Salvation comes through the Jews" (John 4:22), and he wanted her to know that he was the promised Messiah, the one who alone could forgive her sins and give her spiritual satisfaction.

Tips on Talking

Start talking about things the other person understands. Jesus started with a bucket! Next, make sure you show interest in people as people! Jesus cared about the Samaritan woman's personal problems, and she knew it! Don't be sidetracked. The woman wanted to start arguing about which church to go to, but Jesus reminded her that it was the person she worshiped that was important, not the place of worship.

The woman was surprised, for Jews refuse to have anything to do with Samaritans. She said to Jesus, "You are a Jew, and I am a Samaritan woman. Why are you asking me for a drink?"

JOHN 4:9

Don't be shocked. Know your world and what's going on out there; there is a difference between isolation and separation. Jesus was never isolated from sinners, but he was separate from sin. Next, realize that sin is a symptom of the real problem—a soul-thirst only God can quench. Tell people that Jesus is the answer to their thirsty quest. Don't be afraid to talk about salvation, souls, and sin; Jesus did.

Talk naturally. You should be able to talk about your faith as freely as you do about your family. Jesus made spiritual talk easy and comfortable for others, because it was easy and comfortable for him. Be sure not to put on a special voice when you talk about God—use your usual one!

And, finally, don't run after your prospective converts; Jesus didn't. When they've had enough, let them go—but pray for them. And then watch them come back with their friends. What joy! Talking of truth satisfies as nothing else can. You may even conquer your appetite the way Jesus did, just with the fullness of it all!

Take my voice, and let me sing
Always, only for my King.
Take my lips, and let them be
Filled with messages from Thee.

A Heart for Women

"You have had five husbands."

JOHN 4:18

Jesus had a heart for women. The disciples were astonished to find him speaking with a woman, especially a woman of the despised Samaritans—a woman who had had five husbands and who was living with a sixth man at the time she talked with Jesus! Yet Jesus saw her need. She thirsted for relationships to fill her empty life. "Wouldn't you like to have that thirst quenched?" Jesus inquired.

We would do well to ask all thirsty women the same question. With broken marriages behind them, many women are searching for their identity, their happiness in a meaningful union. But you can't quench spiritual thirst with a marriage—however meaningful it may be! "God is Spirit," Jesus reminded the woman of Samaria (John 4:24). His Spirit is like living water and quenches our thirst. "Please, sir," said the woman, "give me some of that water" (John 4:15).

Today we can ask him to do that for us, too. We can simply say, "Jesus, I need you; Jesus, I want you; give me this water." We will need to leave our sinful life behind us as the Samaritan woman left her bucket, but then, like the woman at the well, we'll never thirst again.

Jesus, I thirst—
Quench me;

Jesus, I hunger—
Feed me;

Jesus, I'll tell—
Send me.

WHAT WILL THEY SAY?

Just then his disciples arrived. They were astonished to find him talking to a woman.

JOHN 4:27

Thinking about the story of Jesus and the woman at the well made me realize how many of us live crippled Christian lives because of "what *they* might say." "They" can be Great-aunt Alice, my husband or child, my sophisticated friend, or even the gossip at the women's club. Jesus didn't bother himself with what "they" might say about his conversation with a despised woman because he cared deeply about what God had already said! That's why he made himself of no reputation and humbled himself, and that's why we must do the same. Jesus told us that as the Father had sent him, so he would send us (see John 20:21).

Years ago I got to know a rough street boy. After he became a Christian, he asked me to go with him to talk to his friends. "Where are they?" I inquired.

"In the pub," he answered.

"Oh, I couldn't go in there," I quickly responded. "Whatever would people say?" I was pretty sure that if I were to go into a place like that, the church organist would happen by as I entered with my new friend.

"He made himself of no reputation," God reminded me. "Now go and do likewise." So I went—because I tried to care more about what *he* had already said than what "they" might get around to saying.

"Lord, humble me and may you find me fighting to be faithful, rather than seeking popularity. May I care about *your* reputation and learn to let you care about mine."

WHEN

Death is swallowed up in victory.

1 CORINTHIANS 15:54

Have you ever sat by the side of someone you love who is being slowly swallowed up by death? If you have, you will know how hard it is to believe this verse. How you long for someone to come along and stop it all! If only a great big giant could walk into the room and swallow up death, who is busy swallowing up your dear one! It is all like a dreadful nightmare, except it is many times worse than a bad dream because it's real. On the one hand, you can't seem to wake up and have the shadows disappear, and on the other, you can't go to sleep without having a cloud of despondency follow and surround you so tightly that you can't get your breath.

It was at such a bitter, despairing time as this that I found 1 Corinthians 15:54: "When this happens—when our perishable earthly bodies have been transformed into heavenly bodies that will never die—then at last the Scriptures will come true: 'Death is swallowed up in victory.'" Oh, blessed "when." Oh, gentle promise of God. And who shall there be who is strong enough to digest death? Why, the Lord God—it is he! The Lord God will wipe away the tears from all faces and ransom our people from final destruction.

"O death, bring forth your terrors! O grave, bring forth your plagues! For I will not relent!" he promised (Hosea 13:14). Take courage, dear friend, there is a time—a moment—a "when."

Open Heart, Open Home

> **"If you agree that I am faithful to the Lord," she said, "come and stay at my home."**
>
> ACTS 16:15

When God opens your heart, he also opens your home.

What does it mean to have an open home? First of all, it means *work.* To look after three houseguests in Paul's day meant a lot of hard work for Lydia and her household. Second, having an open home means *worship.* Luke, writing the Acts narrative, tells us about Lydia's prayer life (see Acts 16:13-14). Since Lydia was in the habit of praying even before her conversion, I'm sure she was very happy to have her home used for prayer meetings after she came to know the Lord.

Having an open home can also mean *worry.* After Lydia and many others were converted, Paul got into trouble with the authorities who beat him and his companions and threw them into jail. After a very exciting night, during which God intervened and caused an earthquake to free the prisoners, the jailer and his family were converted; but then the authorities discovered that Paul was a Roman citizen. Being frightened about the repercussions of their actions, the authorities begged Paul to leave their city. And where do you think God's jailbirds headed as soon as they were released? That's right, Lydia's house! Once there, the Bible tells us, they encouraged the believers (see Acts 16:40). I would have thought the believers would have encouraged them! I suppose it works both ways. An open home is a place for mutual encouragement in the Lord!

If our hearts are opened to the Lord, so will our homes be—truly open to all God's children, not just the mighty and popular, but the poor, persecuted, and troubled as well!

Down by the Riverside

> **On the Sabbath we went a little way outside the city to a riverbank, where we supposed that some people met for prayer, and we sat down to speak with some women who had come together.**
>
> ACTS 16:13

Lydia, a Jewish proselyte, a seller of expensive purple cloth, was accustomed to going to the place by the river where the Jews met for prayer and joining the worshipers. We learn that "she was a worshiper of God" (Acts 16:14). The fact that the pious Jews met by the river tells us that there were not the requisite ten Jewish adult men in Philippi to start a synagogue in that Roman colony.

We also can learn a valuable lesson about the sort of prayers God heeds and answers. Lydia was heard by God. Prayer precedes conversion; God hears the prayers of a grandmother concerned for her grandchild, a husband concerned for an unbelieving wife, or simply the pray-er concerned for himself—as in Lydia's or Cornelius's case. It's important to encourage people who are seeking a relationship with God to pray, because prayer also prepares the heart to receive the living Word of God. Paul, having had a vision of a *man* from Macedonia asking him to "come over here and help us" (Acts 16:9), found instead a *woman* who was waiting to listen at the place where prayer was made. He lost no time sitting down and explaining the gospel to Lydia. I love Paul's flexibility!

Prayer truly prepares the heart. The Lord opened Lydia's understanding, and she "accepted what Paul was saying." After she and her household were converted, she begged Paul and his friends to stay with her. The beautiful story of Lydia reaffirms our belief in the power of prayer. We are reminded that prayer precedes conversion, prepares the heart, and stimulates us to ministry.

Logos

But these are written so that you may believe that Jesus is the Messiah, the Son of God, and that by believing in him you will have life.

JOHN 20:31

L*ogos* is the Greek word for "the expression of a thought or concept." God's logos is God's Word. In Revelation 19:13, it is used as the title of the Son of God. The Logos was one who did not merely keep company with the Godhead, but was deity himself (see 1 John 1:1)—one in whom all the treasures of divine wisdom were embodied. This logos became human and lived among us (see John 1:14). "We saw him with our own eyes and touched him with our own hands . . . the Word of life," John said (1 John 1:1). His name is Jesus! He is the Word of life and the light of all people.

The light of the Logos overcame the darkness of a lost world. In fact, Jesus Christ was God's ultimate Word of light for our lost, dark days. Hebrews 1:1-2 tells us: "Long ago God spoke many times and in many ways to our ancestors through the prophets. But now in these final days, he has spoken to us through his Son." God has nothing more to say to us than he has already said, for he has said, "Jesus"!

So if "Jesus" was the most important thing that God has ever said, why don't we listen? Why don't we try to understand what God seeks to communicate to us? If Jesus, God's best thought, is not worth one of ours, there's something wrong! God's Logos came into the *cosmos* that the world should pay attention to him. The apostle John wrote about these things so that we could "have life" (John 20:31).

Doulos

I am John, your brother. In Jesus we are partners in suffering and in the Kingdom and in patient endurance. I was exiled to the island of Patmos for preaching the word of God and speaking about Jesus.

REVELATION 1:9

The *Logos* was sent into the *cosmos*—this present world system—that those who desire light to overcome their personal, dreadful darkness should have it happen! John lived in spiritual darkness until Christ shone into his heart and showed him his Savior. John had been a companion of the light, but when trouble came, he ran off into the darkness of denial and trembled there.

It was Pentecost that made the difference to John. Christ suffered at Calvary, the tomb was shattered, and Pentecost came, bringing the power to be different, to overcome the darkness of doubt and fear. John was transformed by his logos to live in his cosmos as a *doulos*—which means "servant" or "slave"!

It took a lot of time for John to become a powerful servant of Christ. First, he had to learn to be a friend of Jesus. We have to be Jesus' friends before we can be his servants. Yet, once we have been privileged with such a precious partnership, being a slave seems the same as being a friend! One doesn't really know the difference! Sometimes it takes a Patmos experience to turn us into a doulos for him.

The Jesus Connection

Write down what you see, and send it to the seven churches.

REVELATION 1:11

To whom did John write from his island of exile? He wrote to ordinary people who were connected to him because he was connected to Jesus! The Jesus connection is a marvelous thing.

Someone led Janet Smith to Christ. She got sick and was taken to the hospital in the town where I was a student. When I, too, got sick and was taken to the same hospital, I was wheeled down a long corridor by a starched lady with a grim face and laid neatly to rest beside Janet Smith. She led me to Christ. Soon after I got better and went back to college, Penny, a freshman, became my "little sister." As her "big sister," my responsibility was to look after her. I did—I led her to Christ! Penny grew in God, and the next year she led her "little sister" to Christ.

This is what the Jesus connection is—a network of blessing, an intriguing mystery that will all be explained one day. But till then, the joy of being part of it all is enough. Whoever and wherever you are, you can be part of it, too! John didn't let the fact that he was isolated worry him. When he was able to travel and preach, he did; when he couldn't do that anymore, he found a way to continue as God's special agent in the Jesus connection—he picked up his pen and papyrus and went right on with his work!

The Golden Sash

> "I am the Alpha and the Omega—the beginning and the end," says the Lord God. . . . I turned to see who was speaking to me.
>
> REVELATION 1:8, 12

Have you ever wondered what Jesus looked like—what it would have been like to see him? I have. We are not given a physical description of Christ our Lord in his humanity, save that we know he lived within a Jewish body. We do know, however, what he looked like in his divinity. John, the apostle, saw him with his own eyes and tried his best to capture that vision of the glorified Christ for us.

He was told to write what he saw in a book and send it to the seven churches in Asia (see Revelation 1:11). This sight of Jesus would help the disciples in these young churches, who were facing prison, persecution, and death, to be faithful to the end. John also wrote to people who were being told that Jesus was a nobody and assured them that Jesus was a somebody—a poor unknown carpenter on earth but the King in heaven.

He was "wearing a long robe with a gold sash across his chest" (Revelation 1:13). Only the most important people wore long garments and only kings wore golden sashes. In the Old Testament Scriptures, such a sash (sometimes called a "girdle") worn around the waist denoted power and authority. Such sashes were worn by taskmasters. But when the sash was worn around the chest, it denoted faithfulness and affection.

John was in terrible trouble just because he was a Christian, but when he saw the gold sash, he remembered how much he was loved! Do you need to remember that too?

White, White Hair

His head and his hair were white like wool, as white as snow.

REVELATION 1:14

The word *white* is used to emphasize its great importance. Christ's hair was "white like wool," said John. When shepherds sheared the sheep in those days, two sorts of wool were gathered. One was an ordinary off-white wool used for everyday garments, while the other was pure white wool kept to make the most expensive clothes. When Daniel had his vision of the Ancient One, he noted the white, white hair as well:

> I watched as thrones were put in place and the Ancient One sat down to judge. His clothing was as white as snow, his hair like whitest wool. He sat on a fiery throne with wheels of blazing fire. (Daniel 7:9)

White hair speaks of eternity, of Christ's agelessness, of the dignity of his endless days. It gives a feeling of security. Just knowing he's been around that long helps when I feel very young, very inexperienced, and very unsure of myself! White hair says, "I am wise. I understand many things because I have lived forever." Christ's age was no ordinary "off-white" age like yours and mine. His white, white hair tells us he existed before the ages themselves and lives outside of time, wise beyond measure, knowing all things.

He promises us white, white hair, too, one day. That's the sort of hair we shall have in eternity. As he said to John, "I am the living one who died. Look, I am alive forever and ever!" (Revelation 1:18). Because he lives, we shall live also. The disciples in the persecuted churches needed to hear that!

Eyes of Fire

His eyes were bright like flames of fire.

REVELATION 1:14

Christ's piercing eyes penetrated one's innermost thoughts and being. Peter knew what it was like to have Jesus look at him with those eyes "like flames of fire." After Peter had denied him, "the Lord turned and looked at Peter. Then Peter remembered that the Lord had said . . ." (Luke 22:61). When Christ was on earth, he had the ability to look at people and make them remember broken promises and words spoken with conviction but never fulfilled!

Christ in heaven has a perfect view of everything: "Everything is naked and exposed before his eyes. This is the God to whom we must explain all that we have done" (Hebrews 4:13). He sees within as well as without: "People judge by outward appearance, but the Lord looks at a person's thoughts and intentions" (1 Samuel 16:7).

When I was a very small child, I can remember hiding behind a sofa, thinking no one could see me! *Even God is looking for me,* I said to my small self with satisfaction. I grew up to realize God never has to look. He sees me hiding; he comes to me and faces me with what he sees. Trying to hide from God is useless. It is best to acknowledge the things we both see and have him deal with the issues of our life. There is no other sensible course of action to take, for "his eyes [are] like flames of fire."

FEET LIKE BRONZE

His feet were as bright as bronze refined in a furnace.

REVELATION 1:15

When John saw the glorified Christ, he saw that his feet looked like bright bronze. Bronze, an alloy of copper and tin, was used extensively in Old Testament times. This ordinary material was used for the sanctuary (see Exodus 25:3), fashioned into clasps to hold the tent of the tabernacle together (see Exodus 26:11), and to make pillars and carts and a bronze sea for the house of the Lord. After Shishak, king of Egypt, came up against Jerusalem and took away the gold shields that Solomon had made, King Rehoboam made bronze shields to replace them (see 2 Chronicles 12:9-10).

Refined, or "white," bronze was not used for these things because it was extremely costly and heavy. It was too heavy to use for sanctuary vessels that would be moved around or for soldiers' shields that had to be lifted up. John saw that the glorified Christ had feet like refined bronze.

Those feet are capable of trampling the serpent's head (see Genesis 3:15); those feet are capable of trampling down the forces of evil. The risen Lord reminded the church at Thyatira about his feet like polished bronze (see Revelation 2:18). There were Christians there who were flaunting sexual sin that needed stamping out. There is no place for such things in Christ's church. His feet are a salutary reminder of that fact! What needs stamping out of your life?

Words Like Waterfalls

His voice thundered like mighty ocean waves.

REVELATION 1:15

The breakers pound on the shore of the beautiful island of Patmos, scattering surf like crystal stars along the sandy slopes. John, the prisoner, would have been encouraged by the sound of that mighty pounding. It would have reminded him of the rhythm of God's creation, held in order by the one in control. As surely as the waves chase each other ashore, so is God's order established in the world. God's blessings, like the waves, roll inexorably onward.

John was encouraged by his belief that God would chase his plans into being and make sure they reached the point of no return, sweeping their way up the sandy beaches of people's lives. When John "turned to see who was speaking" to him (Revelation 1:12), he struggled for a valid expression of what he had heard. The best way he found to describe the voice of God was to compare it to "mighty ocean waves"—the mightiest surf that ever pounded a seashore, the biggest breaker ever to break loose of its brothers, the wildest wave ever to dash the bed of the ocean.

Next time you stand at a waterfall, think about that. Then, when you get to heaven, you will recognize his voice! Christ's voice was greater than the thunder of the breakers on Patmos and carried with it the force of many waterfalls. It was a voice to be reckoned with. "Anyone who is willing to hear should listen," said John (Revelation 3:22).

The Mystery

He held seven stars in his right hand.

REVELATION 1:16

Jesus said the seven stars were angels or messengers to the churches in Asia (see Revelation 1:20). God is not a divine detective story writer, who sits in heaven, trying to think of ways to muddle us up! He wants to make things plain. He told John that he holds the messengers in his hand; he has a grip on them. Commentators differ as to whether these messengers were heavenly or earthly, but whichever, they were in his hand! He sent them to do his bidding.

It is a comforting thought to me that Christ holds the messengers in his nail-pierced hand. The church is his bride, and he cares about her. A note in the Scofield edition of the Bible offers one of the most natural explanations of the identity of these messengers: "They were men sent by the seven churches to ascertain the state of the aged apostle, now an exile in Patmos (cf. Philippians 4:18); but they may represent any who bear God's messages to a church." Their job was simply to deliver Jesus' message to the seven churches (represented by the seven lampstands).

Those of us who also have the privilege need to make sure Jesus' letters do not get lost in the delivery. People's reaction to the message is not our responsibility, but the delivery of that message as Jesus gave it *is!* Jesus has his hands full with his messengers, but when John fainted at the sight of the glorified Christ, "He laid his right hand on [him] and said, 'Don't be afraid! I am the First and the Last'" (Revelation 1:17). A vision of him will help us to deliver our message.

THE SWORD OF THE SPIRIT

A sharp two-edged sword came from his mouth.

REVELATION 1:16

Hebrews 4:12 tells us that: The word of God is full of living power. It is sharper than the sharpest knife, cutting deep into our innermost thoughts and desires. It exposes us for what we really are.

When Jesus spoke, his words pierced John's soul. The Word of God is like that. The Bible describes it in many ways: honey, sweet to the taste; a hammer that breaks the rock; a light and a lamp to our path; a seed; and a treasure of gold. Ephesians 6:17 tells us that the Word of God is the sword of the Spirit. There's a battle to be fought. Sometimes we fight it with our life, and other times we fight it with our words. When we speak up for Christ in a secular situation, we will find that the sword cuts to the quick. People are hurt by what we say in a way that makes them fight back.

Jesus' message to the church at Pergamum was to "repent, or I will come to you suddenly and fight against them with the sword of my mouth" (Revelation 2:16). They needed to clean up their act and live like Christ.

Jesus has to use his sharp words on Christians sometimes. Once, when I was afraid of losing my reputation if I witnessed, the Lord used the sword of his mouth on me, reminding me that he "made himself nothing . . . and . . . obediently humbled himself" (Philippians 2:7-8). That cured me! It was sharp, and it hurt, but it drove me to my knees and back to him for healing.

Facing It with Jesus' Face in Mind!

His face was as bright as the sun in all its brilliance.

REVELATION 1:16

John had a case of déjà vu. During Jesus' earthly ministry, John, the apostle, had never seen his Master with pure white hair, holding seven stars in his hand, or with a golden sash round his chest, but there is something about his Lord's glorified face that reminded him of a mountaintop experience in his past.

Jesus had asked John, his brother James, and Simon Peter to go with him up a high mountain (see Matthew 17:1). John remembered feeling very proud to be selected to accompany the Master in this intimate way. They had been wondering what Jesus wanted to say to them when suddenly an amazing thing happened. Jesus was transfigured before them. "As the men watched, Jesus' appearance changed so that his face shone like the sun, and his clothing became dazzling white" (Matthew 17:2). As John "turned to see who was speaking" (Revelation 1:12) on Patmos, he remembered the face of Jesus of Nazareth on that mountaintop. This was the same Jesus, now glorified forever! The blinding light of God, shining through Christ's earthly body, had caused Peter and James and John to fall on their faces, and they were terrified (see Matthew 17:6).

Now, years later, John again fell at his feet as dead (Revelation 1:17). John would look into the dark faces of cruel men before his suffering was over, remember his mountaintop experiences, shut his eyes, and see the face of God shining like the sun in its strength. He would find the courage to bear the unbearable, do the impossible, and reflect the light of Jesus Christ in his own face.

What are you facing? Face it with Jesus' face in mind!

If God Sent You a Letter

Write this letter to the angel of the church in Ephesus. . . . But I have this complaint against you. You don't love me or each other as you did at first!

REVELATION 2:1, 4

The risen Lord Jesus asked his servant John, the apostle, who was exiled on a small Greek island, to write some letters to a group of churches for him. And that's how we *know* what Christ thought about the church! He wrote to the believers at Ephesus and reprimanded them because they had lost their zeal and love for him and for each other.

What do you think of the church? Do you consider it outdated, boring, cold? Have you ever stopped to think what Christ thinks of it? He tells us in the book of Revelation. The church is not a building; it is the people who meet inside it. It is not somewhere you go, but something you are!

Love motivates us to serve others. When you lose your love for Christ, you lose your love for unbelievers, too. You even lose your love for fellow Christians. Love always wants to please. I enjoyed my teenagers being in love. They usually wanted to help with the dishes! Love doesn't only *help* with the dishes, love *does* the dishes! Love goes the extra mile, or two or three or four! Love stops asking, "What can God do for me?" and starts inquiring, "What can I do for God?" Love sings in the rain, and love always replies to God's letters!

If God sent you a letter telling you he was upset with you for losing your love for him and for others, how would you respond? How would you answer his letter?

Jesus Promised

Anyone who is willing to hear should listen to the Spirit and understand what the Spirit is saying to the churches. Whoever is victorious will not be hurt by the second death.

REVELATION 2:11

A willingness to suffer often proves the genuineness of love. The small group of Christians who loved the Lord and lived in Smyrna were suffering because they belonged to him. The risen Christ reminded them who he is. "I am the First and the Last," he said to them. "I am the living one who died" (Revelation 1:17-18). That's always a good thing to hear when you may be facing martyrdom!

Smyrna was widely known as the "crown" city because of its beautiful situation, nestled between the gully and the mountains peaks, crowned with the most luxurious dwellings and government buildings. How appropriate of the Lord Jesus, then, to encourage the few frightened believers to be "faithful even when facing death, and I will give you the crown of life" (Revelation 2:10).

It helps to know that the Savior knows about our troubles, doesn't it? "I know about your suffering and your poverty," he says (Revelation 2:9). We do not know if the Christians in Smyrna belonged to the lower ranks, or if their unselfish concern for the underprivileged had left them poor. More likely, their refusal to cheat in business had resulted in their desperate situation! Whatever the reason for their trials, Christ wanted them to know he saw their plight and was preparing a better place for them. What is more, he told them not to fear the journey to the better land, even though the way would lead through prison gates.

Because of Smyrna, suffering believers through the years have been helped to face the first death by believing they will not be hurt by the second! After all, Jesus promised!

Where You Live

I know that you live in the city where that great throne of Satan is located, and yet you have remained loyal to me.

REVELATION 2:13

"Where do you live?" I asked a newcomer to our church. I could see she was pleased I had asked. We are always pleasantly surprised when people take an interest in us, aren't we? That interest is often demonstrated by the question, "Where do you live?"

Jesus knew exactly where the Christians in Pergamum lived. They lived right next door to Satan himself! Pergamum was not a Satan-worshiping city full of witch doctors, but rather a Satan-worshiping city full of priest doctors! The city was famous for its medical library and hospital. It boasted fantastic temples and a theater that seated thirty-five hundred people. Psychiatry and hypnosis were practiced there, and on the top of a huge hill stood the famous temple of Zeus! Was this "Satan's seat," we wonder? In 1871, an altar with the words "Zeus the Savior" inscribed on it was found in that area. We have to wonder what it would have been like to live in a place like that, daring to believe in Jesus the Savior, the Healer, and the Lord of all! Antipas, Christ's faithful martyr, found out what it was like and sealed his witness with his blood. Others would be faithful to their deaths in that place. Still, the risen Christ had some things against his church there. Basically, many were compromising their faith in the face of the opposition. Error had been mixed with truth, and morals had been corrupted. "Repent," commanded Jesus. "Everyone who is victorious will eat of the manna that has been hidden away in heaven. And I will give to each one a white stone, and . . . a new name" (Revelation 2:16-17). Jesus promised he would reveal intimate secrets to those who stand firm, however hard it is!

Rooted and Grounded

The rocky soil represents those who hear the message with joy. But like young plants in such soil, their roots don't go very deep. They believe for a while, but they wilt when the hot winds of testing blow.

LUKE 8:13

"When the going gets tough, the tough get going," so they say. Yet those who do not let the seed of the Word of God take root in their lives, will *get* going, but not be able to *keep* going when the tough times come!

"Nobody told me my Christianity would cause such trouble at home," complained a teenager accusingly. But Jesus was always warning people about the costliness of being his disciples (see Luke 14:26-33).

It's all very well to get worked up at a meeting or a conference and to go home on a spiritual high. But ahead is Monday morning or a husband who doesn't want anything to do with your Christ or maybe a hostile teenager who will laugh at you. What happens when you offend your friends with the great glad news of your conversion? If your life is filled with rocks, and there has been little attempt to cultivate and pull out the weeds and the stones, your profession of faith will never stand up to opposition.

Jesus says his seed will test us and find us wanting if we are all noise and no fruit. When a rootless believer feels the hot sun and burning winds of rejection, he will soon wither away. Let us grow roots downward, so we can bear fruit upward!

Pleasure's Pretty Flowers

The thorny ground represents those who hear and accept the message, but all too quickly the message is crowded out by the cares and riches and pleasures of this life.

LUKE 8:14

Weeds are awful things. Who has ever kept a garden and has not wanted to have a word with Adam about being the cause of all these choking growths? "Cares and riches and pleasures of this life" can very easily choke the spiritual seed God wishes to cultivate. But it doesn't have to be so. God has given us all things richly to enjoy, and it is the love of money—not money itself—that can become an obsession. But there is no doubt about it—there are many beautiful weeds!

My husband's favorite color is yellow. Every spring he smiles with satisfaction at our yellow lawn—a sea of golden dandelions, stretching from boundary to boundary. Our neighbors do not share his joy. In fact, spring is a time I try to leave and return to the house in the dark to avoid a confrontation! Dandelions are pretty but if not dealt with, they will choke the grass and spread to other lawns, causing consternation everywhere.

Pleasures are pretty, too. We need the Sower to test the soil of our life and make sure the seed of truth is growing strongly and is not being choked by pleasure's pretty flowers. A garden is intended to produce fruit. Do we need to give our heavenly Gardener permission to till the garden of our life and rid our soul of weeds?

The Handle Is on Your Side

Look! Here I stand at the door and knock. If you hear me calling and open the door, I will come in, and we will share a meal as friends.

REVELATION 3:20

The Laodiceans were familiar with the famous medical school that had produced a powder for the cure of ophthalmia, an eye disease affecting many people in the East. Again Jesus uses a familiar illustration to open their eyes to spiritual realities. "Buy ointment for your eyes so you will be able to see" (Revelation 3:18), he counsels the unbelieving believers.

Though they think themselves clothed in their religion, Christ tells them they are "wretched and miserable and poor and blind and naked" (Revelation 3:17), pointing out how obnoxious spiritual pride is in God's sight.

But listen—God is counseling his own. Lukewarm they might be, but God's people they most surely are—and he would be a wonder of a Counselor to them, a Mighty God, their Everlasting Father, their Prince of Peace. Jesus offered them his rightness for their wrongness, urging them to dress their spirits in such a garment of grace that they would "not be shamed by [their] nakedness" (Revelation 3:18).

He stands at the door of every lukewarm heart. He wants to come into our uninterested lives and bring his cup of rejoicing with him. He would meet us inside our shallow spirituality and heat our cooling ardor into bright flames of love. Open the door—the handle is on your side!

Enter my heart,
My loving Lord,
Take not a part but the whole—
Quicken my spirit,
Warm my cold mind,
And set me on fire in my soul!

THE "JUST US"

A great wave of persecution began that day, sweeping over the church in Jerusalem, and all the believers except the apostles fled into Judea and Samaria.

ACTS 8:1

When the first persecution arose around Stephen, the Christians were scattered abroad. Acts 8:4 tells us they "went everywhere preaching the Good News about Jesus." In other words, they gossiped the gospel. A good definition of "preaching" is the communication of truth through personality.

Ordinary people fleeing for their lives told other ordinary people along the way the reason they were on the run. This was the way the Good News was carried to the uttermost parts of their world. There were leaders among them, even though the apostles stayed in Jerusalem. But the majority of the people were just like you and me—ordinary folk.

It is the same today. God wants ordinary people to tell other ordinary people about his good news of salvation. The leaders can't do it all. The leaders can help us to know what to communicate, and the evangelists can show us how to lead people to Christ. But if our world is to be reached, it will take every single one of us passing the news on to another.

I was invited to some meetings in Atlanta. I asked the lady who had called to inquire about my coming what church or organization she represented.

"Well," she replied a little shyly and hesitantly, "it's just us." I found out the "just us" was a bunch of God's ordinary people gossiping the gospel. It was a sheer delight to serve them!

WHAT IF?

I had heard about you before, but now I have seen you with my own eyes.

JOB 42:5

I found it quite by accident—a nasty little black mark on my skin. I couldn't remember having seen it before. I showed it to my husband. "You'd better show it to the doctor," he said. My heart beat a little harder. I'd heard about black warts. The doctor said I'd better have it removed that week.

I was frightened. *What if* . . . I wondered, with a rising tide of apprehension. Things were good—so very good. I could say in all sincerity: "The land you have given me is a pleasant land" (Psalm 16:6). Our children loved the Lord, our ministry was prospering. I was young, well, I *felt* young, too young to. . . ! I couldn't say it—not even silently!

I read the book of Job. Job had had it good, too. The lines had certainly fallen to him in pleasant places! He knew the Lord. He believed his Word. He had been an obedient servant. But then, "What I always feared has happened. . . . What I dreaded has come to be" (Job 3:25). Job's family died; his health failed; his business crashed. Only his wife remained, and he could well have wished her gone, so little help she turned out to be! But, oh, at the end he was able to say, "I had heard about you before, but now I have seen you with my own eyes" (Job 42:5).

The wart was removed. It was benign. When I came home and read these verses again, I understood Job a little better. I understood it had been worth my little scare to "see" God in quite a new way. He had sharpened my focus and given me a clear glimpse of glory!

A Radical Change

Come, be my disciples, and I will show you how to fish for people!

MATTHEW 4:19

Jesus always managed to communicate to people where they were. He did not come to Peter and Andrew and say, "Follow me, and I will make you astronauts, or computer experts, or preachers!" He used terms that would be most familiar to them. He wanted them to know there was a cost involved. Commitment meant a radical change. "If you follow me, you will catch people instead of fish," he said. Now *that* was a change!

Peter and Andrew were casting their nets into the sea at the time Jesus called them. The Bible says that "they left their nets at once and went with him" (Matthew 4:20). It must have been difficult for them to drop their heavy involvement with their daily tasks and leave just at that moment. But catching people, in all probability, always will be very inconvenient. Jesus did not tell them to finish the job at hand and come along when they felt more inclined. He called them, and they left their nets and came.

James and John were also busy when Jesus came by. They were not actually casting their nets into the sea but were mending them (see Matthew 4:21). They "immediately" left their aging father, their nets and boats—all that they loved—and followed him.

What are your "nets"? Jesus is asking you to catch men and women for his kingdom. This will involve commitment and a radical change in your life. Will you obey—immediately—like the early disciples?

Upset Plans

> **As soon as Jesus heard the news, he went off by himself in a boat to a remote area to be alone. But the crowds heard where he was headed and followed by land from many villages.**
>
> MATTHEW 14:13

How do you react when somebody upsets your plans? Perhaps you have planned a lovely day at the zoo with the children, when, at the last minute, you get a phone call from work. Someone has called in sick, and you are the only one who can do her job. Or perhaps you have dreamed of a special vacation. The plans are in place, when a distant relative dies and you have to go to the funeral. You get as upset as your upset plans!

Something like that happened to the disciples. They had planned a lovely vacation with Jesus. They had the place all picked out—a resort area on beautiful Lake Galilee.

They needed a vacation! They had just received the terrible news that their dear colleague and friend, John the Baptist, had been cruelly murdered. They had been terribly busy for days—keeping the crowds of people who came to see Jesus in order, helping take the sick to the Master, and controlling the children who got under everyone's feet. Feeding and housing their party and making endless travel arrangements were hard work. How relieved they must have been when they were actually on their way away from it all!

But "it all" met them as soon as they stepped out of the boat on the other side of the lake. Jesus was moved as he looked at the multitude of need. The disciples looked at the multitude and needed to have them *re*-moved! How would you have reacted?

Facing Up to the Supernatural

When the disciples saw him, they screamed in terror, thinking he was a ghost.

MATTHEW 14:26

The disciples "screamed in terror." Even Peter was frightened. We need to take note of the fact that Peter was not afraid of the *storm*. Peter, the intrepid fisherman, knew the Sea of Galilee like the back of his hand. He respected its moods and knew it could be very dangerous at times, but he had experienced storms before. He didn't know, however, if he could handle a ghost!

Have you ever noticed how many folks are totally self-confident until faced with the supernatural? Sometimes you meet people who are not one whit frightened by the storms of life (they've been around) but are petrified when presented with the claims of Jesus Christ!

Are you frightened by things you don't understand? Has someone "put you off" Christianity because he made it sound a bit "spooky"?

Jesus Christ told the disciples not to be afraid of him. He wasn't a ghost. He was and is God, and you don't ever need to be afraid of God—unless, of course, you have never asked him to forgive your sins! Then, you have good reason to cry out for fear.

Perhaps it's time you invited Christ into the boat of your life to handle the storm of your fears about himself. He will forgive your sins. He will bring peace and purpose to your life. You'll be glad that you met him!

Keeping Your Eyes on Jesus

But when he looked around at the high waves, he was terrified and began to sink. "Save me, Lord!" he shouted.

MATTHEW 14:30

Peter, having overcome his fear of Jesus, decided to walk on the water, too! He was wise enough to wait until Jesus told him it was all right to try. Then he clambered over the side of his boat to go to him.

As soon as you get over your fear of the supernatural by recognizing and acknowledging God's lordship over everything in heaven and on earth, you will want to experience that power for yourself. I believe, for example, that Jesus could do extraordinary things. Not only could he heal sick people, he could keep his temper, be unselfish, and always say the right thing.

Can I do what Jesus did? Can I stride over the circumstances of my life in triumph? Can I walk over the waters of worries and fears? Yes, if I keep my eyes on him.

Peter unfortunately forgot who was keeping him afloat and started to look at the reasons he should be sinking. As soon as you do that, you are sunk! Peter had been afraid to face the supernatural. Having overcome *that* fear, he then became afraid he couldn't depend on God to see him through.

It's a matter of keeping your eyes on Jesus, not on the storm. And remember, if you begin to sink, cry out to him. He will put out his hand and save you. It's important to him that you succeed!

"OTHER" BOATS

He was already in the boat, so they started out, leaving the crowds behind (although other boats followed).

MARK 4:36

There was another storm on the Sea of Galilee. Jesus and the disciples were in a boat together. According to Mark, "other boats" went along. We do not know who was in those other vessels; all we know is that they wanted to be near Jesus.

"But soon a fierce storm arose. High waves began to break into the boat until it was nearly full of water" (Mark 4:37). This time, even Peter was afraid of the storm. If the big boat was in trouble, can you imagine what was happening to the "other" smaller boats?

Jesus, meanwhile, was asleep in the stern (Mark 4:38). His frightened men woke him up and accused him of not caring for them properly. "Teacher, don't you even care that we are going to drown?" (Mark 4:38), they asked him. Jesus didn't answer that question, but he stilled the storm, and he told them he cared about their lack of trust! "Why are you so afraid?" he asked them. "Do you still not have faith in me?" The Bible says the disciples "were filled with awe" (Mark 4:40-41).

It always makes more sense to fear the power of the one who can still the storm rather than to fear the power of the storm itself! The other little boats were helped when Jesus stopped the wind and hushed the sea to sleep. Our faith, or lack of it, always affects the little boats that sail by our side. We mothers should remember that!

Jesus' Friends

The members of the council were amazed when they saw the boldness of Peter and John, for they could see that they were ordinary men who had had no special training. They also recognized them as men who had been with Jesus.

ACTS 4:13

Have you noticed how much easier it is to be with Jesus' friends than to be with Jesus? We can go away on a spiritual retreat and never manage to bump into Christ! We are far too busy having fun and fellowship!

What did it mean for the disciples to have "been with Jesus"? It meant they listened to his sermons and helped him help people; they tried to do what he told them to do; they left their homes and their loved ones and became as poor as Jesus had become. They experienced the popularity and the persecution Jesus experienced.

Being with Jesus also meant making some very special friends. Even though the "inner circle" was made up of diverse personalities, the men grew close as they spent time together. Jesus was glad about that. He wanted them to love one another and to enjoy one another's company. But he did not want them to enjoy that fellowship more than friendship with him.

Do you find yourself enjoying Jesus' friends more than your friend Jesus? Give yourself a little test. Count up the hours you've spent with Christian friends this last month. Then count up the hours you've spent with your best friend, Jesus. That should tell you something!

The world will take notice and marvel when we've "been with Jesus," but not necessarily when we've been with Jesus' friends! I love to be with Christian people, but when I begin to love that more than being with Christ, it's time to look at my priorities and change some things!

The Four Seasons

There is a time for everything, a season for every activity under heaven.

ECCLESIASTES 3:1

Life has its seasons. Spring is the beginning—babyhood, childhood, adolescence. Our hands must be held to help us walk with more mature steps. Summer follows—our twenties and thirties. Then comes middle age, a less welcome friend—autumn has arrived. Lastly comes the white, white world of winter—our old age accompanies us home. Each season has its special blessings and problems.

Spring is fun and free, new and exciting. It is bright and fresh and makes us feel a little crazy. We are tempted to do rash things, to experiment, and to live in fast time.

Summer sees us consolidate. Our mistakes lend us help in making better choices. We learn who we are and what we can do.

Autumn finds us reflecting on summer and occasionally wishing for spring. The colors of our character, formed in spring and summer, fall like autumn leaves across the pathways of the people whom we love. Occasionally, a chill wind blows, and we mourn better days when our branches were prettier and didn't threaten to break off in the storm.

Then winter closes in. Sometimes, old age is warm and cozy; we don't want to go outside. We wrap our years around us like a warm old sweater and feel comfortable at last. At other times, we venture outside and romp like two-year-olds in the snow.

There is a "time for everything." Blessed are those of us who see our four seasons through!

Dead on Time!

A time to be born and a time to die.

ECCLESIASTES 3:2

As I grow older, I occasionally struggle with accepting wrinkles, a double chin, a failing memory, and glasses! The day I got my first pair of bifocals a friend of mine (or so I thought!) left me a funny poem:

My glasses come in handy,
My hearing aid is fine,
My false teeth are just dandy,
But I sure do miss my mind!

That didn't help! My husband, seeing my struggle, usually tells me to get my theology straight—I was born at the right moment and will be "dead on time." Therefore, I must stop wanting to reverse the trend! Life has been so good to me, I cling to it. But I have a poor view of heaven if I want to stay on earth.

A friend of mine, my age and dying of cancer, told me people keep asking her if she is angry. "Why should I be angry?" she asked me. "I've had a marvelous life, and heaven will be even better. Sure, I'll miss everyone, and I hope they will miss me, but it's my time, and it's all right." What a contrast to the statement of a girl being interviewed on a TV show about her reaction when she discovered she had cancer. "I hit out at everyone in sight," she said. "It was so unfair! I hadn't had time to do everything I wanted to do. Mostly I was mad at God."

When you know Jesus, you let him wind your watch. When it stops, he gives you a new one with everlasting springs!

Read Time Is Seed Time

A time to plant and a time to harvest.

ECCLESIASTES 3:2

You don't plant seeds in frozen soil. You don't wait until autumn to prepare the ground. You plant seeds in the warm, moist springtime. That way you have a chance to pluck up that which you have planted.

I take every opportunity I am given to tell young mothers these things. It's hard to be a young mom these days. Many a single parent is left to cope with two toddlers. Trying to juggle a job and manage a home leaves little time to plant seed thoughts from God's Word in the moist soil of a child's springtime.

I am convinced the first five years of a child's life are vital. What they learn in these years shapes much of their future. This is the time to talk of Jesus and his friendship and of God their Father and his care. This is the time to share picture books of their Savior and to tell stories that make Bible people walk off the pages and become their friends.

Read time is seed time! It will have to be a priority or it will never get done. The devil will see to that. He hates little children and their springtimes. But if you would harvest a crop of Christian children who would minister to others, and perhaps to you in your old age, you will have to minister to them in their youth!

Prince

A time to kill and a time to heal.

ECCLESIASTES 3:3

We bought a dog and named him Prince. By the time he had belonged to the family two weeks, the family belonged to him! He was a beautiful golden retriever and was supposed to be kept in the backyard. But he made himself at home wherever he would, and we settled down to sixteen marvelous "dog years." He was probably the most disobedient dog in the neighborhood and useless as a watchdog, but we loved him. He was something of a legend by the time we arrived in America. I could write a book about him! Then he got heartworm. I had never imagined there would be a time in my life when I must kill. Was this it?

Being a Christian makes a difference in attitude, even toward animals. After all, God made the animals and gave people dominion over them (see Genesis 1:28). We should show respect to all of God's divine creation by the way we treat it—and that includes animals.

Prince survived his heartworm. It was a time to heal. Years later, when he was old and decrepit, our friends advised us to have him put to sleep. Was *this* the time to kill?

"We must make sure we don't just get rid of him because he's inconvenient," my husband said to me. "He's been a marvelous family friend."

In the end, we knew it was time—time to kill. It was very hard. Animal lovers will understand! But Jesus understood, too! "Nothing exists that he didn't make" (John 1:3), and that includes Prince!

God's Wrecking Ball

A time to tear down and a time to rebuild.

ECCLESIASTES 3:3

How can a Christian know what it is to rise triumphant unless she has first fallen down, defeated? "The way to *up* is *down,* and the way to *down* is *up,*" someone has said. I do believe that the way to *up* is down. It's a matter of taking time to let the Master Builder demolish the old building so a new structure can rise on the old site!

Have you ever gazed in awe as a massive wrecking ball cracked the walls of a condemned apartment house and flung the bricks in the air, sending the structure to destruction in a cloud of choking dust? Have you ever wondered what could take the place of that familiar old building? Then you pass that way in a little time and see the modern replacement, which often makes the memory of the old distasteful.

It takes time to build the new in the place of the old. Therefore, "those who become Christians become new persons. They are not the same anymore, for the old life is gone. A new life has begun!" (2 Corinthians 5:17).

God can demolish the old life. Some of us need to be broken. He will have to use a very big wrecking ball on some of us! Not until that happens will there be the possibility of being built up again—a new house, a habitation fit for the Lord!

Balance

> **A time to cry and a time to laugh.**
>
> ECCLESIASTES 3:4

Listening to some people talk, you get the impression that tear ducts are supposed to dry up the moment you become a Christian. But there is a time to weep. Jesus wept, you will remember.

Looking at some people's faces, you get the impression that at the moment they are born again, Christians' mouths are frozen into a line of disapproval. But there is a time to laugh. We laugh when we celebrate life. I believe Jesus laughed, too.

Sometimes speaker after speaker will bring messages of consolation and testimony after testimony of victory over horrendous odds. The impression is given that you cannot get to know Christ properly unless you have had the worst possible experiences in life!

But there is a balance in life, which the Scripture above speaks about. There is a time when it is perfectly permissible for the Christian to weep. In fact, there are some situations that demand such a response from God's children. There is far too much injustice in our world to stay a dry-eyed disciple. On the other hand, you love Jesus no less if you enjoy a season of celebration. There *is* a time to laugh; thank God for that! Use it to go on your way rejoicing. Utilize that freedom from trouble to lift the spirit of the one whose time it is to weep!

Tender Time

A time to grieve and a time to dance.

ECCLESIASTES 3:4

Jesus said that it's hard to mourn when the groom is with you. On the other hand, it's hard not to mourn when the groom is taken away (see Matthew 9:15)! When the wedding is in full swing, it is time to dance. If the groom were to die, it would be time to mourn.

I heard a true account of a wedding of two young Bible school students who really loved the Lord and were preparing to serve him together. On their way to their honeymoon hotel, the groom was killed in a car crash. How soon the dancing turned into mourning!

Sometimes the two things come so close to each other it shatters the soul. The parents of the young man who met such an untimely death did not believe their son's home call was some freakish accident. The Christian doesn't believe in accidents of that magnitude. Actually, there is no such thing as "untimely" death for the Christian, for we believe there is "a time to die" (Ecclesiastes 3:2).

Time is a kind cushion, separating the good days from the bad days, preparing us for change. Time heals. Time gives us perspective we've never had before. Time taken for grieving eventually helps us to dance. Time taken for dancing helps us to prepare ourselves to grieve. Time ripens us, like cheese, making us sharp. Time does not usually demand such instant adjustments as in this sad incident of such unexpected death. But when such things do happen, tender time takes care of the wounds.

The Disappointment Stones

A time to scatter stones and a time to gather stones.

ECCLESIASTES 3:5

Perhaps the meaning of these phrases about stones refers to the way an Eastern gardener prepares to till his vineyard. These vineyards are often hacked out of the steep sides of the vales. The ground in Israel seems to be made of stones of every shape and size. There is a season when the owner of the vineyard has to clear the ground of stones, and other times when he needs to gather, for some useful purpose, the very stones he has thrown away.

A young missionary would travel many months on end teaching and preaching, so his time at home, though very important, was fleeting. His wife would make all sorts of plans, only to find her life littered with the stones of disappointments. There would always be some responsibility her husband had to fulfill, and her plans would be spoiled. Picking up her disappointments and throwing them at her mate solved nothing! It was time to cast the stones of disappointment into the corner of her life.

As time went on and the fruit of Christian perseverance began to grow in the cultivated ground, the young wife tentatively began to build a watchtower in her mind with the disappointment stones. From that tower she could watch for her husband to come home and prepare a suitable celebration.

There *is* a time to scatter stones, and there *is* a time to gather stones together. I know—I was that young wife!

A Special Fast

A time to embrace and a time to turn away.

ECCLESIASTES 3:5

Our sexual appetites need to be under control. We do well to make our God the God of our loves. *Eros* must be mastered by *agape* in obedience to the law of the Lord. We cannot go around sleeping with whomever we will and expect God to smile. The place for the full expression of the Christian's sexuality is within the boundaries of marriage—which are designed to nurture love to full maturity.

The Bible teaches us that fornication (sex before marriage) is sin. Adultery (extramarital sex) is also sin. Jesus, face-to-face with a woman taken in the very act of adultery, forgave her, but said, "Go and sin no more" (John 8:11). Once you have been face-to-face with Jesus, your sexuality must be subject to his commands.

The sexual act speaks of a commitment to a forever relationship with another human being and therein lies its wonder and enjoyment. How, then, can casual sex be part of a Christian lifestyle? For the couple who follows Christ, there is "a time to embrace and a time to turn away." We are not to withhold our bodies from our mates, using our sexuality as a weapon, but rather are to use our bodies to bless (see 1 Corinthians 7:3-5).

There are times, however, that God calls some of his children to a ministry that entails considerable separation for the kingdom's sake. Such has been our case. I would testify to the fact that as we have "fasted" in this area, God has given special grace for this special calling. But then he is a special God!

A Time to Worship

A time to search and a time to lose.

ECCLESIASTES 3:6

Do you know how to live with little or much? Paul said he knew what it was "to live on almost nothing or with everything" (Philippians 4:12). Job knew, too. "Should we accept only good things from the hand of God and never anything bad?" (Job 2:10). When Job's world crashed around his ears, he

> stood up and tore his robe in grief. Then he shaved his head and fell to the ground before God. He said, "I came naked from my mother's womb, and I will be stripped of everything when I die. The Lord gave me everything I had, and the Lord has taken it away. Praise the name of the Lord!" (Job 1:20-21)

The Bible goes on to say, "In all of this, Job did not sin by blaming God" (Job 1:22).

When trouble comes our way, many of us tear our hair out and collapse in a whimpering heap like Job, but few of us fall to the ground before God in worship. Worshiping means acknowledging God's worth. When trouble strikes, most of us don't think God is worth much! Job's wife told Job to curse God for causing him to suffer (see Job 2:9).

While sin stalks our earth, there will always be a time to lose. We shall lose our health and our friends. Some of us may lose a wife, a husband, or even a child. But there will be times to gain as well. Not only will we gain new spiritual insight through our trials as Job did, but some of us may well have years of blessing. God does give us all things richly to enjoy! Whether we have almost nothing, or whether we have everything, we must worship. Then all will be right.

THE GRATEFUL SHELF

A time to keep and a time to throw away.

ECCLESIASTES 3:6

I like to keep everything—tied up with pretty string or filed away in colored folders or packed in boxes. I'm like my mother. When my mother died, I did not relish going through her house and disposing of her goods. What a job that was.

I was prepared for tears but not for the things that triggered them. I thought when I saw her favorite worn chair or her beloved teakettle or her walking cane, it would get to me. But it was the sight of dozens of little unimportant things wrapped up in plastic bags and sealed with rubber bands that finished me off. Even as I write this, I am crying. But that's all right—there's a time to remember!

My sister and I felt like reluctant thieves, rummaging through someone's personal belongings. It was horrible. But it had to be done. There's a time to keep, but there's a time to throw away—and that time had come.

As we went about our necessary work, closed up in the silence of our deep sorrow, I realized how precious a time this was for both my sister and me. This was a time we could take "mother memories" and wrap them up more carefully than even the little plastic packets we found, tie them with the strings of love, and place them safely on the grateful shelf of our hearts. It was a time to throw away, but it was a time to keep as well, and we held each other, my sister and I, and thanked God for motherhood and daughterhood, sisterhood and family!

THE STITCHES OF FORGIVENESS

A time to tear and a time to mend.

ECCLESIASTES 3:7

"A time to tear" refers to the rending of garments in an outward show of distress or repentance. Reuben, returning to the pit where Joseph had been held, found him gone and tore his clothes in distress (see Genesis 37:29). "Jacob tore his clothes and put on sackcloth. He mourned deeply for his son for many days" (Genesis 37:34), believing him dead.

Later, after God had miraculously preserved Joseph and he had become Pharaoh's right-hand man, his brothers, seeking food for the family, were tricked by Joseph, who had a cup put in Benjamin's sack. The brothers discovered this, "tore their clothing in despair, loaded the donkeys again, and returned to the city" (Genesis 44:13) to seek the mighty man's mercy. If the men in the family knew what "a time to tear" was about, surely the women in the clan knew what "a time to mend" was all about! They must have dreaded their menfolk's coming in for supper!

Seriously though, we are talking about a custom that dramatically demonstrated inward mourning and sorrow. But as is often the case with outward signs of inward things, the ritual eventually took the place of the reality.

Joel, the prophet, had to call Israel to true repentance.

> That is why the Lord says, "Turn to me now, while there is time! Give me your hearts. Come with fasting, weeping, and mourning. Don't tear your clothing in your grief; instead, tear your hearts." Return to the Lord your God, for he is gracious and merciful. He is not easily angered. He is filled with kindness and is eager not to punish you. (Joel 2:12-13)

Joel knew that when we rend our heart and not our clothing, God sews it up for us with the stitches of forgiveness.

Taming My Tongue

A time to be quiet and a time to speak up.
ECCLESIASTES 3:7

I have a problem. I often open my mouth simply to change feet! I'm always saying the wrong thing!

I remember once going to hear a visiting preacher at our church. I was delighted to see two unfamiliar ladies in "my pew." Our church was small, and visitors were a rarity. I hoped the preacher would be good, and they would like the service and come again. The visiting preacher was not bad—he was terrible!

I watched the visitors carefully. The younger lady, looking embarrassed, glanced at the older one. As soon as the service was over, they rose to leave. I leaped around the pew, welcomed them profusely, and said I hoped they wouldn't judge the fellowship by this one visit.

"The preacher is usually very good," I said as quietly as I could. "I don't know where this man came from."

"I do," said the older lady icily. "He's my husband."

"And he's my dad," added the younger woman balefully.

This was definitely a time I should have kept quiet. Other times, I have kept quiet when I knew I should speak up!

"Who makes mouths?" (Exodus 4:11) God asked Moses, when he was busy telling God he wouldn't be a good speaker. God knew he could be and should be: "Now go, and do as I have told you. I will help you speak well, and I will tell you what to say" (Exodus 4:12).

My tongue needs teaching, too. I need the Lord God to instruct it when to speak and when to stay silent. I need to use it, to ask him to touch it, and tame it, and turn it into an instrument of blessing!

The Spoiler

A time to love and a time to hate.

ECCLESIASTES 3:8

We know there is always a time to love, but is there ever a time to hate? I believe there is a legitimate case for hating whatever it is that spoils love.

What wife beater does not hate the temper that controls him? What alcoholic wife does not despise the urge to reach for the bottle that is ruining her home and her relationships? There is definitely a time to hate that which destroys love. If we hate sin enough, we might be motivated to seek God's help to turn from it and be different.

God hates sin. He hates it because he knows sin is a spoiler. Jesus showed us God's heart when he turned on the Pharisees, hating their hypocrisy and pride. "I hate pride" (Proverbs 8:13), said the Lord. God hates lying, divorce, and all sorts of abuses of human rights. He hates cheating and sexual perversion.

Yes, there is a time to hate. The problem comes when our love does not contain the element of hatred. False love allows anyone to do anything to anybody regardless of the consequences. False love even loves what God hates!

"God has given me this wonderful love for this married man," a woman told me.

"Nonsense," I replied. "He wouldn't. God hates adultery."

True love hates the thing that spoils it. True love has rules, and it confronts, disciplines, and shows itself strong in sticking to principles. True love is honest and open, willing to sacrifice itself, being first and foremost concerned with the loved one's highest good. There is a time to love. It's now!

An Enemy Worse Than Hitler

> **A time for war and a time for peace.**
>
> ECCLESIASTES 3:8

It was a time of war. I was small, very insignificant, and extremely frightened. I sat on a little stool, looking up into the darkening sky at the searchlights seeking shapes—sinister shapes of war and hate and death. I didn't understand why the shapes might drop bombs all over my garden, my daddy's cabbage patch, and my mummy's washing machine, but I knew if I didn't run into the air-raid shelter, they would drop bombs all over me as well!

My mother explained that an evil man called Hitler was trying to conquer the world, someone had to try to stop his gobbling up all the nations on the globe. Then I dimly understood that sometimes there's a time for war.

After it was all over and I was grown and at college, I came across a book of photographs that had been taken in places called Belsen and Auschwitz. Then I understood more fully why I had had to run into the air-raid shelter, why my daddy had had to fight, and why my friend's uncle had been killed.

Now I am middle-aged, and it's a time of peace. My Bible instructs me to pray for peace in our time. If there is peace, we can attend to God's work and try to reach the half of our world that has never once heard about the Prince of Peace, Jesus Christ. When we live in a time of peace, we don't need to spend every waking moment in the business of survival as we do in wartime. We can attend to those in the grip of an enemy worse than Hitler—Satan himself, who would gobble up people's souls. We can spend time caring for souls. We can fight the devil, for there is a time for war!

Timing

God has made everything beautiful for its own time.

ECCLESIASTES 3:11

God has painted time with changes. The kaleidoscopic movement of innumerable processes will be seen in the end as "beautiful for its own time." It may look a mess up close, just as putting your face too near a big painting will distort your view of it. Stepping back puts it in better perspective. One day we will step back, look at the finished canvas of life with the Artist by our side, and see it in all its beauty and completeness.

The same thought inspired some unknown author to write:

Not till the loom is silent,
And the shuttle ceases to fly
Will God unveil the canvas,
And show the reason why
The black threads were as needful
In the weaver's skillful hand
As the threads of gold and silver
In the pattern He has planned.

Ecclesiastes 3:11 goes on to say, "He has planted eternity in the human heart." People who have a worldview from a worldly perspective will fail to see beauty in black threads. All will be meaningless to them.

But for those of us who have eternity in our heart, it is another matter. We are given faith to believe that "people should eat and drink and enjoy the fruits of their labor, for these are gifts from God" (Ecclesiastes 3:13). And it is the grace of God that will enable us to leave the explanations of the dark threads till heaven. This faith will help us to rejoice and to enjoy our life.

To everything there is a season: a time for this and a time for that. There is a time to ask God to put eternity in your heart—now! Ask him.

A Hymn Called "Forever"

And I know that whatever God does is final. Nothing can be added to it or taken from it.

ECCLESIASTES 3:14

God made man, and as Derek Kidner said in his book *A Time to Mourn and a Time to Dance,* "God has no abortive enterprises or forgotten men!"

God did not make the world, throw it into space, and then wonder where it went and what was happening to it. "Whatever God does is final"! What's more, "Nothing can be added to it."

People, however bright, cannot possibly create another world just like the present one. Whatever we can do—even of considerable value, wrought with incredible ingenuity—can never "be final" or eternal if we believe only in the now. If we are earthbound in mind and spirit, we cannot comprehend a God who foreknows all and overlooks nothing.

The frustration and emptiness of doing things that are only for now must lead some honest people to ask questions. What joy to tell the seeker that whatever God does is final and lasts forever.

He forgives me—that's final and it lasts forever. He will not suddenly change his mind. He loves me forever, and he changes me forever, refusing to let me jettison my preparation for life in another dimension. He gives me family who are forever: a forever husband, two forever sons, and a forever daughter. He sends me forever friends and helps me engage in forever pursuits.

Final and forever have already forgotten now. They linger for eternity; their joys expand, filling the universe, singing a hymn.

THE LIBRARIAN

All Scripture is inspired by God and is useful.

2 TIMOTHY 3:16

The Bible is like a library. It has a historical section, a poetry shelf, and a collection of wisdom literature. There are practical helps for daily living. If you are musically inclined, there is a section just for you. If you like human interest stories, there are lots of biographies and autobiographies. There are even books that look into the future!

When you visit a library, you need to know how it is arranged so you can quickly select the material of your choice. Take some time to sit down with God's Word and familiarize yourself with its layout. Then try to read something from each section in the course of the year, so you will have a balanced view of the whole.

The Holy Spirit is like the librarian. His job is to answer your questions, see to your complaints, and encourage you to become an accomplished reader. In the end though, *you* have to sit down and read the book. The librarian cannot do that for you; neither can the other people who use the library!

Many of us treat our Bibles as we treat our public libraries. Some of us never even bother to get a card. Oh, we believe in libraries (and the Bible), but we think they are just for people who like that sort of thing.

Others of us start a book, never finish it, and find ourselves fined for keeping it too long. That's a shame! It will always cost you if you make a habit of doing that! It will cost you the encouragement, wisdom, and instruction that are available to you. Become a book lover. Read in God's library today.

The Stamp of Authenticity

And I suppose that if all the other things Jesus did were written down, the whole world could not contain the books.

JOHN 21:25

Some people say the Gospels contradict themselves. They tell us there are discrepancies and differences.

If you saw a fashion show with three of your friends, and then you all came home and talked about it, would you all recount the same thing in exactly the same way? Of course not! You would describe the same "happening" from a different perspective. This is how the four Gospel writers came to record the same events a little differently.

Their reasons for writing played an important part, too. Matthew wrote for the Jews. Knowing his people were looking for a king, he wrote about Jesus as the Kingdom Man they were looking for. Mark, on the other hand, wrote primarily for the Romans. He presented Jesus as the Servant Messiah, knowing that the Romans knew all about servants! Luke wrote for the Greeks, and banked on the Greeks relating to their mythology. He emphasized the God-man character of Jesus. John wrote for all the rest of us, emphasizing the humanity and the divinity of our Lord.

The Holy Spirit used these men's personalities and diverse writing styles in the accounts as we have them. No wonder there were differences—but the important thing to remember is that the message is the same! The writers may have conveyed the Good News with contrasting style and color, and with different motivation, but the divinity of Christ, the redemption of mankind, and the resurrection from the dead were similarly revealed through their pens. The variations of their Gospels only stamp them with authenticity!

God's Roses

Instead, God deliberately chose things the world considers foolish in order to shame those who think they are wise. And he chose those who are powerless to shame those who are powerful.

1 CORINTHIANS 1:27

Here we have a description of God's VIPs. The Bible does not say there will be *no* wise, mighty, or noble people at all among God's special servants. There will, in fact, be a *few* (see 1 Corinthians 1:26), but the majority of God's chosen ones will be like you and me—nobodies! Paul explains the Lord's strange choices by showing us that God's glory will be enhanced against such a dim landscape!

I have two containers for flowers. One is an old clay pot, the other is a beautiful cut-glass vase. Occasionally, I receive a lovely bouquet of roses. If I put them in the vase, the glory is shared. If I put them in the pot, attention is drawn to the blossoms. "What beautiful flowers!" exclaim my visitors, ignoring the container.

God chooses such earthen vessels that his glory may be better displayed. In fact, he has told us that he will not share his glory with another. He insists on receiving the honor due his name.

Sometimes I want to be the cut-glass vase and draw attention to myself. I have to be reminded that my sense of importance lies in the miracle of God's choosing me. He placed his roses in my vase. In this lies my value. What use is a vase without flowers?

Humility Is Grown in the Desert

"Are you really the Messiah we've been waiting for, or should we keep looking for someone else?" Jesus told them, "Go back to John and tell him about what you have heard and seen."

MATTHEW 11:3-4

Humility is grown in the desert. John the Baptist cultivated a wilderness lifestyle. He would rather do without "things" than do without God. Humility is modeled after other godly people.

John's model was Elijah. John came in the spirit and power of the great Old Testament prophet! Elijah lived in the desert, too. He was conscious of his own shortcomings. When his faith faltered, he cried out to God, "I am no better than my ancestors" (1 Kings 19:4).

John had his shortcomings as well. At one point in his life, when he had been put in prison, he had horrible doubts about Jesus. He was tortured with thoughts that perhaps he had made a terrible mistake. Maybe Jesus was not the Messiah after all. Had he baptized the wrong person? Perhaps he had said all the wrong things in his sermons!

Humility is asking questions; not being afraid to send a message to Jesus and ask him to help with doubts. That's what John did, and Jesus gave him assurance and encouragement at once.

If we have humility, we know we can tell Jesus when we're weak. Humility helps us to be strong, even when we are in a prison of death, doubt, or despair.

Prideful people won't ask. They try to figure it all out for themselves. But, then, pride doesn't live in the desert with God.

A Sense of Destiny

He will be a man with the spirit and power of Elijah.

LUKE 1:17

If you are going to be great for God, you will need a sense of destiny. John the Baptist had a sense of destiny. In fact, when the Jewish leaders of the day came to ask him what he thought about himself, he answered in the words of the prophet Isaiah, "I am a voice shouting in the wilderness, 'Prepare a straight pathway for the Lord's coming!'" (John 1:23). He had taken time out to meet with God and find out what he was supposed to be doing with his life. He appeared very sure of his role in God's plan and purpose.

Do you have a sense of destiny? Do you know what you are supposed to be doing? "How do I find that out?" you may ask.

How did John find it out? He found out from the Scriptures and by prayer and fasting. He knew his Bible well enough to be familiar with Malachi 4:5, which says Elijah must come before the Christ. He also knew that this did not mean Elijah would be reincarnated. When the priests and Levites asked him if he was Elijah, he said no (see John 1:21). He understood that it *did* mean there would be one sent to prepare people's hearts for the King and his kingdom, and he believed himself to be that man. I'm sure his parents had had a lot to do with his discovering his destiny; they must have told him the angel had referred to Elijah's prophecy when speaking of him.

Ask God to show you your mission in life. He will.

The Voice

Look, I am sending my messenger before you, and he will prepare your way before you.

MATTHEW 11:10

Do you know what your gift is? Are you a voice, a hand, an ear, or an eye? Knowing is the first step, doing is the second.

John the Baptist knew he was "a voice" (John 1:23). He knew his gift was strong, easily heard! He preached mighty sermons in the open air, and no one had any difficulty listening and understanding. John's sermons were not designed to win friends. In one sermon, he called some of the people snakes; others, hypocrites; and he finished up with a punch line about God's chopping them up and using them for firewood (see Matthew 3:7-10).

Another time he was hauled in front of Herod. He knew the king had the power to put him to death. But he also knew he was called to be "the voice." So he looked the king right in the eye and said, "It is illegal for you to marry your brother's wife" (Mark 6:18). Now of course the lady in question did not like his saying that and decided to silence him once and for all.

Sometimes it's dangerous to be a voice. At other times it's damaging to our relationships or our reputations. But if we're a voice and have to make headway in people's lives so Jesus can enter, there's no option. We have to speak up so they have the chance to clear up the mess.

Knowing what we should say is one thing. Saying it is another.

THE COST OF CRYING IN THE WILDERNESS

The soldier beheaded John in the prison.

MARK 6:27

It's hard to say the right thing as John the Baptist did. I often think about him, standing in front of Herod. John could have given him a nice little comforting sermon and been out of prison and back with his bushes in the desert before he knew it. But he didn't.

I was traveling back home to Milwaukee on a Saturday night, and the plane was delayed. A group of Englishmen were chatting together in the airport. I made myself known to them, and one of them said to me, "We are on our way to Milwaukee. What is there to do there?"

I told them my city was full of interesting things to do. "There are some super restaurants," I burbled enthusiastically.

"We're not interested in eating," they informed me. After telling me where their interests lay, I told them I didn't know where they could go to indulge in those sorts of activities! I began to wish I hadn't gotten involved.

"What do *you* do on a Sunday then?" one of them asked me.

I thought of John the Baptist. I could have answered the man (I was sure his name was Herod), "Oh, I go for a jog," or "I read books," or "I ski with the children." All of that would have been true, but I knew I had to tell him what I *really* do on Sundays. It was hard, but I stepped out of my prison of fear and told him that I always spent a part of each Sunday in worship.

My "Herod" effectively silenced me, too—but in rather a less dramatic way. He just walked away. But I had managed to lift up my voice and cry in the wilderness. I was glad.

LETTING GO

Right here in the crowd is someone you do not know, who will soon begin his ministry. I am not even worthy to be his slave.

JOHN 1:26-27

Andrew was at first a disciple of John the Baptist. John pointed him to "the Lamb of God who takes away the sin of the world" (John 1:29), and walked away from companionship. That must have been hard to do. Andrew left John to follow Jesus.

Sometimes we have to let go of our friends so they can stop depending on us and begin a ministry of their own. As far as God is concerned, you are greatest when you give your friends to Jesus.

Helping someone move on to other ministries is a little bit like teaching a child to ride a bicycle, running alongside the little one, holding to the back of the seat. But at some point, you have to let go. The child will never learn to ride unless you take your hands away, and you will have a heart attack if you keep holding the back of the seat!

The difficult thing is to know when to let go. John knew. When Andrew followed Jesus that day, he may have wobbled for a few feet without John's support, but within a very short time, he brought his brother, Peter, to Christ!

The Right Group of Disciples

Then John's two disciples turned and followed Jesus. . . . Andrew, Simon Peter's brother, was one of these men who had heard what John said and then followed Jesus.

JOHN 1:37, 40

What does it mean to follow Jesus, to be his disciple, to forsake it all? What did it mean to Andrew? Andrew forsook his old friend, John the Baptist. Following Jesus meant leaving the familiar behind and learning something new.

Sometimes we immediately reject a new thought or philosophy of religion because it's not what we are used to. If we have been brought up Anglican, being born again seems to belong to the Baptists! If we have been raised Baptist, singing psalms appears ritualistic.

Andrew learned that he didn't need to reject the things John had taught him but simply add the living Christ to the truth he already knew. For Andrew, that meant forsaking the company of John's disciples for the company of Jesus' disciples. Maybe you need to do the same. Make sure you are in the right church—a place where Christ is honored, where the Word is taught, and, above all, where he would have you to be. For some, their church is right; for others—like Andrew—a change is necessary. Ask him to show you what to do. Being among the right group of disciples is part of discipleship.

The Best Man

Talk about pressure! Jesus' disciples were baptizing just around the bend of the river from the place John was baptizing. Can you imagine Jesus setting up a church on your block? What would that do to your congregation?

Teacher, the man you met on the other side of the Jordan River, the one you said was the Messiah, is also baptizing people. And everybody is going over there instead of coming here to us.

JOHN 3:26

John's answer is an example to all Christians who struggle with jealousy when their ministry is threatened by someone else: "I am filled with joy at his success" (John 3:29).

How can you say "I am filled with joy" when you are losing people to another church? Maybe you are leading a Bible study. Some "new kid on the block" begins a meeting the same night as yours. One by one your people disappear. How do you handle that? Or you are teaching an elective seminar at a convention. Six women come into your room, while the speaker across the hall has to ask you for some of your empty chairs!

John said, in essence, "Jesus is my friend. He is the bridegroom, and the best man never competes!" We need to remember that we are only and ever the "best man." The one who must get all the glory is Jesus. If he chooses to diminish my responsibility and give it to another, that is his prerogative. After all, it is his wedding!

John lived by a very simple principle: "He must become greater and greater, and I must become less and less" (John 3:30). When we live by the same principle, we, too, will be able to say, "I am filled with joy."

The King Is Coming

Prepare a straight pathway for the Lord's coming!

JOHN 1:23

John the Baptist said he was the servant sent before the King to prepare the pathway. What did he mean? When Eastern kings and emperors visited their realms, a servant was always sent ahead to prepare the pathway. Torrential downpours often caused roads to cave in and mountains to slide down onto the highways, blocking traffic. The servant's job was to make sure the highways were repaired, with all the holes filled in, so the way was fit for the king!

This custom was familiar to the people of John's day. So when John cried out, "Prepare a straight pathway for the Lord's coming," the meaning was unmistakable. The people knew their national road in Israel needed repair—the Jews served Rome. The people had family problems—personal paths to clear up, too. Their lives were a mess of rubble that needed attention. The Jews knew that Isaiah the prophet had said that when the Messiah came, he would restore all things (see Isaiah 11:12). John told them the King was coming, and it was time to pick up a shovel and get to work.

Repentance is taking up a shovel and showing God you mean business. It's being sorry enough to make restitution where possible. Then the King will come!

YOUR OWN HOMETOWN

Then Jesus returned to Galilee, filled with the Holy Spirit's power. Soon he became well known throughout the surrounding country. He taught in their synagogues and was praised by everyone.

LUKE 4:14-15

Jesus started where he was. He began in Galilee. He did not start in Rome, or even in Jerusalem. He came out of the desert and began his ministry in the "surrounding country."

Many of us come to Jesus wanting to serve in Rome, or at least expecting to do something big in Jerusalem. But if we follow his example, we must do what he did—start in the "surrounding country." Start in church. Join a fellowship of believers and take the opportunities it offers. Jesus "taught in their synagogues."

"Well, now," I seem to hear you say, "I'm not Jesus! If I could preach like him or even like John the Baptist, I'd offer my services to my local congregation!" But even though Jesus was the best preacher in the world, people didn't always appreciate his sermons!

The Bible says he was "praised by everyone," but a day or so later when he preached in his own home church, he ran into trouble. "No prophet is accepted in his own hometown" (Luke 4:24). All who heard that particular message were so angry with him, they tried to throw him over a cliff (see Luke 4:29)! You don't learn to minister by finding ready-made situations with no opposition. You learn as Jesus learned, by starting in the surrounding region, even in your own hometown!

The Silent Years

Jesus got his training for the ministry at home, in Nazareth. We know very little about those thirty "silent years." We do know Joseph died (though we are not sure when), making Jesus head of his earthly family, the breadwinner. He lived as a part of a small country community and plied a trade. These years belong to Mary and to Jesus' brothers and sisters. Apart from these things, we know nothing.

Philip went off to look for Nathanael and told him, "We have found the very person Moses and the prophets wrote about! His name is Jesus, the son of Joseph from Nazareth." "Nazareth!" exclaimed Nathanael. "Can anything good come from there?"

JOHN 1:45-46

The Gospel writers respect the silent years and do not intrude. Jesus used that time to prepare himself for his spiritual calling.

Do you live in a Nazareth? Perhaps you feel that there is nothing special about your hometown. Maybe your family is an ordinary one, which does pretty routine things. You have a so-so job and your life goes on its way, uninterrupted with much trauma. Did you know that these "silent years" are important?

The mundane atmosphere of your Nazareth does not mean you need to be a mundane Christian. "Nazareth living" can be a test of your commitment to Christ. If God called you to leave home and begin to serve him today, would you be ready? Seminaries do not servants make! Nazareths do! If these are your silent years, make sure they are busy ones. If you cannot serve God in Nazareth, he will never send you to serve him anywhere else.

Nazareth Living

Then he returned to Nazareth with them and was obedient to them; and his mother stored all these things in her heart.

LUKE 2:51

Jesus knew how hard it is to serve at home. At age twelve, he reminded his parents, "You should have known that I would be in my Father's house" (Luke 2:49). He then went home to Nazareth and was subject to them for another eighteen years. Jesus of Nazareth served the Lord his God for thirty-three years, the vast majority of which he lived at home. I believe he wanted to know what that was like so he could help you and me.

Jesus learned to minister to his father and his mother, to his brothers and sisters, and to his friends and relations. He worked with them and for them. He took his share of the daily doings in a Christlike way! And I believe he gave us a good picture of a balanced lifestyle—three years talking and thirty years living!

We tend to think of Christian service as "platform duty"—speaking, preaching, videotaping, conferences, that sort of thing. But divine services are conducted three times daily at my kitchen sink!

If you have just come to faith in Christ and are wondering what you can do for Jesus, do what he did and learn to do it heartily and well. Serve the people you live with, the folks who belong to you. Make no mistake about it—it counts! When Jesus cried out from the cross, "It is finished" (John 19:30), he spoke of the work of redemption. Thirty years of Nazareth living had been an important part of that!

A Great Place to Grow

So Jesus grew both in height and in wisdom, and he was loved by God and by all who knew him.
LUKE 2:52

Home is a great place to grow. Jesus grew at home in four different ways. First of all, he grew in height. Home is a great place to play, to eat, to sleep, to develop a healthy physique. This is all preparation for God's plan for your life.

Second, Jesus grew in wisdom. You gain wisdom and insight for yourself at home. You watch your mother and your father parenting, whether they do it right or do it wrong!

Third, Jesus was loved by God. The family is intended to be the place you learn the fundamental tenets of your faith, but the church is intended to supplement and deepen that knowledge. Jesus and his family always went to the synagogue (Luke 4:16).

Fourth, Jesus was also loved by all who knew him. We grow in favor with people when we live at home in a manner that honors him. If I am an angel in church but a devil at home, what is the use of that? Home is an ideal place for the sort of growth that shows us how to get along with people. What better people than my brothers and sisters can teach me that! Home is a great place for breeding character—either good or bad.

Jesus increased in four ways—intellectually, physically, spiritually, and socially. Yes, home is a great place to grow!

Going On

Let us press on to know him!

HOSEA 6:3

A call to follow Jesus involves commitment. Sometimes people can remember the exact time and place they committed their lives to Christ. "It was at a meeting," says one. "A Billy Graham crusade," says another. "At my mother's knee," adds a third. Others cannot remember the exact moment they accepted Christ. Stuart, my husband, was a little boy of seven when he asked Jesus into his life. I was a big girl of eighteen when I did. Some of our friends who are children of Christian parents cannot remember a time they did not love and trust Jesus.

The important thing is to be sure you know him now, rather than be able to recite when it happened. "Is it happening now?" you should ask yourself. For those raised in believing families, an initial commitment as a child usually leads to a full commitment in later years. Somehow, the child needs to be sure his beliefs are really his, not an extension of his parents' faith.

When we look at the call of the disciples to follow Jesus, we see three things—an introduction to Jesus, an investigation of Jesus, and ongoing instruction by Jesus. Do you know you really *know* Jesus rather than just know *about* him? Have you investigated and understood the Christianity you have embraced? Are you being instructed by him now? Being a disciple means going on to know the Lord. Are you going on, or have you gotten stuck somewhere along the way?

Getting In Deep

Now go out where it is deeper and let down your nets, and you will catch many fish.

LUKE 5:4

Jesus had already called the disciples to himself. At this point in the Gospel story, they were working with Jesus in their spare time while trying to keep up with their fishing business. Then one day Jesus used Peter's boat as a pulpit and "sat in the boat and taught the crowds from there" (Luke 5:3).

I wonder what the sermon was? Maybe it was about forsaking everything and following him.

After the sermon, the Lord told Peter to launch out into the deep. Peter did what he was told, even though he was somewhat skeptical. After all, as he told the Master, "We worked hard all last night and didn't catch a thing" (Luke 5:5).

But because Jesus, the maker of fishes, told them where to fish, they caught many. More important, Jesus caught a lot of committed men! Simon Peter was astonished, afraid, and ashamed of his confusion. All who were with him, including James and John, felt the same way. "And as soon as they landed, they left everything and followed Jesus" (Luke 5:11).

There comes a time when you have to launch out into the deep. Some of us paddle around the shallows all our life. It's time we took a risk and began to do what Jesus tells us to do. Once we are out of our depth, we will be astonished, too. We will want to forsake all—even our boats, our beloved ones, and our most familiar things—and follow him to the ends of the earth.

Thirty Years Later

Don't be afraid! From now on you'll be fishing for people!

LUKE 5:10

For many people, a call to follow Jesus is all they ever hear. They never hear his Spirit say that it's time to launch out into the deep. One reason they do not hear is that they make sure they are not listening! Jesus will not use a megaphone. You will be safe if you stay out of earshot. But if you stay close to him, you will be bound to hear the commissioning call of the Lord.

Very soon after I accepted Christ, he asked me to let him use the boat of my life to preach from. This necessitated my moving out a safe distance from the shore. After catching some fish (what a thrill!), I was hooked myself! Once you have caught men and women for Christ and his kingdom, there appears no sane alternative under heaven. You have to forsake all and follow him!

The first time I led someone to Christ, the joy and astonishment was enough to make me decide there was nothing in life I would rather do. Whether I continued to teach to support myself or depended on the church for my full salary appeared a minor consideration. The most important decision was full commitment to the art and technique of fishing for people for the rest of my days. I couldn't wait to start and, thirty years later, I have absolutely no plans to stop! It's marvelous, fishing with Jesus!

The Seed

A farmer went out to plant some seed. As he scattered it across his field, some seed fell on a footpath.

LUKE 8:5

"Anyone who is willing to hear should listen and understand!" (Luke 8:8), said Jesus. He was telling a story about a farmer sowing seed. "The seed is God's message," he said (Luke 8:11). The speaker can control the message but cannot control the hearers. The hearers evaluate the Word of God as they receive it from the preacher.

All too often the personality of the preacher gets in the way, and the hearers end up evaluating the preacher, not what he said. If you dislike the man, you probably will have little respect for his message. Yet Jesus said when his farmers—or preachers—scatter the seed, we should receive it.

In a little English churchyard, there stands a tall, beautiful oak tree. There is nothing strange about that, until you realize it is growing right through the middle of a grave! The force of life was so strong that it split the stones in two as the tree pushed upward toward the light. What dynamic power in a tiny acorn!

There is similar power in the seed of God. When sown in good soil, though buried underneath concrete, it will break through. The first thing we need to do is receive the seed sown by the preachers God has given us. We must listen to God's message and stop testing it. We must realize it is testing us!

Pathway Thinking

As the farmer sowed his seed, he inadvertently dropped some on the hard path that wound through the cultivated areas. Jesus compared this picture to the minds of "pathway people" who receive the Word of God without understanding (see Matthew 13:19).

The seed that fell on the hard path represents those who hear the message, but then the Devil comes and steals it away and prevents them from believing and being saved.

LUKE 8:12

The mind is the avenue through which truth travels to our heart to give us spiritual experience. If the soil of our mind is like pathway soil, nothing will take root, and the seeds of the fruit of truth will not be carried along into our understanding. The wind of other concerns will blow it away before it has time to be translated into sense.

Satan stands by the pathway person's mind. He watches the seed fall and snatches it away like a ravenous bird. He doesn't want that person to believe the message and be saved, so he will distract in any way he can (see Mark 4:15).

Pathway people do not believe they need Jesus Christ. They may not accept the fact that he is divine or relate him to themselves or their dilemma. In fact, pathway people do not even believe they are in a dilemma. They never listen in church. They fill their minds with thistle fluff that will not trouble them or with weed seed that will never bear a useful plant. They believe anything that is comfortable, acceptable, and even respectable.

The seed tests such soil and condemns it. It is frightening to think that we can choose to fill our mind with such pathway soil. What a huge responsibility!

Good Soil

> **But the good soil represents honest, good-hearted people who hear God's message, cling to it, and steadily produce a huge harvest.**
>
> LUKE 8:15

The Bible says, "The way to identify a tree or a person is by the kind of fruit that is produced" (Matthew 7:20). The authentic Christian hears and receives the Word of God, makes sure the roots of that seed go deep into her thinking, weathers the storms of opposition, and does not allow worry weeds or pleasure's pretty flowers to choke the fruit that is inevitable if the conditions are right.

When the Bible talks about fruit, it is referring to character (see Galatians 5:22-23). If we fill our life with good soil, we will need to bring forth his fruit "with patience." Character is not grown in a single night. It takes a long time to learn self-control and love, to live peaceably with all people or to suffer long and patiently.

Finally, a word of caution: It is the Sower who will judge and test the soil. That is not our job. The fruit should give us a hint as to where people stand. But in the last analysis, the Savior will decide.

I dreamt death came the other night
and heaven's gates swung wide.
An angel with a halo bright
ushered me inside.
And there to my astonishment stood folks
I'd judged and labeled
As "quite unfit," "of little worth,"
and "spiritually disabled."
Indignant words rose to my lips but
never were set free,
For every face showed stunned surprise;
No one expected me!

They Couldn't Do It

I begged your disciples to cast the spirit out, but they couldn't do it.

LUKE 9:40

Jesus' disciples "couldn't do it." They wanted to, but they "couldn't"! Have you ever felt like that? Have you faced a troubled parent, wanting to say something—yet nothing would come out of your mouth? Or have you wanted to do something to relieve a sufferer but haven't known the right course of action? That "couldn't" feeling is very frustrating indeed.

But Jesus was frustrated, too. "You stubborn, faithless people . . . how long must I be with you and put up with you?" he said (Luke 9:41). He told the distraught father to bring the child to him. Jesus then rebuked the unclean spirit and healed the child, delivering him to his father (Luke 9:42). The disciples waited until they could get the Lord Jesus alone to ask him why they could not cast out the demon (see Matthew 17:19). Jesus replied that their faith was at fault. "You didn't have enough faith," he told them (Matthew 17:20).

That's a very challenging thought. If I cannot do something because I lack the faith in God to do it, I must ask him to help my unbelief. He will, of course. He wants us to dare to believe we can move mountains if we trust God to intervene on our behalf. What mountain were you unable to move today? Jesus says you could tomorrow! Do you believe him?

Asking Jesus the Right Things

In your glorious Kingdom, we want to sit in places of honor next to you.

MARK 10:37

Isn't it surprising that James and John had just had a mountaintop experience, yet they hit rock bottom in the valley only a few days later? They had seen Jesus transfigured before them, then they had come down into the valley and heard the Lord rebuke their brother disciples for their lack of faith. Perhaps they despised their friends.

After all, James and John believed that Jesus could do anything. Hadn't they themselves just heard the voice of God affirming him? How strange, then, to find the brothers behaving in such a childish way. A little while later, believing themselves to be Jesus' favorites, they requested that he keep a chair just for them on each side of his heavenly throne. The Bible says that "when the ten other disciples discovered what James and John had asked, they were indignant" (Mark 10:41).

Oh, be assured, the ten will *always* hear it! Competitive spirits don't ever whisper; they shout! They are bound to be heard! Jesus must have been frustrated all over again; this time, with James and John! He reminded them that unbelievers compete with each other, but disciples must not (see Mark 10:42-43). "And whoever wants to be first must be the slave of all" (Mark 10:44). Later on, he knelt down, wrapped himself with a towel, and washed their feet (see John 13:1-17).

We must be careful to ask Jesus the right things. If we watch how he lived in the Gospels, we will begin to know instinctively which prayers are out of order. We mustn't frustrate the Lord!

Coping with Privilege

Master, we saw someone using your name to cast out demons. We tried to stop him because he isn't in our group.

LUKE 9:49

We are supposed to learn humility on the mountain! Jesus took his three special friends up the Mount of Transfiguration to teach them humility. They were supposed to see how great Jesus was and how small they were. Visions of God should do that to us and not result in a sense of our own importance!

The nine disciples at the foot of the mountain could not help a family in trouble. James and John could not cope with privilege. It went to their heads. It wasn't long before they were telling the Master to forbid "outsiders" a ministry. When we begin to think that we are the only ones who have a corner on the truth, we are in trouble. Jesus said, "Don't stop him! Anyone who is not against you is for you" (Luke 9:50).

Some of us have been blessed beyond measure. We come from Christian homes and have been taught the Bible from our youth. We have listened to God's best on radio and TV. We have bookcases full of excellent Christian literature. We have peace in our country and may worship freely. Much has indeed been given to us, and much will indeed be required!

God requires our toleration of those less privileged. We are to support the weak, encourage the ignorant, disciple the undisciplined, and discern gifts in others. We are not to forbid a ministry! We are to use our privilege to the advantage of others!

The New Recruits

The Lord now chose seventy-two other disciples and sent them on ahead in pairs to all the towns and villages he planned to visit.

LUKE 10:1

Jesus had spent a very frustrating time with his twelve specially chosen men. If I had been Jesus, I would not have felt like choosing another seventy-two! If the twelve represented the best, Jesus must have worried about the new recruits! But the Lord worked with raw material, and he never gave up!

When I am training others to go out and serve God, I gain help from the Lord's example. He went right ahead choosing people to do his work, trusting them with ministry, and dealing with their failures. After the twelve had failed, disappointed, and frustrated him, the seventy-two returned rejoicing! "Lord," they said, "even the demons obey us when we use your name!" (Luke 10:17).

Fancy the seventy-two doing better than the twelve! That must have been a humbling experience for Jesus' closest disciples. I wonder how they handled that! Can you handle someone else's success? When a younger Christian succeeds where you have failed, can you rejoice?

Jesus was delighted! He said, "O Father, Lord of heaven and earth, thank you for hiding the truth from those who think themselves so wise and clever, and for revealing it to the childlike. Yes, Father, it pleased you to do it this way" (Luke 10:21). New recruits should delight us. It's the old recruits that can give us a hard time. Old or young, we need to remember we are part of Jesus' army. If we would only stop fighting each other, we may get around to winning the war!

UNTIL HE FINDS US FAITHFUL

When James and John heard about it, they said to Jesus, "Lord, should we order down fire from heaven to burn them up?"

LUKE 9:54

When our children were small, they wore retainers on their teeth. They were corrective braces that had to be removed when eating, and when the family was in a restaurant, they posed a little problem. The children learned to slip the braces out of their mouths and wrap them in a napkin until they had finished their meal.

One day on the way home after a meal of hamburgers, David shot over the front seat, nearly causing an accident. "I left my retainers on the table!" he gasped. We turned around and retraced our steps. When we inquired about the braces, we were led into the yard behind the restaurant and shown fourteen pails of garbage! Somewhere in one of them lay David's retainers, wrapped in the napkin!

After foraging through three garbage pails of refuse, we found our treasure! The thing that kept us going was the knowledge that among all that gook was a precious piece of metal!

When God deals with us, he must feel like we felt that day. But he keeps searching through the garbage in our life until he finds the precious faith in him he is looking for. He searches through our failures until he finds us to be true to him. If we have faith to trust him to be our Savior, he knows we can have the faith to obey him as our Lord. He will go on searching our soul until he finds us faithful!

The First and Finest Missionary

As the Father has sent me, so I send you.

JOHN 20:21

God had one Son, and he sent him to be a missionary. "For God so loved the world that he gave his only Son" (John 3:16). Jesus' mission was to go on a cross-cultural journey to tell the people he found about God. He left his home and family, traveled a long way, and identified with the people. He learned their language, ate their food, wore their clothes, and endured their sicknesses. He lived among the poorest folk in the obscurest village, and understood the deepest needs of the community.

But he also kept abreast of the national and international news and was articulate in expressing his biblically based views on the issues in focus. After thirty years of preparation, he began his preaching, teaching, and healing ministry. He went about doing good. He drew large crowds of people to hear his sermons, yet he always had time to listen and love the individual.

In the world's eyes, he failed in his missionary endeavors and was crucified for his trouble. But in God's sight, his mission was gloriously accomplished, and he returned home to a marvelous welcome and a grand reward. He paid the ultimate price a missionary is ever asked to pay—laying down his life for his God on the foreign mission field. But like other humble servants that followed after him, he lives forever in heaven, surrounded by his converts. Jesus was the first and finest missionary!

The Morning of Our Lives

Go into all the world and preach the Good News to everyone, everywhere.

MARK 16:15

God is a sending God. We need to remember that. He sent Abraham into a strange and foreign land. He sent Joseph into Egypt. He sent Moses into Canaan, and he sent a continuous stream of prophets into all sorts and conditions of places. "From the day your ancestors left Egypt until now, I have continued to send my prophets—day in and day out" (Jeremiah 7:25).

I have a marvelous picture of God, getting up early in the morning to pack lunches for his missionaries and get them on their way! The descriptive language of the verse lends us help in realizing God's eagerness to send aid.

God is a sending God because He is love, and love sends. It is the nature of love to give sacrificially, to involve itself in flying to the side of the needy ones. God sent the twelve disciples, and he sent seventy-two more after them. After the Cross and Resurrection, he sent women to tell men he was alive. After Pentecost, he sent us to tell others who haven't heard God's good news of salvation. God sent his people to tell a story—an old, old story, a good story, a gospel story.

"Therefore, go and make disciples of all the nations" (Matthew 28:19), he told his followers. The word *nations* is *ta ethne,* from which we get the word *ethnic*. Jesus told us that every ethnic group must hear the gospel. That means we will need to get up in the morning of our life and get going! We shall also need a badge of authority if we are to accomplish what must be done. Our heavenly Sending Agency will not leave us without credentials.

A Fire of Coals

> **When they got there, they saw that a charcoal fire was burning and fish were frying over it, and there was bread. "Bring some of the fish you've just caught," Jesus said.**
>
> JOHN 21:9-10

Simon Peter had seen something like this before—a net full of fish that had been caught miraculously (see Luke 5:1-7). The disciples had toiled all night and caught nothing, but a man had stood on the shore and commanded them to throw the net on the right side of the ship (John 21:6). They brought up 153 large fish in their net, yet the net was not torn (John 21:11).

"It is the Lord!" John exclaimed to Peter (John 21:7). At that, Simon Peter got dressed (he had stripped off his outer garment to fish) and promptly dived into the water to get to shore and face Jesus. When he got there, he found a fire ready to cook breakfast. Peter must have found it hard to look into the Lord's face. The smell of that smoke was an acrid reminder of another fire, in Caiaphas's courtyard (see John 18:18). He had been haunted by the memory of Christ's eyes ever since. Peter had been frightened and had denied him with oaths and curses, and Jesus had turned and looked at him. Peter remembered what Jesus had said (Luke 22:61). Now Peter remembered again!

Jesus remembered, too, but he had come to tell Peter that he was forgiven. He was to leave his nets forever. It was time to change his profession from fisherman to shepherd (see John 21:16). A simple communion was held on the shore that day. After it was over, Peter was restored and ready to obey.

A Spirit of Competition

After breakfast Jesus said to Simon Peter, "Simon son of John, do you love me more than these?" "Yes, Lord," Peter replied, "you know I love you." "Then feed my lambs," Jesus told him.

JOHN 21:15

Peter left his beloved blue, blue Sea of Galilee, his nets, his fish, and all that was dear to follow Jesus. But Peter left something more important than all of these things—his spirit of competition!

When he and Andrew had been business partners with the sons of Zebedee, there had always been a sense of competitiveness. James and John and old Zebedee had managed to do better than Peter and Andrew, but Peter knew fishing. What's more, he had the physique. Look who pulled the net ashore with 153 fishes in it (see John 21:11)!

But Jesus asked Peter for that competitive nature on the seashore. Breakfast had been eaten, and Jesus asked, "Do you love me more than these [the other disciples]?" Peter had been sure he loved the Lord more than all the other disciples put together. Why, he had even told the Lord so in front of them! But after three denials, he had to humbly admit he had not beaten the others to it, in the matter of loving!

If we are to shepherd the Lord's sheep together, there is no room for a spirit of competitiveness—the sort of spirit that says I am more loving or more capable than others. We need to cooperate in brotherly love if the sheep are to be fed. Do you need to give your competitive nature to Jesus?

Something for Nothing

Once more he asked him, "Simon son of John, do you love me?" Peter was grieved that Jesus asked the question a third time. He said, "Lord, you know everything. You know I love you."

JOHN 21:17

Discipleship is not giving something for nothing; discipleship is giving nothing for something! Peter had nothing to give Jesus except his failure. Jesus took it, forgave it, and said, "Feed my sheep." When you have just made a total idiot of yourself in front of your friends, your enemies, and, indeed, the whole world, how incredible to hear Jesus commission you to serve him again!

Peter had served Jesus for three years. In his opinion, he had been giving him something for nothing. Hadn't he given Jesus the benefit of his strong body and personality, his time, his energy, his enthusiasm? *And all for nothing,* Peter must have thought proudly to himself. He had not charged Jesus for his services or demanded special rooms or treatment when they traveled together.

But after the Cross, Peter was a broken man. He had denied his Lord and had followed him afar off. He came to realize discipleship is not giving something for nothing; discipleship is giving nothing for something!

Jesus loves us when we fail. We come to the end of our fleshly effort to be something or to do something and lay our nothings in his hand, and he gives them back to us, dressed in something new. He gives us hope for the future, a job to do for him, a sense of being needed after all, his power to overcome, and a great sense of worth. Now that's something!

Thank you, Jesus!

Having Breakfast with Jesus

Several of the disciples were there—Simon Peter, Thomas (nicknamed the Twin), Nathanael from Cana in Galilee, the sons of Zebedee, and two other disciples. Simon Peter said, "I'm going fishing." "We'll come, too," they all said.

JOHN 21:2-3

A Christian call involves commitment to a person—Jesus Christ. Commitment involves a commission to a cause. A commission, or a sense of calling to a cause, without a commitment to the person of Christ, has nothing to do with Christianity.

There are many worthy causes in the world. But let us never mix them up with the Christian cause. When Jesus says, "Follow me," he calls us first and foremost to a relationship with himself. As we follow him, he leads us into a needy world and directs us to tasks specifically designed for us.

When Jesus called Peter to follow him, Peter had to make an initial decision. He had to say, "Yes, I will," or "No, I won't." He said yes. He committed his life to Jesus. After Jesus was crucified, Peter went back to his fishing. He realized that without a personal ongoing relationship with Christ, the cause was meaningless. When Christ talked with Peter by the Sea of Galilee, he restored that relationship and commissioned him to feed his flock.

The Acts of the Apostles is the record of the results of that meeting. In Acts, we see Peter committed to the cause of Christianity because he is committed to the person of Christ.

Are you trying to serve the cause without having met the Christ? It won't work. Have breakfast with Jesus. Meet him by your seashore of failure and listen to him. Then do what he tells you to do. You—and your world—will never be the same again.

The Cost of Giving Our Choices to Jesus

But when you are old, you will stretch out your hands, and others will direct you and take you where you don't want to go.

JOHN 21:18

Discipleship not only involves a call, a commitment, and a commission; it involves a cost—the loss of our independence. Our responsibilities take hold of our rights and lead them to places we would not choose to go.

Jesus spoke of this to Peter. Peter was crucified upside down. That surely was not the way Peter would have chosen to die! But he had no choice. When we are truly his disciples, Jesus makes our choices for us.

The thing that matters most to us is freedom—to dress ourselves as we wish, to come and go when we please, and to use our hands to shape our own destiny. Yet in one sentence, Jesus told Peter that discipleship would cost him all these freedoms. Another would dress him; cruel men would force him to walk to a dreadful, inverted cross, where his hands would be stretched out and his freedom to hold his own destiny, crucified.

Not all of us will be called to glorify God by such a death. But we are certainly called to glorify God by our life. Commitment costs. Yet we need to remember the cost will be rewarded with a crown. When Jesus had finished talking with Peter about this matter, he said to him, "Follow me" (John 21:19). Peter gave his choices into the hands of Jesus and obeyed. Will we?

THE POTTER AND THE CLAY

He is the Potter, and he is certainly greater than you. You are only the jars he makes! Should the thing that was created say to the one who made it, "He didn't make us"? Does a jar ever say, "The potter who made me is stupid"?

ISAIAH 29:16

It was said of the disciples that they "turned the rest of the world upside down" (Acts 17:6). Yet, they actually turned it right side up! People who know Jesus do that.

People who don't know Jesus may be described as pots that turn themselves upside down on the potter's wheel and tell the potter to take his hands off their lives. "He [God] doesn't know what he is doing," they say.

The disciple knows the Potter, who molds marred lives over again, keeping one hand inside the pot and the other outside. He knows a pot is only as good outside as it is inside.

The disciple knows that, to function, he will have to be fired in the kiln. The number of firings depends on the pot's use, but the good Potter watches the clay carefully. When the color comes up in its "character," he will remove it. It will not be left in the heat to crack.

Disciples have a wonderful relationship with God through Christ—as close as an earthly potter to his clay. Don't turn yourself upside down on the wheel; let him turn you right side up!

Acceptance—The Key to Usefulness

> **And yet, Lord, you are our Father. We are the clay, and you are the potter. We are all formed by your hand.**
>
> ISAIAH 64:8

Discipleship involves call commitment, commission, cost, and character change. You need not change your entire personality—just the things that spoil your character. You learn to handle yourself by accepting yourself as God has made you.

Our daughter is very intense. She wishes she could "hang loose" like her younger brother. A friend helped her by telling her God would not change her personality but would help her to come to terms with it.

Before the pot is ever begun, the shape of the vessel, the type of clay, and the color are all recorded in the Potter's manual. In his mind, he has finished the pot and has it sitting on a shelf before he ever begins to form it (see Psalm 139:13-16).

God wants us to find out how he made us, and then he wants us to accept it. When you become a disciple, the Potter doesn't change *who* you are but *what* you are *without Christ*. For example, Matthew the tax collector was good with money. Without Christ, he cheated everyone; with Christ, he used his money to good purpose, throwing evangelistic parties in his home (see Matthew 9:9-10)! Simon the Zealot believed in military might. After he met Christ, he put all that zealous energy into bringing in a spiritual kingdom instead of an earthly one. He didn't change his personality—the Potter simply used who he was to better effect.

Discipleship means changing your mind about sin and changing your mind about yourself. Acceptance is the key to usefulness.

All Things

> **Those who become Christians become new persons. They are not the same anymore, for the old life is gone. A new life has begun!**
>
> 2 CORINTHIANS 5:17

When I was eighteen, I became ill and was taken to a hospital. Maureen, the nurse assigned to me, immediately made me worse! She was impatient, rude, and very brusque. She would never stand and chat and didn't appear to care whether I lived or died. Then she became a Christian. God tempered her impatience into swift efficiency and transformed her brusqueness into briskness. She still didn't chat very much, but that was because her sense of integrity didn't allow her to talk on the job. She did come back in her spare time, though, and gave herself to her patients. All things had become new, though Maureen's personality was the same. God did not change who she was but what she had been without Christ.

When I found the Lord, he showed me I must stop bossing everyone around. There were ways to get things done without treading on everyone's toes! He showed me how to change my "bossing" into leadership capabilities and to channel my creativity into reaching teenagers in trouble.

Before I knew Jesus, I used my creative energies to organize wild parties and to think of crazy things to do that no one had ever tried before! As a Christian, I wrote plays, trained teenagers to act in them, and took them into places where we could reach young people with methods that had never been tried before.

Jesus will change the direction of your life, channel your energies, and bring the uniqueness of your personality into play.

GRUMBLERS' GRIPE

The people soon began to complain to the Lord about their hardships; and when the Lord heard them, his anger blazed against them.

NUMBERS 11:1

Moses was the pastor of the "First Church of the Wilderness."

This popular church had thousands of members, but many of them were chronic complainers who displeased the Lord. The mixed multitudes, or the rabble who were with them, started it all (see Numbers 11:4). They didn't like anything about the church—the location or the preacher—and they said so. Every church has to contend with the rabble-rousers. The problem is, their grumbling grows, and, before you know it, the members have begun to grumble, too!

What did the members of Moses' church have to complain about? They complained about the manna they were eating. Soon they began to pine for the good old days!

It's hard for a pastor to cope with that sort of talk. When church people begin to talk about the previous pastor or to pine for the food they were fed at their last church, there is little he can do about it. Complaining, grumblers' gripe, is caught like measles. Once started, it spreads like wildfire. It can become very discouraging.

Moses fell into the trap that many pastors fall into. He caught the disease and began griping, too. The Lord is displeased with such behavior; he gripes about gripers, and that should be enough to stop it!

A Butcher's Shop in the Middle of a Desert

I can't carry all these people by myself! The load is far too heavy!

NUMBERS 11:14

Moses had a terrible sense of isolation born of desperation. He felt that he was carrying the burden of the whole world on his shoulders. His ministry had become a punishment instead of a privilege.

"Why are you treating me, your servant, so miserably? What did I do to deserve the burden of a people like this?" he asked the Lord (Numbers 11:11). Moses was angry. "It isn't fair!" he raged. "Why should I have to take this? I don't need it!" Moses felt isolated from God and also from his people. "Are they my children?" he asked the Lord (Numbers 11:12). "And they are so unreasonable! Why, they expect me to find them a butcher's shop in the middle of the desert!" Moses almost became irrational with the weight of it all. "I'd rather you killed me than treat me like this. Please spare me this misery!" he cried (Numbers 11:15).

God answered Moses' complaint. He didn't baby him, defend himself, or let his servant off the hook. He simply gave Moses the solution to his problem. He advised him to delegate his responsibility, pointing out that there were plenty of good men around who could be trusted to share his heavy charge with him. He told Moses to choose leaders who had proved themselves and to set them apart for the ministry (see Numbers 11:16-17). God promised that he would give them the same spirit of power and enabling that he had given to Moses himself.

Delegation is one answer to effective ministry. A shared ministry results in shared blessings.

Burnout

I have had enough, Lord.

1 KINGS 19:4

Elijah was the pastor of the "First Church of Mount Carmel." I don't know about you, but I would have loved to have belonged to Elijah's church. There was always something exciting going on with such a pastor in the pulpit. He was a showman who managed to get the entire country out to one of his crusades. His church sat on the top of a mountain range, so there was plenty of room for everyone.

Elijah loved visual aids. On this particular occasion, he challenged the leaders of the popular cults of the day to a prayer contest. He won after preaching a pretty fiery sermon with dramatic results (see 1 Kings 18:18-40)! Many people were added to Elijah's church that day, and the 450 subtractions rid Israel of all its prophets of Baal! Then he climbed a high hill and prayed one of his powerful prayers. It had been three years since Elijah had prayed such a prayer, and God had shut up the heavens in response. God answered this prayer by sending rain (see 1 Kings 18:41-46).

Unfortunately, pastors like Elijah are liable to burn out. After running miles in the rain in front of Ahab's chariot (anyone else would have walked or asked the king for a ride!), Elijah fell flat on his face—spiritually speaking, that is! He burned out!

Ahab's wife, Jezebel, threatened him, and he ran into the desert, told God that he had had enough, and asked for permission to die. Successful, dynamic preachers are liable to burn out. They need help. They need Jesus to touch and heal them like he touched and healed Elijah.

Building a Talk

> **I will show you what it's like when someone comes to me, listens to my teaching, and then obeys me. It is like a person who builds a house on a strong foundation laid upon the underlying rock. When the floodwaters rise and break against the house, it stands firm because it is well built.**
>
> LUKE 6:47-48

Building a talk is like building a house. The house—and the talk—must be built on the rock—on a good foundation! All talks given to God's people should be "built on the foundation of the apostles and the prophets. And the cornerstone is Christ Jesus himself" (Ephesians 2:20).

The themes of our sermons, Sunday school lessons, and Bible studies should be founded on sound doctrine taken from the Bible. Jesus said it's a wise person who builds his or her life on such a foundation. If only all so-called biblical talks were biblical, what a difference that would make!

After laying the foundation of our message, we should take heed to the design. We should ask ourselves some questions: Who's going to live in the house? Is the talk for glamorous ladies, blue-collar workers, or a bunch of junior high kids? Sometimes people give messages and build houses as if everybody's needs are the same. If you design a house, you usually design it with a particular family in mind. So it should be with a spiritual talk!

Who is going to live in the house? Who is going to hear the talk? If the elegant, then it must be appropriately furnished. If the street boy, it must have the basic needs and comforts. If the very young, it must be bright and attractive. Building a talk is like building a house—it takes an awful lot of time and trouble!

The Marriage House

Anyone who listens to my teaching and obeys me is wise, like a person who builds a house on solid rock.

MATTHEW 7:24

Jesus said that if we do what he says, we will be like a person who builds a house on a rock. Many people are building their homes on the sand, laying the foundation for their marriage on human love alone. They think, *It's love that makes the world go round*. Therefore, their love for each other will keep their relationship going. They promise each other that their love will last forever, but such promises are often like building a house on the sand.

People shift like the sand, changing their minds and their promises. We are sinful, fallible people, and no matter how sincerely we mean what we say, we lack the necessary rocklike quality of utter reliability. Love—human love—doesn't last forever. That is because it is invariably tinged with selfishness. We want our needs met, and when our partner doesn't meet them, we look around for someone else who will. We all too soon forget the promises we made and start promising someone else our love if *they* will meet our needs!

No wonder the house falls down. Jesus' Word is reliable; it will last forever and ever. When he promises us something, we can know he means what he says. What better foundation for the "marriage house" than wise words and sure promises? He promises us that he is committed to our marriage relationship. If we are committed to him and he is committed to us and to our love, we can stand firm and laugh at the storm!

Building

> **A person . . . builds a house on a strong foundation.**
>
> LUKE 6:48

The foundation of all relationships is laid in God's Word. *Agape* love—the sort of love that puts the loved one's interests first and fuels the fire of faithfulness—is that foundation. God's love can be traced throughout the Bible as he reveals himself to people. Agape promises can be fully trusted. God promised to care for Adam and did so even when Adam, who had promised to care for God, didn't!

Love tells us how to behave when we succeed and when we fail. Love instructs, rebukes, commands, and warns. Love's words are strong. We "hear" those words when we read the Gospels and listen to Jesus talking.

Building is hard work. When Stuart and I lived and worked in England, we decided to build our own house. Experts laid the foundation of our house for us, and we were to build on that foundation. The unmade house arrived on two trucks in bits and pieces, but it was all there. It looked like a giant children's construction kit—the kind you buy the family for Christmas. At first we were bewildered. After all, we were amateurs who had never built a house before! But the designer knew all about that, and he provided a master plan. It was imperative that we follow it.

If we begin to build on the foundation that has already been laid, our "marriage house" will begin to take shape. It's a wise couple that builds in such a way.

The Drawing Board

"For I know the plans I have for you," says the Lord. "They are plans for good and not for disaster, to give you a future and a hope."

JEREMIAH 29:11

The planner of our prefab cedar house had made provision for amateurs. As we unloaded the frames off the two huge trucks, we matched the numbers of the frames against the plans and fitted them into place. The plans were so detailed it seemed certain we could get the house built in no time. We worked with a will, becoming blasé to the point of carelessness. We didn't run to the master plan laid out on the drawing board quite so often. We began to think we could do it on our own.

It was pretty obvious we had made a mistake, however, when we got to the last frame and discovered a two-foot gaping hole in the wall with no frame to fit it! "We'd better get back to the drawing board," said my husband.

Who of us knows how to build a "marriage house"? How can we be sure we are building it right? Do you remember how earnest you were in the early days of your marriage? Did you grow blasé, thinking you knew how to build the marriage house without consulting the plans? When did the gap appear, showing you that something had gone sadly wrong? Maybe you discovered it in the bedroom or perhaps in the living room or even in the nursery. Do you need to get back to the drawing board?

The Communication Gap

The Lord God called to Adam, "Where are you?"
GENESIS 3:9

One of the gaps we may come across in our "marriage house" is the communication gap. Perhaps we are not very good with words—we're the strong and silent type. Or then again, we may have tried to talk to our partner, but there hasn't seemed to be too much common ground. When you don't have common interests, what is there to communicate about? Let's go back to the drawing board!

God is seen in the beginning of days, walking and talking with his creatures. He created man and woman and made them capable of communication with God, with their own kind, and with the world around them. Communication was to be a mountain that they could scale and explore to discover all that the Creator had made available to them. When sin entered their hearts, communication with God stopped. But God took the initiative to restore it. "Where are you?" he called out to Adam, knowing full well that the man was ashamed and in hiding. He forced a confrontation on the issue and insisted on talking it over.

When there is a communication gap in the marriage house, we need to go back to the plans and remember we were created to communicate. If something has severed the lines of communication with another, we need to be godly (or God-like) and take the initiative, finding ways to fill in the gap. There is no substitute for walking and talking in the garden with your loved ones. Whatever it costs—it must be done.

The Generation Gap

We who believe are carefully joined together, becoming a holy temple for the Lord.

EPHESIANS 2:21

Another problem we may discover in our "marriage house" is the generation gap. Sometimes older members of the family who live in the marriage house fail to understand younger members. Grandma may fail to appreciate her granddaughter's choice of clothing, or a son may not appreciate Dad's taste in music.

When our children were growing up, our very different tastes in music caused us to begin to listen to our radios in isolation. But that is not what "family" is all about. So instead of scattering to different corners of our home to do our own thing, or each using a pair of earphones, we took turns listening to one another's music over the evening meal.

Father insisted we could all choose whatever music we wished, as long as we felt perfectly free to comment on each other's choices. That stimulated plenty of communication, and understanding was born around that family table! As we explained our choices of music, we began to see the generation gap closing.

Do you have trouble with a relative who seems to live in another dimension? Don't be discouraged. When you find a generation gap in your house, hunt around for the right frame to fit it.

WINDOWS

> "Let there be light," and there was light.
>
> GENESIS 1:3

All houses need windows. It's a dark, forbidding home that admits no natural light to wake us up in the morning.

One of the windows that lets light into the "marriage house" is the "honesty window." My husband has always insisted upon an honest openness between family members. Lies have been treated as intruders to be reprimanded severely and chased out of the house.

Another light source is the "humor window." Laughter lights up dark moments, bringing sweet relief to tense, tired faces.

Then there is the "happiness window." Who would want to live in a house without happiness? The virtuous wife enriches her husband all the days of her life (see Proverbs 31:11-12). What's more, "she laughs" (Proverbs 31:25). Her husband praises her in front of his friends and colleagues, saying that she is an excellent wife (see Proverbs 31:28-29). To excel in bringing happiness into the lives of your loved ones is excellence of a precious sort.

The secret is that this woman "fears the Lord" (Proverbs 31:30)! When you fear the Lord, you open the windows of your house to honesty, humor, and happiness.

When we built our wooden house in England, we were delighted to see that the designer had provided many windows in the structure. In fact, the living room was made up of two huge walls of windows. He knew how important those apertures were.

Do you and I know how important windows are in a marriage? Perhaps it's time for us to do a little remodeling.

A Godly Heritage

But as for me and my family, we will serve the Lord.

JOSHUA 24:15

Joshua had made up his mind. Knowing he was responsible to give an account of his life to God, he had decided to serve the Lord. What was more, as head of his household, he had set himself the task of leading and influencing his family to do the same.

David said, "I will be careful to live a blameless life" (Psalm 101:2). The word *blameless* does not mean that David considered himself sinless; rather, it means he was determined to be mature. He strove to grow up into God.

We can never make our husband accept Jesus Christ as his Savior. We must never try to force a decision for Christ out of a pliable child. But if we have a high and holy desire that our life and the lives of those for whom we are responsible should honor God, we can create an environment where God can work.

I often talk to women who envy the godly heritage of others—a heritage they themselves do not have. They seem to think that those born into Christian homes have had a somewhat unfair advantage. "Why, with all those godly grandpas and grandmas and aunts and uncles littering their lives, no wonder their children turned out OK!" they say.

Don't let other people's blessings paralyze you. *Start* a godly heritage. Let it begin with you. Say as Joshua said, "As for me and my family, we will serve the Lord"! If you determine, as David did, to "lead a life of integrity in [your] own home" (Psalm 101:2), God will respond. If you are quiet a moment, you may even hear him whisper, "I will honor only those who honor me" (1 Samuel 2:30).

WHAT'S IN A NAME?

Name him Jesus.

LUKE 1:31

If you have children, you'll know what care goes into the choosing of a name. God the Father took inordinate care in naming himself. It was of vital importance. God explained his character by the use of his names. In Judaism, names denotes the type of personality a person has.

Judaism and Christianity seek to explain God to us. These religions are concerned with ideas. In fact, in the first chapter of John, we learn that the idea who had all the other ideas in the universe was born on our planet!

Words explain ideas, and Christianity staggers the thinking person with the concept that the "Word" (one of God's names) dressed himself in a man's body and greeted us on Christmas morning. In the Old Testament, the written Word had spoken about the living Word, who would come with this divine explanation of all things. When he did come, just as he promised he would, he assured us that we could trust his word. He didn't say, "I'm a truth," "I'm a part of the truth," or "I think I'm the truth." He said, "I am the truth" about God, the world, and everything else you'd like to know about.

Nature shows us a little of the might of God but often gives an imperfect picture. People can show us a little of God as Christ shines out of their lives, but people are not perfect either, so the picture is still indistinct. Only God's Word is safe—revealing him by his names and telling us to dare to believe that God has spoken to you and to me.

Elohim

In the beginning God created the heavens and the earth.

GENESIS 1:1

Used twenty-five hundred times in the Old Testament, the name *Elohim* reveals the mighty strength of God. *El* is the Hebrew word for "strength," while *alah* or *oah* means "faithfulness." What is God saying to people who want to know what he is like? He is saying, "I am almighty, faithful, and strong."

God's faithfulness begins afresh each day (Lamentations 3:23). God is always fresh, never stale. We can depend on it!

The Bible is not a scientific textbook but a book about faith. It does not tell us how the heavens go, but how to go to heaven. But it does tell us who makes the heavens go, and who knows how, and who upholds it all "by the mighty power of his command" (Hebrews 1:3).

Elohim meets us in Genesis. In the beginning of days and nights, flowers and trees, fish and mammals, he tells us by his name that he is the Creator of it all. God is strong enough to make myriad universes and faithful enough to keep them all spinning safely at the right speed.

And what does this name mean to me? It gives me confidence. It tells me that if God made the world, he can make my world spin around with a little more order than I've managed to create in it! It gives me something—someone—I can depend on. If God is perfect faithfulness, renewing his pledge to me morning by morning, I can go to sleep in peace evening by evening. Elohim can be known; Elohim can be trusted; Elohim is there!

Jehovah-Yahweh

> **I will be with you, and I will protect you wherever you go.**
>
> GENESIS 28:15

When God appeared to Jacob he called himself *Jehovah*, the *Elohim* of Abraham (see Genesis 28:13). The name *Jehovah* was first used in Genesis 2:4 when God made man. The title speaks of the special relationship between God and Israel.

When Moses talked with God and asked his name, God replied, "I AM" (Exodus 3:14). Jehovah told Moses he had heard the people of Israel crying because of their Egyptian taskmasters and had chosen to redeem them. "I am all that you will need as the occasion arises," he promised Moses. He is all that is needed as our occasions arise as well!

He cares when we are in bondage to some earthly taskmaster. Perhaps food or some other appetite has us whipped, and we long to be free. Yahweh has revealed himself as our Redeemer from all bondage.

It is exactly at this point that some reject Christianity. The idea of God's relating to them in a personal way is too much for them. Somehow the concept diminishes him in their thinking. People feel that if God can be known, this brings him down to their size; if he is their size, why do they need him? But knowing someone does not necessarily mean knowing all about that person. The pot knows the feel of the potter's hands, but because it is not the potter, it cannot possibly fully fathom its creator's mind. Jehovah-Yahweh wants us to know him. His name assures us that he made us capable of knowing enough to experience his salvation.

JEHOVAH-JIREH

Abraham named the place "The Lord Will Provide."

GENESIS 22:14

As people realized that God really was interested in their personal lives, they began to look for evidences of his intervention on their behalf. The name *Jehovah* spoke of God's involvement in people's lives. Many patriarchs recognized his hand of mercy and blessing in their circumstances. There are eight compound names of Jehovah that explain God in a fuller sense.

We come across the first in Genesis. God tested Abraham's faith by asking him to sacrifice his son Isaac as a burnt offering. Incredibly, Abraham set out to do so. Taking Isaac with him to Mount Moriah, he said to the young men who accompanied them, "Stay here with the donkey. . . . The boy and I will travel a little farther. We will worship there, and then we will come right back" (Genesis 22:5). Notice he said, "*we* will come back." He had faith to believe that even if he did kill his son, God would raise him from the dead. After all, God had told him Isaac was a very important part of his plan of redemption for the whole world.

As Abraham raised his knife to kill Isaac, the angel of the Lord called to him from heaven and stopped him. "Now I know that you truly fear God. You have not withheld even your beloved son from me" (Genesis 22:12). Abraham saw a ram caught in a thicket and sacrificed the animal instead of Isaac.

Because God had provided himself a sacrifice, prefiguring Calvary, Abraham called the name of that place *Jehovah-Jireh*, meaning "The Lord Will Provide." At that point, Abraham understood a little bit more about God's redemptive character.

JEHOVAH-RAPHA

For I am the Lord who heals you.

EXODUS 15:26

If the name *Jehovah-Jireh* revealed God's concern for people's spiritual health, the name *Jehovah-Rapha* revealed his gracious concern about Israel's physical health. Moses led the children of Israel to a place where they saw God heal bitter waters, making them fit to drink (see Exodus 15:23-25). God then used this as a little object lesson, saying:

> "If you will listen carefully to the voice of the Lord your God and do what is right in his sight, obeying his commands and laws, then I will not make you suffer the diseases I sent on the Egyptians; for I am the Lord who heals you." (Exodus 15:26)

It was at Marah, which means "bitter," that God showed the children of Israel that he was the source of all health.

Does God really care if I am sick? Does he notice when my child's life is threatened by some dreaded disease? Nowhere does Scripture tell us he will heal *all* people of *all* diseases; but he will heal *many* people of *many* diseases. There is no health without the healthy God. In his wholeness, we find a measure of health on earth and a full measure of health in heaven. Revelation 21:4 tells us no one is ever sick in heaven.

God heals, of that there is no doubt. Sometimes he allows the body to heal itself, and at other times he miraculously quickens the process. Either way, he is Jehovah-Rapha, the healing God! This should be enough to turn our bitter waters to sweet.

Jehovah-Nissi

Moses built an altar there and called it "The Lord Is My Banner." He said, "They have dared to raise their fist against the Lord's throne, so now the Lord will be at war with Amalek generation after generation."

EXODUS 17:15-16

The children of Israel were beginning to get the picture—God loved and cared for them. He would provide a lamb to take away their sin. He would bless their obedience with a measure of health. In the midst of a fierce battle, another facet of Jehovah's character was revealed: He insists on having his people be a holy people. He said, "You must be holy because I, the Lord your God, am holy" (Leviticus 19:2).

While Joshua fought with Amalek in the valley, Aaron and Hur went up with Moses to the top of a hill overlooking the battle. Moses had his staff, representing Jehovah's power, in his hand. When Moses held the staff high, that power was applied to the battle, and Joshua prevailed; but when Moses' arm tired, Amalek prevailed (Exodus 17:11). In the end, Moses sat on a rock while Aaron and Hur supported his arms, and the battle was won. The banner of victory was flown over the place of conflict, and Moses named the alter he built there *Jehovah-Nissi,* "The Lord Is My Banner."

The Amalekites represent the selfish nature in all of us that God fights and puts to death. God has sworn he "will be at war with Amalek generation after generation." Jehovah will not rest until we are like him.

Jehovah-Shalom

> **And Gideon built an altar to the Lord there and named it "The Lord Is Peace."**
>
> JUDGES 6:24

The Lord provides, heals, and serves as my banner. What is more, Gideon discovered that he is peace. The Midianites were harassing Israel and destroying and plundering its crops. Gideon must have been scared to bits because he was threshing wheat in a winepress, and no one normally does that (see Judges 6:11). People usually threshed wheat on the top of a hill so that the wind would carry the chaff away.

The angel of the Lord came and sat under a tree and watched him. After a bit the angel said, "Mighty hero, the Lord is with you!" (Judges 6:12). (He must have said that with a smile!) Then the angel of the Lord told Gideon he was going to use him to save Israel from the Midianites.

If you think Gideon was frightened before, you should have seen him then! He began to come up with all sorts of excuses. Then the angel of the Lord revealed his power. Realizing that he had been arguing with God himself, Gideon was paralyzed with fear. Then the Lord said to him, "It is all right. . . . Do not be afraid. You will not die" (Judges 6:23).

Fear petrifies, punishes, and paralyzes us. Fear of what others may do to us, fear of what we cannot do for others, or fear of what God may do to us if we do not do for others—all can be dealt with by Jehovah-Shalom, who is our peace.

Jehovah-Tsidkenu

"For the time is coming," says the Lord, "when I will place a righteous Branch on King David's throne. . . . And this is his name: 'The Lord Is Our Righteousness.'"

JEREMIAH 23:5-6

Many of us look back to the good old days. But Israel was told by Jeremiah to look forward to the good new days that lay ahead. Jehovah himself would provide not only a lamb for an atoning sacrifice but a hope for the future. Psychologists tell us people cannot function without hope. Yet many people today feel a hopelessness that never seems to go away.

Without Christ there is no hope for the future because he is the future. God holds the future as surely as he holds the past and the present. He is working his purposes out. He knows the plans that he has for us: plans of good and not of disaster. Without God, without Christ, without hope, we are lost people, groping in the dark for some meaning to life.

"The time is coming," says the Lord, when he will provide one who will put all things in their proper place. Rights will be respected and wrongs redressed. There will be salvation and security for God's people. This is our hope. There's a new day coming for the believer.

Jehovah-Tsidkenu gives us that new day, that hope, that future. Do you feel hopeless? "Hope in God" (Psalm 42:5).

Jehovah-Sabaoth

> **Who is the King of glory? The Lord Almighty—he is the King of glory.**
>
> PSALM 24:10

"The Lord Almighty is here among us" (Psalm 46:7). God is the Refuge for his people and the Conqueror of nations. God commands a heavenly host—spirits that battle the abounding evil that threatens us.

God shows us his power, not only through his personal intervention, but by sending individual members of his host to empower, console, or encourage us in our earthly pilgrimage. People do not always recognize such heavenly visitors because they have the ability to appear as humans. Many of us have perhaps "entertained angels without realizing it!" (Hebrews 13:2). Usually the people in Scripture became aware that they were involved in an angelic visitation. Gideon didn't realize that the angel of the Lord (a pre-Incarnation appearance of Jesus himself) was God until he suddenly disappeared (see Judges 6:21-22). An angel strengthened Daniel after Daniel recognized his heavenly visitor:

> "Don't be afraid," he said, "for you are deeply loved by God. Be at peace; take heart and be strong!" As he spoke these words, I suddenly felt stronger and said to him, "Now you may speak, my lord, for you have strengthened me." (Daniel 10:19)

The heavenly host sang a cantata at Christ's birth, succored Christ after his temptations, and hovered around his cross to rescue him if he called. They rolled away the stone on resurrection morning and "sat on it" (Matthew 28:2)!

The hosts of the Lord are marvelous—but not nearly as marvelous as the Lord of hosts!

JEHOVAH-SHAMMAH

And from that day the name of the city will be "The Lord Is There."

EZEKIEL 48:35

There is a day coming that will never end. There is a day coming when we shall see God face-to-face. There is a day coming when we shall not have to teach people to know the Lord; they shall all know him. There is a day coming when he will be there, and we will be there—forever.

God revealed himself to Israel through his names. The name *Jehovah* speaks primarily to his intention to be involved in our life. The last chapter of Ezekiel promises that Jehovah also intends to be involved in our death.

There is a day coming! Oh, the joy when death is but a step of faith into the daylight of that city of God's permanent peerless presence!

JEHOVAH BE PRAISED!

When "I was not," Jehovah created me.
When "I was," Jehovah redeemed me.
When I was ashamed, Jehovah-Jireh forgave me.
When I was sick, Jehovah-Rapha made me well.
When I was tired of losing my battles, Jehovah-Nissi won them for me.
When I was frightened, Jehovah-Shalom frightened my fear away.
When I was lonely, Jehovah-Shammah promised to take me to His home
to stay.

Without Jehovah I am nothing;
I will be nothing; and there
is nothing
ahead.

With Jehovah I have all that I
need as the occasion
arises!

Jehovah be praised!

El Shaddai

When Abram was ninety-nine years old, the Lord appeared to him and said, "I am God Almighty; serve me faithfully and live a blameless life. I will make a covenant with you, by which I will guarantee to make you into a mighty nation."

GENESIS 17:1-2

What's in a name? Comfort, instruction, and an invitation to trust what is revealed! "I am God Almighty," said El Shaddai, the God who is enough—the breast, the succorer, the fruitful one.

This was news to Abraham, but he needed some good news at that moment. He was well aware he was ninety-nine years of age and well past the time to be able to have "millions of descendants" (Genesis 17:6); even one would be a miracle! Yet God was telling him that he would have a child! The fact that his wife was no spring chicken herself added to his confusion. Abraham knew he had a grand opportunity to find out if God was as big and as powerful as his name! And find out he did. Abraham believed El Shaddai, and Sarah conceived! God told Abraham that he was the nourisher, the fruitful one, the supplier, the one who satisfies, and Abraham and Sarah found it to be so.

What impossible situation are you facing? Does it seem as "dead" as Sarah's womb, as unlikely as a ninety-nine-year-old man producing a child? El Shaddai would tell you he can bring life into deadness.

> Abraham never wavered in believing God's promise. In fact, his faith grew stronger, and in this he brought glory to God. He was absolutely convinced that God was able to do anything he promised. (Romans 4:20-21)

God performs the things he promises to perform!

Someone We Could Trust

And Abraham's faith did not weaken, even though he knew that he was too old to be a father at the age of one hundred and that Sarah, his wife, had never been able to have children.

ROMANS 4:19

I was teaching in a tough part of Liverpool and had just taken my life in my hands. It was my turn to do playground duty! As I watched those little rascals being themselves, I thought of the churches, mine included, in the area. There was nothing remotely on their wavelength. The situation seemed hopeless. Dead churches don't reach lively kids.

Then I read about El Shaddai. Could the God of life and fruitfulness, who caused a baby to be born to two old people, cause life to spring out of deadness for these children of the twentieth century? God had revealed that fact of his person and power to me, but could I dare to believe he would do for me what he did for Sarah? Would he give me spiritual children in the barren womb of my own situation?

I timidly told him I believed that what he had promised he was able to perform! Then I went ahead in trust and started a club for the kids.

Confused and frightened, old before their time, they had not understood about El Shaddai, the God who would satisfy them. But they came, they listened; they believed, and though my "seed" was not nearly as numerous as Abraham's, life sprang out of deadness, and God was delighted! The kids and I were delighted, too. We had found someone we could trust!

ADONAI

You call me "Teacher" and "Lord," and you are right, because it is true.

JOHN 13:13

"I saw the Lord. He was sitting on a lofty throne, and the train of his robe filled the Temple," said Isaiah (Isaiah 6:1).

Adonai speaks of master-ownership. "You call me Adonai and so I am," said Jesus Christ to his disciples. God revealed his ownership of us through Israel and expects our obedience and respect.

There are good masters and bad masters. God is a good Master—one who makes sure his servants are properly cared for and reimbursed for their services. Paul delighted to call himself a slave and to serve the Lord Christ, never doubting that God was his Master and marveling at the rewards of his servitude.

Do you ever worry that Christianity will reduce you to servitude? I have news for you—it will! But it will turn out to be glad and willing service—a voluntary offering. You will soon count it a privileged calling.

Our Master is Master of the universe, of the people in it, and of their destiny. He is Master of our earthly masters. He is Master of our situations, Master of our trials and our joys. He is the Master Master!

I hear people talking about making Jesus Christ Lord or Master of their lives. They cannot do that. They cannot make him what he is already. He is Adonai, and you and I had better get around to acknowledging him as such.

The Devil Is No Gentleman

Take my life, for I am no better than my ancestors.

1 KINGS 19:4

Satan picks his moments! He does not wait until we return from a holiday in Hawaii to hit us with depression! He waits until he sees us at our lowest ebb, then kicks us in the stomach. The devil is no gentleman!

He knows us pretty well. He has done his homework and understands our weak spots. He did not tempt David with an ugly woman or offer Eve a rotten apple. Perhaps he knew Elijah could cope with a weak man like Ahab but would be threatened by a strong woman like Jezebel. Be sure, Satan chooses his strategy with care. He wants, above all else, to see us fall flat on our face and consider committing suicide.

Satan is well aware that God's servants are most vulnerable after great victories. When the evangelist sees people stream to the front of the church; when the preacher accepts a record number of new members into the fellowship; when the writer completes an overnight best-seller; when the soloist's heart-rending number has everyone in tears—watch out! Look around for Jezebel!

In one way or another, Satan will try to capitalize on God's victories. He knows that, at times like these, we are off our guard and become proud or complacent. Make no mistake—the devil is no gentleman!

Having Lunch with Jesus

Get up and eat some more, for there is a long journey ahead of you.

1 KINGS 19:7

Jesus looked at Elijah, lying totally exhausted under the broom tree, and set about restoring him. He knew his prophet had just been through a colossal strain and was utterly spent both physically and spiritually. He attended to those needs in that order. He touched Elijah, got out his frying pan and teakettle, and made him some lunch!

Arranging Elijah's stone pillow a little more comfortably, Jesus settled down to wait until Elijah woke up again for supper! The prophet was so exhausted, he didn't even wake up after sleeping for hours. Knowing his tired servant still had a long journey ahead of him, Jesus woke him up with some marvelously gentle words.

Sometimes we expect God to shake us awake and tell us we are naughty prophets and we'd better shape up or ship out. But he knows when the journey is too much for us, and he wants us to feel his touch of tender concern and, in the strength of that encouraging nourishment, continue on our way to restoration.

Sometimes we give trite spiritual answers to people's physical problems. Jesus knows all about the weaknesses of the flesh. He borrowed a body and lived in it for thirty-three years—a body that got hot and tired and sick, a body that felt thirsty and hungry and experienced pain, a body that needed to have some place to lay its head so it could sleep.

What are you doing here, Elijah?

1 KINGS 19:13

After Elijah had journeyed for forty days and nights, he found a cave to lodge in. But God had no intention of letting him stay there too long. He gives us room to make mistakes and time to mend, but he will not allow us to lick our wounds forever. He knows they will never heal that way.

Calling Elijah outside onto the mountaintop, God sent the wind, earthquake, and fire along to keep him company. The noise was frightening. The voice of the storm reminded Elijah of the angry voices of Jezebel and her cohorts. The Lord's voice could not be heard because of the tempest. After the wind had blown, the earth had quaked, and the fire had died down, there came a gentle whisper. Elijah recognized God's still, small voice immediately and wrapped his mantle around his ears! Was this to shut out the sound? Perhaps he knew what God wanted to say, and he didn't want to hear it.

I'm sure in that moment he realized that the fire of Jezebel's wrath had frightened him so much that it had distracted him from the gentle whisper of God: "What are you doing here, Elijah?" God will not leave us in our caves of self-pity. He comes to take us out of such places of despair and back into service. A new commission followed, and Elijah turned his back on his cave and returned to serve the Lord his God. Whose voice are you listening to? The loudest one? God does not always speak through a megaphone!

You Don't Kill a Giant Every Day

David heard these comments and was afraid of what King Achish might do to him.

1 SAMUEL 21:12

Saul had been rejected by God, and Samuel had anointed David king. The young shepherd boy was sent by his father to see how his brothers were faring. They were with Saul, fighting the Philistines. When David arrived, he saw Goliath defying God's people, so David bravely slew him.

Saul took him to his palace as his servant but became madly jealous and tried to kill him. Warned by Saul's son, Jonathan, that his father meant business, David ran away, and his troubles began!

David became a fugitive, persistently hounded by King Saul. He visited Nob, where the holy shrine was, and using lies and deceit persuaded the priest to feed him and give him Goliath's sword. Then he traveled to the camp of Achish, the king of Gath, and threw himself on his mercy. It was a wonder that Achish did not recognize Goliath's sword around David's waist. The servants of the king wanted no part of him, and David feigned madness to escape.

David had killed the king's giant, yet he ran away from the giant's king! How can you do so well one day and so badly the next? I know, don't you? David gives me courage to know you don't kill a giant every day. Some days the giant gets you, and you fail—badly—but as David learned, God loves you just the same!

THE YEAR OF FAILURE

But the Lord will redeem those who serve him. Everyone who trusts in him will be freely pardoned.

PSALM 34:22

Have you ever been really disappointed with yourself? David was. He must have felt that he had really let the Lord down. Looking back to his brave beginning with Goliath, he may have found himself fearing he never again would attain such spiritual heights.

After he escaped from the Philistine king, he hid in the cave of Adullam and penned Psalm 34. He was able to say, "I prayed to the Lord, and he answered me, freeing me from all my fears" (Psalm 34:4). One of those fears must have been the fear of failure.

He reminded himself that: "Those who look to him for help will be radiant with joy; no shadow of shame will darken their faces" (Psalm 34:5). Was he thinking back to his desperate measure at Gath when he had scrabbled on the gate with his fingernails and had let saliva flow down his beard? If he came back to trusting the Lord, he told himself, his face would be ruddy and radiant again!

The fear of failure can keep you in a cave of self-recrimination forever. Or it can drive you to the one who said: "The Lord will redeem those who serve him. Everyone who trusts in him will be freely pardoned" (Psalm 34:22).

A missionary returned from the field in disgrace, leaving a broken marriage and a broken missionary career behind her. She told me, "I'm frightened to try again. I can't take another failure." A good dose of Psalm 34 helped her confess her transgressions to the Lord, who forgave the guilt of her sin (see Psalm 32:5). She found out that failure is never final.

THE FEAR OF THE FUTURE

Let the Lord's people show him reverence, for those who honor him will have all they need. Even strong young lions sometimes go hungry, but those who trust in the Lord will never lack any good thing.

PSALM 34:9-10

David had seen lions; he had killed old lions and watched the cubs starve to death. But he knew God was "an indestructible lion," and as his "cub," David would never go hungry while God was looking after him!

Life is unpredictable, isn't it? Nobody's job is secure anymore. Even presidents of large corporations cannot be certain they will be retained.

David knew what it was like to be a king one day and a fugitive the next! He had lost a job as shepherd, a job at Saul's palace, and his position as captain in Israel's army. Yes, David knew what it was to feel very insecure about the future, even to the point of wondering if he would starve to death! "The righteous face many troubles, but the Lord rescues them from each and every one" (Psalm 34:19).

He who taught us to pray "Give us our food for today" (Matthew 6:11) keeps a full larder for his hungry children. Of course, he expects those of us with laden baskets to share with those with empty stomachs. God used the priest Ahimelech to feed David. He doesn't send bread from heaven any more than he sends pennies. He wants us to be part of the answer to others' needs.

God Is Always within Earshot

> **The eyes of the Lord watch over those who do right; his ears are open to their cries for help.**
>
> PSALM 34:15

David had the answer to all of his afflictions. He sat in his cave and counted his blessings. Blessings are very threatening to afflictions. Troubles tiptoe out of the door when praise tiptoes in. David began to praise God for being God, which is an excellent idea when you can't praise him for what he has allowed to happen in your life!

David said, "I prayed to the Lord, and he answered me" (Psalm 34:4). He believed God was near enough to hear his cry. We need to remember that when trouble comes, God is always within earshot.

We talk of him as if he is present, but we secretly think of him as absent! "The Lord is close to the brokenhearted," insisted David (Psalm 34:18). A broken heart may feel only its brokenness, not his nearness. It's what we *know* of God, not what we *feel* of him, that brings his healing presence to our damaged life.

"Where is God when it hurts?" cries the rejected wife, the mourning husband, the lonely teenager. God is near. David wrote in another place, "Do not stay so far from me, for trouble is near" (Psalm 22:11). When David insisted on believing trouble was near, God insisted on being nearer.

"But if I could only see him, feel him," we say. Will you believe he is near when you can do none of those things? If you will, you will be well on the way to growing faith in the soil of your troubles. After all, what is faith for? When we count the blessings of his nearness, sorrow and sighing flee away.

Fear of a Family Feud

O my son Absalom! My son, my son Absalom! If only I could have died instead of you! O Absalom, my son, my son.

2 SAMUEL 18:33

There's nothing like a family feud to crush your spirit! David knew all about that. To the boy David, a giant's wounds were nothing compared to the hurt his older brother Eliab's angry words caused.

> "What are you doing around here anyway? . . . What about those few sheep you're supposed to be taking care of? I know about your pride and dishonesty. You just want to see the battle!" "What have I done now?" David replied. (1 Samuel 17:28-29)

You get the picture: a long-standing family problem—a big brother with a complex about his little brother, perhaps. Something like that can break your heart. Much later in his life, David was to have his heart broken yet again by another family feud. This time it was to be his own son—his favorite son—Absalom, who would steal away the people's hearts, pursue his father to death, and try to seize his throne.

If anyone could talk about being brokenhearted, it was David. But, oh, "the Lord is close to the brokenhearted; he rescues those who are crushed in spirit" (Psalm 34:18). After David had mourned for Absalom, perhaps he took that psalm out of the scroll shelf and reminded himself of the words he had penned.

Which of us does not know what it is like to lie awake all night worrying ourselves sick over members of our families who are at odds with each other? No one can hurt you like your family can. If such is our case, we can do the same as David!

EITHER WAY, IT WILL BE ALL RIGHT!

Then Elisha prayed, "O Lord, open his eyes and let him see!"

2 KINGS 6:17

For the angel of the Lord guards all who fear him, and he rescues them" (Psalm 34:7), David exulted, warming to this theme! David believed the angel of the Lord was captain over the heavenly host. He would have appreciated hearing about Elisha's experience!

Elisha was in trouble with the king of Aram, who dispatched men, horses, and chariots to Dothan, where the prophet dwelt, to capture him. When Elisha's servant got up in the morning, he saw the army with their horses and chariots surrounding the city. (I wonder if it was a Monday morning!) "Ah, my lord, what will we do now?" he cried. "Don't be afraid!" Elisha answered him. "For there are more on our side than on theirs!" Then God opened the servant's eyes, and he saw "that the hillside around Elisha was filled with horses and chariots of fire" (2 Kings 6:15-17).

Christ, who is the captain of the Lord's host, encamps around those who fear him. Sometimes the captain commands those unseen hosts to intervene, as in Elisha's case, and a miracle of deliverance takes place. At other times, in God's infinite wisdom, the heavenly host is restrained. But it's still a comfort to know they are there!

Whether one of the angels leaned out of his heavenly chariot and clobbered David's enemies for him, or simply pulled him up alongside and deposited him safely in heaven, David knew that, either way, it would be all right!

LAZINESS

The following spring, the time of year when kings go to war, David sent Joab and the Israelite army to destroy the Ammonites. In the process they laid siege to the city of Rabbah. But David stayed behind in Jerusalem.

2 SAMUEL 11:1

At the time that kings went forth to battle—David stayed at home! David had become lazy. The Bible says, "Late one afternoon David got out of bed after taking a nap" (2 Samuel 11:2)! A king who's kingly doesn't take naps in the day of battle. He gets up early and puts in a productive day's work.

I'm sure the devil was on the spot immediately, trying to think up a way to exploit the situation. Laziness invites Temptation to tea and listens to his proposals. If we allow self-indulgence to contribute to the conversation, we are in for a load of trouble.

We can be lazy physically, giving into our body's demands instead of practicing self-control. We can be lazy socially, refusing to make the effort to reach out to Christians and build ourselves some solid friendships to support us in our hour of need. We can be lazy spiritually and forget to read the Bible and pray—especially when things appear to be in good order.

David's forces had destroyed the Ammonites and were besieging Rabbah; the battle was going well. Perhaps David thought he would take it easy. Maybe he considered himself too old for war. But laziness caused him to lose a fight on the home front. Think of David and be aware of laziness!

Loneliness

She is Bathsheba, the daughter of Eliam and the wife of Uriah the Hittite.

2 SAMUEL 11:3

Yes, indeed, this was Bathsheba, Uriah's wife. Her husband was at the battlefront, and like countless other women in Israel, Bathsheba was lonely, frustrated, and vulnerable. She was also very beautiful.

Loneliness does strange things to you. It tells you it's not fair to be alone and you don't need to be too picky as long as you're satisfied. Loneliness can make you do wild things, quite contrary to your Christian character. Loneliness tells you that you *have* to have companionship, even if it is illegitimate! If a chance of companionship comes along, there's a real danger of the possibility of the companionship being more important than the companion.

But King David was not just any man! King David was good looking, a poet, a man's man, and a ladies' man! He was a hunk of a catch. But then all that is understandable. The devil isn't stupid. He got Bathsheba when she was most vulnerable, and he sent along a handsome king. What were her chances of resisting such advances?

It's hard when your husband is away, isn't it? It's tough when he's out of town for even a few days, to say nothing of when he's walked out of your life forever! But loneliness does not give us permission to be promiscuous; it gives us opportunity to overcome temptation and grow stronger in the Lord. Who is sufficient for these things? I am—"in Jesus Christ our Lord" (Romans 7:25).

THE POWER TO SAY NO!

As he looked out over the city, he noticed a woman of unusual beauty taking a bath.

2 SAMUEL 11:2

Did you know that we are responsible for our response to temptation? If we believe that, we may not yield quite so quickly, and certainly we will not want to be a temptation to anyone else. If I sin in response to someone's tempting me, that's bad, but if I initiate a temptation and cause both of us to sin, that's even worse!

Bathsheba tempted David. She knew that clothes (or their absence) could say what she wanted to say. Things haven't changed much! We need to watch how we dress and be conscious of the messages clothes send. We would do well to look in the mirror before we go out into our world.

It's hard to face our motive and ask ourselves honestly, "Now just *why* did I do it, or say that, or dress like that?" It's hard to admit that I am capable of doing anything deceitful! But, "the human heart is most deceitful and desperately wicked. Who really knows how bad it is?" (Jeremiah 17:9).

"I'll never be unfaithful to my husband," vowed a young wife. Within five years, she was living with her boss. It's easy to say, "I'll never be unfaithful," if we never have the chance! Those who meet the opportunity know the battle that ensues. They know they are capable of sin. The marvelous thing about being a Christian is that at such times, God says he'll lend us the power to say no!

Lust

> He sent someone to find out who she was, and he was told, "She is Bathsheba, the daughter of Eliam and the wife of Uriah the Hittite." Then David sent for her; and when she came to the palace, he slept with her.
>
> 2 SAMUEL 11:3-4

When Satan introduces laziness and loneliness to lust, he's in business. Of course, Bathsheba could have said no, but she didn't. The Bible simply says "she came." Just like that!

A clue to Bathsheba's character lies in the fact that she had just taken her bath in full view of her neighbor's house (2 Samuel 11:2)! She must have known the king was home, and I can't help thinking she sent him a very simple message that said, "I'm vulnerable, reachable, and available. Come and get me!"

I believe all women know how to convey that message. I also believe every woman knows how *not* to! God has provided us tongues and feet for such times. Tongues can say no and feet can "run from . . . youthful lust" (2 Timothy 2:22).

When I came to Christ at the age of eighteen, I was told by a good friend to start to look boys straight in the eyes. Being intensely anxious to please Jesus, I searched my Bible for confirmation of that advice. I found it in the book of Job. "I made a covenant with my eyes not to look with lust upon a young woman" (Job 31:1). Job made a promise to God. I knelt and told God I'd like to make a promise about my eyes, too. What a difference that prayer made.

When the messengers come, send the right message back—whether it be by letter, a phone call, or a long, level look! You don't have to comply!

God Would Spare Us

Have mercy on me, O God, because of your unfailing love. Because of your great compassion, blot out the stain of my sins.

PSALM 51:1

Being sorry doesn't always change the thing you are sorry about. David was sorry he had sinned with Bathsheba. But being sorry didn't bring their baby or Uriah back from the dead. Being sorry didn't mend Bathsheba's broken heart either.

"You may be sure that your sin will find you out" (Numbers 32:23). This should caution us to watch our p's and q's! God will forgive murder, but the grave stands, a still and silent testimony to the act. God will forgive the adulterer, but he may lose his wife to another man. God will forgive the teenage drug addict, but the child's mind is destroyed and his or her perception impaired. There *are* consequences to sin.

Absalom, David's favorite son, revolted against his father, raped David's wives in public, and tried to kill him. Did Absalom's behavior reflect his father's sexual license?

Joab, David's lifelong friend and trusted general, had received David's message: "Station Uriah on the front lines where the battle is fiercest. Then pull back so that he will be killed" (2 Samuel 11:15). Did Joab's later decision to follow Absalom reflect his disillusionment with King David?

You reap what you sow. God will forgive you, but the clock cannot be turned back. The far-reaching results of sin are appalling, and God would spare us.

Truly Sorry

> **The sacrifice you want is a broken spirit. A broken and repentant heart, O God, you will not despise.**
>
> PSALM 51:17

God sent Nathan to tell King David that he had seen what David had done to Uriah and was angry with him. David's repentance was immediate. "I have sinned against the Lord," he cried out (2 Samuel 12:13). He was not angry with Nathan, or with God, but at himself!

True repentance is being angry at yourself in the right way. Many of us are angry when we're found out—with the person who finds us out or with the one with whom we sinned. When God sees us truly angry with ourselves for sinning, then he accepts our confession. A truly broken and repentant spirit he will *not* despise. As soon as David confessed his sin, Nathan discerned that the king was really sorry and said, "The Lord has forgiven you, and you won't die for this sin" (2 Samuel 12:13).

Being repentant means you allow God to speak to you about sin. You don't argue; you listen! God is our judge. David acknowledged that fact: "You will be proved right in what you say, and your judgment against me is just" (Psalm 51:4).

Being repentant means you agree with your own conscience. It is in this inward place that God makes us to know wisdom! "You desire honesty from the heart" (Psalm 51:6). Let's face it, we *know* when we have sinned. We can also know that he will forgive us if we want him to.

With whom are you angry? Why? Shouldn't you rather be angry with yourself for sinning? Wouldn't you like to hear God say to you, "The Lord has forgiven you"? You'll hear him say it, if you are truly sorry.

Guilt Doesn't Know Any Songs

Forgive me for shedding blood, O God who saves; then I will joyfully sing of your forgiveness.

PSALM 51:14

When we are truly sorry, and truly forgiven, guilt cannot blanket our souls with depression anymore. Guilt smothers, whispering in our ears, "Don't try again; you'll fail." Or, "The thing you did is unforgivable; you'll never recover from it."

After you have been angry with yourself for hurting God and those you love, and he has forgiven you, you have to forgive yourself. After all, true repentance has led to true confession, which must lead to true freedom from guilt. "Forgive me for shedding blood, O God," cried David. David wanted his heart to sing again, but guilt doesn't know any songs! He longed to tell others that God was right and he was wrong, but guilt sealed his lips. Guilt wants you to go on being angry with yourself forever.

We may experience guilt because we *are* guilty. This helps us become angry with ourselves and confess our sin. When we hear God tell us he forgives us, we can stop being angry with ourselves. God can and will save us from the guilt and power of sin. Some people live all their lives forgiven, yet guilty. "I don't *feel* forgiven," said a despondent single. "How can I get out from under all this guilt?"

Ask God to forgive you for nursing guilt when he has dealt with it all. Dare to believe that the God of your salvation has saved you, not just from sin, but from guilt as well!

Renewal

Create in me a clean heart, O God. Renew a right spirit within me.

PSALM 51:10

The word *renew* conjures up the promise of a fresh start, a new day, daffodils, and spring. In this context, it also carries with it the sense of permanent renewal. "Renew a right spirit within me," David prayed. David did not want God to renew him for a passing moment or a day. He wanted to know a steady spirit of commitment for the rest of his life. "Don't take your Holy Spirit from me," he pled (Psalm 51:11). David wanted desperately to experience a steady resolve to follow God's pathway.

God's Holy Spirit will lend our spirit his renewing, willing steadiness. David prayed that the Holy Spirit would not be removed from his heart. No believer of the present church age needs to pray that prayer. Christ promised his own that the Spirit would "never leave you" (John 14:16).

But we, like David, need to constantly seek God's face, conscious of our need for a daily cleansing from sin and renewal of his power to continue. Are you tired of constantly coming short of his expectations, others' expectations, and even your own expectations? When you ask him to renew a right spirit within you, he will lend you his other self to help in renewing your resolve, restoring your joy, releasing your lips, and receiving your praise!

Mothers need renewal. Sometimes they give up believing their children will ever make it. They give up their hope of maintaining their own steady love, unbroken by temper or careless care. Mothers understand David's prayer. They echo it every day, and God hears and answers with an eternal *yes!*

A New Ministry

Then I will teach your ways to sinners, and they will return to you.

PSALM 51:13

A new ministry begins when we have a new sense of cleansing and renewal. After all, we have something new to share.

David knew that. Once God had forgiven him, he knew he could better teach repentance and renewal to other transgressors like himself.

Somehow someone on a platform is set apart from those in the audience. However, if the speaker is able to share the listeners' experiences, it helps the audience to identify. When I came out the other end of a long, dark tunnel of loneliness, experiencing depression and disgust with myself, I was ready to share my lessons with others still in the tunnel. As I began to speak, I hesitantly admitted my failures and then discovered that many women identified with and responded to me. They felt I was just like they were—which of course I was!

When I shared the fact that I looked under the bed when I was alone at night, I found instant rapport! I was not proud of my lack of faith, simply truthful. The secret, of course, is not only to share one's shortcomings but the answers! As we present the God of our salvation—from sin, failure, and fear—then sinners *will be* converted! It's neat to tell people that God can help them get into bed without looking under it! If God has cleansed you anew, he has a new ministry for you. Accept it.

My Heavenly Oscar

After all, what gives us hope and joy, and what is our proud reward and crown? It is you! Yes, you will bring us much joy as we stand together before our Lord Jesus when he comes back again. For you are our pride and joy.

1 THESSALONIANS 2:19-20

Did you know that there will be an awards day? When it comes, crowns will be given to God's faithful servants. When Paul speaks of a crown of rejoicing, he is talking about the evangelist's crown! That will be the reward for those who have faithfully preached the gospel or have led people to Christ.

What other awards will be given? There will be a crown of righteousness which will be given to all who have been eagerly looking forward to his second coming—all who love his appearing (see 2 Timothy 4:6-8)! You could call this crown a crown of readiness!

The shepherd's crown will be received by those who have cared well for the flock of God (see 1 Peter 5:1-4); a crown of endurance for those who have resisted temptation; a crown of life for the martyrs who have lost their lives for the sake of the gospel. Christ encourages such sacrificial servants: "Remain faithful even when facing death, and I will give you the crown of life" (Revelation 2:10).

Have you ever watched the Oscar presentations? I have and have been struck by the way every recipient takes the platform to thank the people who have made it possible for them to win. When the heavenly Oscars are presented, all of us will want to take our opportunity to thank the ones who made it all possible—the Father, the Son, and the Holy Spirit!

A Windbreak

> **Look, a righteous king is coming! And honest princes will rule under him. He will shelter Israel from the storm and the wind.**
>
> ISAIAH 32:1-2

This passage is an oracle about the coming King. It speaks of his own qualities given by the Spirit of the Lord, but also speaks of the same Spirit in the character of the King's subjects.

If the King be king of my life, then I shall be a windbreak! Each person will be like a shelter from the wind. In his strength, I can stand in the middle and be a windbreak. What is a windbreak? Most of us are familiar with the word *windbreaker*. The dictionary tells us it is an outer jacket that prevents the worst of the weather from getting through.

Do you know anybody against whom the stormy gales of adversity are raging? I think of a friend whose husband will not speak to her. Her children are hostile. She knows and loves the Lord, but she lives alone in a house full of strangers who have but one thing in common—their name.

Since no one speaks to her, she desperately needs someone to talk to. When we meet each other, we stop to chat or take time out for a cup of coffee. Occasionally, I meet her husband, and he talks to me. More accurately, he talks *at* me. Somehow he feels better once he's unloaded, and he goes home to his wife and asks her to pass the sugar at breakfast! Now, that's progress, and she calls me to rejoice. I have been a shelter, a windbreak, and I am glad!

A Watershed

He will refresh her as a river in the desert.

ISAIAH 32:2

A watershed is a ridge off which water flows. Its usefulness lies in its ability to divert streams to dry places.

When we think of water, we think of the Holy Spirit. Jesus said that "the water I give them takes away thirst altogether. It becomes a perpetual spring within them, giving them eternal life" (John 4:14). He also said, "If you are thirsty, come to me! If you believe in me, come and drink! For the Scriptures declare that rivers of living water will flow out from within" (John 7:37-38). By this, he meant the Spirit.

In myself, if Christ by his Spirit does not live in me, I have no power to refresh people who thirst inwardly for eternal things. But if he does indeed live within my heart, I can become a watershed, diverting the water of life in the appropriate direction.

When I first came to Christ and had my own needs met and my inner thirst satisfied, I realized my friends were thirsty, too. I prayed I would become a watershed.

One of my best friends asked me to play tennis. She knew something had happened to me and was curious. In between "love-fifteen" and "love-thirty," she asked me to explain my new satisfaction. I had the great joy of diverting some of the living water over her! Before we got to game point, Jesus had won, and she was as drenched with delight as I was. She was well on the way to becoming a watershed, too!

Do As I Do

Strengthen those who have tired hands, and encourage those who have weak knees. Say to those who are afraid, "Be strong, and do not fear, for your God is coming to destroy your enemies. He is coming to save you."

ISAIAH 35:3-4

Another interesting thing about watersheds is that water has to flow over them before they can divert it anywhere else! Am *I* drinking daily of the Spirit before I run about my neighborhood telling others to drink daily, too? It's the easiest thing in the world to say, "Do as I say, and not as I do!"

My schedule of speaking engagements is full. I spend much time preparing my messages. It's hard sometimes to make sure it is my own before it becomes anyone else's. If the water has not flowed over me, I will not see it flow over others.

I had been preparing a message on prayer. I had a good outline: three points—all beginning with the same letter so that people could remember them; some excellent illustrations to let some light into the structure of the talk; and, of course, lots of Scripture passages. I wanted very much for the ladies to get the point.

As I put the finishing touches on my talk, I glanced at the clock. It was very late, and my family was long since in bed and asleep. I tumbled into bed and then tumbled out again! I had almost forgotten the water needed to flow over me before I could be a watershed for others! I needed to pray! Are you telling people to do as you say or to do as you do?

A Wall

Not only can I be a windbreak and a watershed, I can be like a wall of rock—a solid piece of permanence rising up out of a weary land. Notice I said "like" a wall of rock. God is the Rock. David told the Lord he loved him for his rocklike qualities (see Psalm 18:1-2). He knew he could rely on God's rocklike permanence, eternal strength, and stability as a refuge for his frail human nature.

The cool shadow of a large rock in a hot and weary land.

ISAIAH 32:2

This was a favorite theme of the king. David lived much of his life in the rocks of the Holy Land. When he was chased by his enemies, he knew what it was to run into the crevasses and caves and find shelter there. He could always rely on the caves being in exactly the same place he had left them! They seemed to be eternally reliable.

"I love you, Lord; you are my strength," sang David. "The Lord is my rock, my fortress, and my savior; my God is my rock, in whom I find protection" (Psalm 18:1-2). We all need such a wall of permanence in our life. We need to lean back and find the granite firm against our back. Sometimes we need to find a crevasse in the rock and hide ourselves from our enemies.

The prophet Isaiah tells us when our Rock is King, we become like a shadow of the Rock to others. A shadow is an image of a body intercepting the light, an inescapable companion. Do others look at you and me and see us as shadows of our Rock within the weary land? Are we his inescapable companions?

Do for Us That We May Do for Them

And he will say to me, "You are my Father, my God, and the Rock of my salvation."

PSALM 89:26

Children need to see a rock-like quality in their parents' characters. They need to see us as shadows of the Mighty Rock. They need to feel the permanence of our positions on moral matters, for example. Sometimes they run to us, looking for security, like David ran into his caves.

Friends need us to be a shadow of the Mighty Rock, too. Fickle friends are not friends at all. Is there a sense of permanence about us? Do our friends always know how they will find us?

Husbands need to know us as a shadow of the Mighty Rock as well. The solid stability of our commitment to Christ our Rock, smitten for us and out of whom flows rivers of living water, will be a sure and settled sign of our permanence. They will know they can rely on our word; they will trust our promises, and that means much in a weary land.

The world is a weary wilderness. People walk at a fast pace in deep sand; they get dreadfully tired. There's nothing quite as exhausting as trying to run through loose, dry sand, especially under the cruel heat of the sun! Children play with children in the shifting sands of changing times; friends struggle in the sinking sands of complicated relationships; husbands and wives come home at the end of a day, worn out with making desert deals.

"God, make us shadows of our Rock! Do for us that we may do for them!"

King Jesus

If Jesus is King of my heart, then he will reach out of my life to conquer other lives. He must make my choices, direct my heart's affairs, choose my friends, assign me duties. He must be sovereign.

Open the window of my mind, Lord.
Breathe the breath of life through
cobwebs of carnality.

Send the sacred sounds that touch
my sleeping senses,
kissing faith awake.

Overtake my harried heart;
Set it down and speak to it
until it listens.

Touch my tongue and stop its
stammering journey.
Bring it home to clarity
till
fluent faith proclaims
Thy kingliness.

Make my ministry Your home,
That my earth knows Your rule
of righteousness.

Manage my little world,
rule it from Your throne
King Jesus!

Look, a righteous king is coming! And honest princes will rule under him. . . . Then everyone who can see will be looking for God, and those who can hear will listen to his voice. Even the hotheads among them will be full of sense and understanding. Those who stammer in uncertainty will speak out plainly.

ISAIAH 32:1, 3-4

Not Just Idle Words

So Moses recited this entire song to the assembly of Israel. . . . My teaching will fall on you like rain; my speech will settle like dew. My words will fall like rain on tender grass, like gentle showers on young plants.

DEUTERONOMY 31:30; 32:2

Doesn't that sound as though you are about to be so thoroughly soaked with satisfaction you'll never be thirsty again? What beautiful words! Those of us who teach must want to fall on our knees before this verse! Moses had a message that would thoroughly refresh his hearers. Part of this fresh message was the concept of God as our Rock.

The picture of God as our Rock is firmly embedded in the ground of the Old Testament. Moses says that God is a perfect Rock, a faithful God who does no wrong. He is always right, and we must measure our little ideas of rightness against his eternal truth.

Moses mourned the times the children of Israel rejected the Rock, their Savior, and his ideas of rightness. Deserting the Rock who fathered them, Israel became like other nations whose dependence on lesser rocks had let them down—nations whose rock had sold them. "But the rock of our enemies is not like our Rock, as even they recognize," he reminded them (Deuteronomy 32:31).

Moses sang a fresh song, calling his people to a renewed commitment to the Rock of their salvation. When he had finished he warned, "These instructions are not mere words—they are your life!" (Deuteronomy 32:47). Have you deserted the Rock who fathered you? Return to him. You can depend upon his renewal.

He Is Our Joy

Go and do what I say. For Saul is my chosen instrument to take my message to the Gentiles and to kings, as well as to the people of Israel. And I will show him how much he must suffer for me.

ACTS 9:15-16

When I came to faith in Jesus Christ, I came to realize I had been saved to serve. I'm glad I understood that fact soon after my conversion. However, I had the distinct impression that serving was going to cause me a lot of suffering. After all, hadn't God warned the great apostle Paul that he was to suffer much for the cause of Christ?

And I met many believers who looked as though they had eaten pickles every day since they became Christians! They had dark, sour faces—saved, but sour. Others seemed very, very sad—for no apparent reason! Yes, I decided, belonging to Christ must be a very somber business indeed.

These people reminded me of Nehemiah. Nehemiah was the king's cupbearer, a Jewish prisoner of war, who was serving a monarch who would not allow anyone to look miserable in his presence. One day Nehemiah received some bad news. He couldn't help looking sad, and the king was furious. "Why are you so sad? You aren't sick, are you?" he demanded (Nehemiah 2:2).

The king couldn't imagine anyone's being anything less than ecstatic while serving him. Come to think of it, I can't imagine anyone being sad in the presence of King Jesus either. Even if suffering is allowed, there is no excuse for sour, sad faces. After all, he has promised to be our joy.

GOD'S MEDICINE

A glad heart makes a happy face; a broken heart crushes the spirit.

PROVERBS 15:13

A smile on your heart means a smile on your face. Some people wear their hearts on their sleeves. What goes on inside, shows up outside. Have you ever asked a junior high daughter to help you with the housework? Her face tells the story. Her heart is definitely not in it!

When your heart has Jesus as its guest, it smiles. How can it do anything else? When your heart houses the one who is our joy, it cannot help grinning at grief, laughing at loads, and smiling at sorrows. Even when we are called to suffer, we cannot be sad or sour because we discover that we have been saved to sing! Even if you can't sing very well, you can make a joyful noise—that will do (see Psalm 100:1)!

"But," you may object, "how can I even smile when I'm suffering, much less sing about it?" Look at Jesus! Can you look at Jesus and remain sober? When I'm in trouble, and I meet him in the secret place and he smiles at me, that mends my heart so I can mend others. He sets my heart singing!

"A glad heart helps and heals" (Proverbs 17:22, Moffatt). Or, as the King James Version puts it, "A merry heart doeth good like medicine." Now that's the sort of medicine our sick society needs. There is joy in serving Jesus, and when merry missionaries and contented Christians dispense their smiling medicine in an unsmiling world, we are in business.

Hanging Up Our Harps

But how can we sing the songs of the Lord while in a foreign land?

PSALM 137:4

The children of Israel were captives in the land of Babylon. They had been carried into a situation that they would never have chosen for themselves.

By the rivers of Babylon, the captives sat down and wept and hung up their lyres (harps) on the willow trees (see Psalm 137:1-2). There is no sadder picture than harpless harpists! The problem was aggravated by the Babylonians tormenting the children of Israel with the words "Sing us one of those songs of Jerusalem!" (Psalm 137:3).

Somehow unbelievers expect those who claim a relationship with the Music Maker to make music at all times. Even when they are in "a foreign land!"

Perhaps you know how the children of Israel must have felt. Did your husband become an alcoholic after you got married? Have you had to move again and again to "foreign" situations, away from friends and familiar things because of your husband's job situation? Have you hung up your harp?

I remember moving from the city to the country—a foreign land as far as I was concerned! I am a city girl, and I could see little to sing about in a country environment. I hung up my harp. But Jesus came along, reached up, and took it down again. "These people need to hear my music," he said quietly, giving me back my instrument. "You don't hang up your harp without permission, and I haven't given you permission!"

So I began to play, in a minor key at first, but then in major chords of triumph. I sang my "captors" one of the songs of Jersualem. I don't know if they liked it, but Jesus did!

The Annual Family Reunion

Worship the Lord with gladness. Come before him, singing with joy.

PSALM 100:2

"Joy is a question of obedience," explained a friend of mine. She was helping me to discover that I was saved to sing! It helped me greatly to hear that God had commanded me to be joyful.

She showed me a passage of Scripture (see Deuteronomy 28) that contained a list of God's expectations. If his people fulfilled them, God promised them happiness. If they disobeyed and did not serve the Lord with "joy and enthusiasm for the abundant benefits" they had received (Deuteronomy 28:47), they were promised misery and tears. The choice was theirs. The choice is ours, too. To obey or not to obey—that is the question!

We not only are commanded to serve our God, but to serve him with joy. The idea of offering God "joyful" service is embodied in the thank offerings of the Old Testament. A thank offering in many contexts was the virtual synonym of the peace offering, and the general idea of the peace offering indicated a person's right relationship with God, good fellowship, gratitude, and obligation.

God was pleased to accept thank offerings. They looked good to him. They were not only offered at the end of famine or pestilence or war, but when a new king was installed, at a time of spiritual renewal, or at harvesttime. They were offered when lepers were cleansed and even at the annual family reunion! Now, when I can make a thank offering for *that,* I'm really doing well!

When I can serve those closest to me and serve them joyfully, I'm in business. I have to admit, it will take an act of obedience on my part, but that's all right, for joy is a question of obedience!

The Altar of My Pride

Enter his gates with thanksgiving; go into his courts with praise. Give thanks to him and bless his name.

PSALM 100:4

Our immediate family seems to be made up of individuals with extraordinary strength of character. Each person is a strong, independent creature with ideas all his own. As our family circle widens, it reveals more of the same! Grandmas and grandpas, aunts and uncles, and in-laws all seem incompatible, yet are called by God to love and understand each other. That annual family reunion can be quite a challenge, can't it?

In Old Testament times, thank offerings always were connected with communal affairs and usually were made at their culmination. Perhaps God knew the problems that would arise at Christmas, Thanksgiving, twenty-fifth wedding anniversaries, christenings, or graduations! Maybe he knew he would have to command us to be thankful if he ever was going to see us appreciate each other.

It really helps to face an ornery relative and have to search our mind for something to give thanks about! It helps to talk to a difficult cousin and have to apologize to her for some misunderstanding or another. I can always thank God for my growth in humility because of that!

Whenever you face a difficult relative, try a thank offering. Don't let anyone go home without knowing how thankful you are for them. And remember, thank offerings and peace offerings go together! Don't let the sun go down on your wrath without having made a peace offering on the altar of your pride. Such offerings bring to God the smell of a sweet savor.

The Nazirite

Then the Nazirites will shave their hair at the entrance of the Tabernacle and put it on the fire beneath the peace-offering sacrifice.

NUMBERS 6:18

It's great when God sets your heart singing. But how can we keep in tune and not go off-key? One way is to understand that a singing heart is a separated heart. Some have gotten things a little mixed up and believe separation means isolation. Jesus told us we must be separate from sin but a friend of sinners.

The Nazirite understood the joy of separation. One of the things he did when he took a vow was to promise not to drink any wine. Wine was the symbol of natural joy (see Psalm 104:15). By doing this, the Nazirite was saying that there is a devotedness that finds all its joy in the Lord.

The Nazirite did not cut his hair, either. Long hair was considered a disgrace (see 1 Corinthians 11:14). By abstaining from cutting his hair and beard, the man was saying that he was willing to bear disgrace for the Lord's sake. A Nazirite could take a vow for as long as he wished. When he fulfilled his vow, his hair was ceremonially shaved and his beard trimmed and then burned under the thank offering. There was great joy in that final ceremony, not because the period of separation was over, but because the Nazirite was expressing his gratitude for the joy of the experience itself!

There *is* a joy in separating ourselves unto the Lord. The Nazirite knew that holiness meant happiness.

Knowing Is Joy

> **Acknowledge that the Lord is God!**
>
> PSALM 100:3

Joy comes through obedience, separation, and knowledge. When you have to do something you are frightened of doing, like flying in a small aircraft, then it's what you know that will determine how you feel! Joy comes through knowing you will not die until God is ready for you to die!

The psalmist told us we can make a joyful noise to the Lord when we know the Lord is God (see Psalm 100:1)! Do we believe that God holds the whole world in his hands? If so, then that knowledge can filter down through our brain to our emotions and gently untie the knots in our stomach.

When you are asked to stand up in front of a crowd of people (especially people you know well) and give a speech, it's what you know that will help you at that time. You know that "God, who calls you, is faithful; he will do this" (1 Thessalonians 5:24)! There is great joy in knowing that!

When you are having your in-laws stay for the weekend, it's what you know that will help you to look forward to the visit with gladness. You know that the Holy Spirit will shed his love abroad in your heart for your relatives. "Hallelujah; I need that," you mutter!

God is my mighty Creator, Provider, Redeemer. Knowing that he *is* gives me a joyful expectation that he will be all that he is in my particular situation. There is great joy in knowing he will simply be himself and help me be myself, while others are busy being themselves! Knowing is joy!

Striving with the Spirit

My Spirit will not put up with humans for such a long time.

GENESIS 6:3

God gets upset with us. He wrestles with us, showing us how to live, move, be, and worship him. He does this as he does anything big—by his Spirit.

In Genesis days, "the Spirit of God was hovering over" the surface of the earth (Genesis 1:2). The angel who announced the Incarnation told Mary, "the Holy Spirit will come upon you" (Luke 1:35). The adult Jesus, "full of the Holy Spirit . . . was led by the Spirit" (Luke 4:1) into the wilderness to be tempted by the devil for forty days. In his temptation, Jesus resisted Satan in the power of the Spirit. Jesus, "by the power of the eternal Spirit . . . offered himself to God as a perfect sacrifice for our sins" (Hebrews 9:14). He was raised from the dead by the Spirit (see Romans 8:11). He works with the Spirit in regeneration, bringing eternal life to men and women.

But men and women do not always allow God's Spirit to have his way in their lives. Whenever God does anything big, he does it by his Spirit. One of the biggest things he does is change self-seeking people into servants! That takes as much power as was manifested in creation! In fact, that is just what the Bible says: "Christians become new persons. They are not the same anymore, for the old life is gone. A new life has begun!" (2 Corinthians 5:17).

It is the Holy Spirit's work to strive with us to bring that creative regeneration about in our life.

Lying to God

> **Then Peter said, "Ananias, why has Satan filled your heart? You lied to the Holy Spirit."**
>
> ACTS 5:3

In the versions of the Bible that I first read, the Holy Spirit was often referred to as the "Holy Ghost." Before I became a Christian, I thought the Holy Ghost was a sheet-shrouded spook who haunted old English graveyards! After I became a believer, I listened to friends and was more confused than ever. Was the Holy Ghost a feeling, a subject for conferences, a vague eminence, or what? As I read the Bible, I discovered the Holy Ghost was a person—in fact, the third Person of the Trinity.

I also found I could treat him as a person. I could resist him (see Genesis 6:3), insult him (see Hebrews 10:26-31), stifle him (see 1 Thessalonians 5:19), and grieve him (see Ephesians 4:25-31). The most sober realization and conviction of all dawned upon me as I read Acts 5:1-11—I could lie to him!

The story tells of Ananias and Sapphira, who sold a piece of property and laid the proceeds at the feet of the apostles. Their sin lay not in the fact that they only brought half of the price, but that they *said* they brought all of it!

How often have I lied to the Holy Spirit? I thought. "You have all my time," I had told him when I first became a believer, yet that was just not true. "You have all my money," I had intoned in a pious platitude at a prayer meeting. "Not so," the Spirit whispered in my ear! "You have all my heart," I had promised many, many times.

How glad I am God does not deal with us as he dealt with Ananias and Sapphira. If he did, I would not be writing this book! The Holy Spirit is a person, and I need to apologize to him and ask his forgiveness.

THE VEIL

We can boldly enter heaven's Most Holy Place because of the blood of Jesus. This is the new, life-giving way that Christ has opened up for us through the sacred curtain, by means of his death for us. And since we have a great High Priest who rules over God's people, let us go right into the presence of God, with true hearts fully trusting him.

HEBREWS 10:19-22

In times past, the priest was the mediator between God and Israel. Since the Resurrection of Christ, *he* alone is the "one Mediator who can reconcile God and people" (1 Timothy 2:5). He is our High Priest. Israel's high priest would enter the Holy Place, where God dwelt, and offer the blood of a lamb as a sacrifice for the people, that they might be made one with God.

When Jesus' flesh was rent on Calvary, the veil or curtain that hung across the entrance into the Most Holy Place was also rent in two, making entrance into God's presence possible. We can call God "Father" and come freely before him to "find grace to help us when we need it" (Hebrews 4:16).

When our children were growing up, their father traveled a great deal. When he returned, he needed to catch up with mountains of work that were always waiting for him. Since his study was at home, I tried to keep the door shut and the children outside! But he would always open the door and tell me to leave it that way. "I want the kids to know I am always accessible to them," he would say. The children would run in and out whenever they had a need or a want, a kiss or a hug for Daddy.

That is how our Father in heaven would have it, too; Jesus made that possible!

The Illustrated Edition

And this is the way to have eternal life—to know you, the only true God, and Jesus Christ, the one you sent to earth.

JOHN 17:3

"Mommy, what is God like?" inquired a typical grade-school child. What would you have said? How can you put the ocean in a thimble, a camel through the eye of a needle, the whole earth in a bucket? Where do you begin and where do you end? God is vast, yet we know he can be known. After all, Christianity is a religion of revelation.

But only God can let us know who he is and what his desires and laws are. The gospel—or Good News—is that he has done just that. There is no excuse for you or for me or even for a child of the age of understanding to say we haven't seen God's power, because "from the time the world was created, people have seen the earth and sky and all that God made. They can clearly see his invisible qualities—his eternal power and divine nature. So they have no excuse whatsoever for not knowing God" (Romans 1:20).

Go for a walk in the park, ski down the crystal slopes, count the stars on a clear night, watch the trees change dresses for the fall—you'll see him there.

God's Word is written on our heart, too—impressed upon our consciences (see Romans 2:15). And in case we misread his message within, he wrote his desires on ten tablets of stone and someone copied them so we have them clearly in our own language in our own Bible (Exodus 20).

Christ is the illustrated edition of that law. God's last Word—"I am God"—he said again and again. People believe because of the life that he lived and the death that he died and the Resurrection he accomplished. "What is God like, little child? Look at Jesus!"

Proving Its Promises

Your word is a lamp for my feet and a light for my path.

PSALM 119:105

"Can we trust our Bible?" a student asked me.

"Oh yes," I said happily.

I remain sure that we can. I was able to tell her that, even though we don't have the original manuscripts, thirteen hundred pieces of very ancient copies of the originals are in the British and Vatican museums. Archaeologists have become the Bible's friends, explaining puzzle after puzzle of the past and revealing by the discoveries of their spades that many of the so-called contradictions are mere difficulties.

The Bible claims that its writers were inspired; Christ himself endorsed the Old Testament over and over again. Prophecy, which is history written in advance, came to pass, proving the uniqueness of the documents. But above all, the Bible is relevant, proving its promises to the ones who will approach and claim them for themselves.

It is a lamp and light to our way. When we are in the dark, we can switch the Scriptures onto our problems and see the answer.

The Bible is a fire, burning its rebukes into our mind. The text hits us like a hammer, breaking our hard heart into pieces (see Jeremiah 23:29); like a sword, pricking our consciences (see Ephesians 6:17); and like milk, nourishing our infant trust until we learn to lean harder on Jesus. It's like a seed that grows within us (see Luke 8:11-12), and like honey to our taste! It's a sweet word when we're sour, and a satisfying meal when we're hungry!

"Yes," I said to my student, emphatically. "We *can* certainly trust our Bible!"

MONDAYS

"Good morning, Lord. It's Monday morning!"

"I know."

"I don't do very well on Mondays. I'm exhausted after the day of rest!"

"Mondays don't bother me at all. All days are alike to me."

"Don't you ever get that Monday-morning feeling, Lord?"

"On Monday, I was bringing order out of chaos. It was a good day! Exhilarating!"

"Well, I never feel exhilarated on a Monday morning. But tomorrow is another day. I'll get around to bringing some order out of the chaos around the house then!"

"You only have today. No one has tomorrow!"

"But Mondays are down days, Lord. Everyone grumbles about Mondays!"

"My children don't have to do what everyone else does. Monday can be a beginning sort of day. Now, what do you think needs beginning in your life?"

"I suppose a new attitude about Mondays."

"That's better."

"Create a new attitude in me, Lord."

"I will. Now, let's go and brighten up somebody else's Monday."

In the beginning God created the heavens and the earth. The earth was empty, a formless mass cloaked in darkness. And the Spirit of God was hovering over its surface.

GENESIS 1:1-2

TUESDAYS

And so it was. . . . This happened on the second day.

GENESIS 1:7-8

"Good morning, God."*

"Good morning, my daughter."

"Where have you been?"

"Right here."

"I couldn't find you. Why do you hide?"

"I don't hide."

"Then how is it I can never seem to see you clearly?"

"You're not looking in the right places."

"God, why have you been silent?"

"I haven't."

"But I can't hear your voice."

"Try turning off the television."

"But it's Tuesday. I go to church on Sundays."

"I don't live in church."

"God?"

"Yes?"

"Why isn't Christianity more exciting?"

"Because you've settled for mediocrity."

"What's that?"

"Safe faith."

"But I want my faith to be exciting."

"Then follow me."

"Where?"

"Take my hand; just follow me."

"I will, Lord. Help me to see you more clearly, to love you more dearly, to follow you more nearly day by day."

Wednesdays

Hello, God. It's Wednesday."

"That's right."

"You were busy that first Wednesday, weren't you?"

"Yes."

And God said, "Let the waters beneath the sky be gathered into one place so dry ground may appear." And so it was.

GENESIS 1:9

"Seas and seeds, mountains and trees; I'll bet you couldn't wait until the weekend to recover."

"Six days a week are set apart for your daily duties and regular work."

"I work a forty-hour week myself, and Wednesdays are boring."

"Why?"

"Because they're middle things, and I'm either thinking about Mondays or looking forward to Fridays. We call Wednesday 'bump day.'"

"No wonder you are bored."

"Well, what are Wednesdays for?"

"I used it to build on Monday's and Tuesday's work, to consolidate gains, to develop new skills."

"That sounds like hard work."

"It was."

"God?"

"Yes?"

"I don't like my work very much."

"Did you ask me about it before you took the job?"

"No. I didn't think you'd want to be bothered."

"I chose my Wednesday work. I could have helped you choose yours."

"That would have been good, God. Let's talk about it. Maybe Wednesdays can be different from now on."

Thursdays

For God made two great lights, the sun and the moon, to shine down upon the earth. The greater one, the sun, presides during the day; the lesser one, the moon, presides through the night. He also made the stars.

GENESIS 1:16

"Good morning, God. You made us a night-light on Thursday, didn't you?"

"Yes, I did."

"And the warm sunshine so I could get a good tan."

"Well, I did have other things in mind!"

"Oh, really?"

"Why do you look in the mirror so much?"

"To see if I'm getting wrinkles."

"Why is that so important?"

"Because if I'm pretty, people will like me."

"What happens if you're pretty but vain?"

"People won't mind as long as I'm pretty."

"I mind."

"But men won't!"

"Are men more important than I am?"

"Sometimes. No offense! God?"

"Yes?"

"Why is my nose so big?"

"It fits your face."

"Why is my face so big?"

"It fits your body."

"Why . . ."

". . . is your body so big? I could have made you a pygmy, but I thought you'd like living in America!"

"Oh, God, I don't want to think so much about my body, but it sort of expects it."

"It rules you."

"I'm sorry! God? Make me two great lights, will you? One to rule my day and one to rule my night. Shine in me."

FRIDAYS

"Good morning, God!"

"Hello, my child."

"I'm going fishing today; it's Friday."

"I know. On the first Friday, I made the fish you are going to catch."

So God created great sea creatures and every sort of fish and every kind of bird. And God saw that it was good.

GENESIS 1:21

"Fridays are fun! God?"

"Yes?"

"Do you want to come with me?"

"Thank you."

"It is all right to have fun, isn't it? I mean, Christians can, can't they?"

"Surely!"

"God?"

"Yes?"

"My friends have brought some beer."

"I can see it."

"Well, fish catching is thirsty work!"

"Really? I didn't need beer when I made them!"

"Oh, er, well, yes! I won't have any, of course."

"Why? You did last Friday!"

"How do you . . . were you peeking?"

"I see everything."

"Oh, dear!"

"It wasn't a pretty sight. I hope your friends don't know you're a Christian."

"Oh no, God, I haven't told them!"

"I thought not!"

"God, I don't know how to have fun as a Christian. Show me how."

"I'd love to. We'll start this week. See! You've got one of my fish on your line!"

SATURDAYS

"Now it's my turn! It's Saturday, and Saturdays are for me!"

"Why are you so grumpy?"

"Oh, God, there's the phone. My sister wants me to baby-sit for her kids today! Little brats!"

"They're sweet children!"

"Little brats."

"Their daddy left them, remember?"

"But Saturday! Why Saturday?"

"Your sister needs a rest."

"I need a rest."

"How selfish you are."

"I chose to stay single; she chose to marry the wrong man. Why should I have to suffer because of her mistake?"

"It takes such little things to upset you. Whatever will happen to you when real trouble comes?"

"God, I don't like feeling like this. Make me like you. Help me take responsibilities as a trust. Grow me up. Settle me down. Slap my hand when I need it—like today."

"I will. I love you too much to let you grow up sour and cold and spoiled."

Then God said, "Let us make people in our image, to be like ourselves. They will be masters over all life—the fish in the sea, the birds in the sky, and all the livestock, wild animals, and small animals." So God created people in his own image; God patterned them after himself; male and female he created them.

GENESIS 1:26-27

SUNDAYS

On the seventh day, having finished his task, God rested from all his work.

GENESIS 2:2

"God, this is your day, isn't it?"

"Yes, my daughter, it is."

"What do you want me to do today? Just tell me, and I'll do it."

"Let's go to church."

"I was afraid you'd say that! God?"

"Yes?"

"Do you really like the organ?"

"Well—"

"I mean, organs and harps and things always leave me cold."

"I like to hear you sing."

"Me? Why, I've got a voice like a cinder under a door."

"True."

"Then how is it that you like to hear me sing?"

"It makes me happy because you haven't had much to sing about since your husband walked out on you."

"That was great, God. I'm glad we went."

"I'm glad you liked it."

"Did you hear that girl ask me to a barbecue tomorrow night?"

"Yes. I told her to ask you."

"Thank you, God! I think I'll go."

"Good."

"She didn't even ask me about my divorce! Do you think she would have asked me if she knew?"

"She would have asked you!"

"Thank you for Sunday, God. It's been marvelous. Come on, week! We're ready for you, God and I!"

Coping with Criticism

What about me? Have I been faithful? Well, it matters very little what you or anyone else thinks. I don't even trust my own judgment on this point.

1 CORINTHIANS 4:3

How I wish I could say that! I have to confess that, when I am criticized, it is never a very small thing to me. It is a *huge* thing!

Having spent fourteen years in the pastorate, I understand what it feels like to be judged by others! Usually I run the gamut: indignation—"How dare they?" self-pity—"How could they?" and paranoia—"How *many* are they?" In no time flat, the whole thing gets totally out of perspective, and I am effectively hindered in my service for the Lord!

Paul was able to say that criticism mattered "very little" to him. This in no way means the apostle arrogantly considered himself above reproach. But he did not fall into the trap of believing *everything* that *everyone* said about him. In fact, "I don't even trust my own judgment on this point," he continues.

Once I have come through my first defensive, hurt reaction to criticism, I usually tend to accept it as true. After all, I know myself pretty well. "I am not perfect and just haven't wanted to admit it," I tell myself sternly.

Then I remember how Paul put the whole thing into perspective for us. "It is the Lord himself who will examine me and decide," he said (1 Corinthians 4:4). The Lord Jesus is the One who sits in the judgment seat. Woe to me if I join him and begin to judge myself or those who judge me! I can go to him for his Word and submit to *his* assessment. In doing so, I will find rest!

If You Don't Want to Paint, Get off the Ladder

Keep on praying.

1 THESSALONIANS 5:17

A teenager was given a bucket of paint, a paintbrush, and a ladder, and was told to paint his house. He didn't want to do it, and simply stood on the ladder with all the wherewithal but no action. After a while, his mother came outside and shrieked, "If you don't want to paint, get off the ladder!"

He reminded me of myself—the ladder was like my access to God; the paint, color that I might apply to the dilapidated house of my world; and the paintbrush, the activity of prayer. I have a feeling that sometimes God would like to shout at me, "If you don't want to paint, get off the ladder!"

A Christian who doesn't pray is as ridiculous as a painter who doesn't paint! Why is it that Christians do not pray? I believe it is a matter of the will—a question of *won't* instead of *can't*. The boy on the ladder could have applied the paint and made the difference to the house, but he didn't want to!

"How do you start to want to?" you may ask. You will need to pray about that! You can't work up the want yourself, and others can't work it up for you. God "will give you your heart's desires" (Psalm 37:4) if you ask him.

The house is in truly terrible shape. Access to God has been made possible by Jesus who, by his death, provided us the ladder. Now he is patiently waiting for us to decide if we "want" to paint!

The Good Old Days

Lord, I am coming.

PSALM 27:8

In a way, I long for the good old days when I was not under daily pressure to produce a message, write an article, finish the chapter of a book, or counsel someone in trouble. When I first came to Christ, I enjoyed a special relationship with God that was as natural as breathing. I met with Jesus for no other reason than to meet with Jesus! The words I read in Scripture were for *me,* not for a women's gathering, church staff, or Sunday school class. I would take my hymnbook and worship. One of the favorite hymns of those unhurried days said:

Speak to me by name, my Master.
Let me know it is to me.
Speak that I may follow faster
With a step more firm and free,
Where the Shepherd leads the flock
In the shadow of the rock!

"Let me know it is to me, Lord," I would pray, and then I'd turn with delicious expectancy to my Shepherd and his green, green pastures and his still, still waters.

One of the hardest things for a Christian worker to do is to make sure the good old days never end! I find I have to struggle for that sense of "What do you have to say to *me?*" every day of my life. But it is certainly well worth the struggle.

Troubled Women

Rachel named him Naphtali, for she said, "I have had an intense struggle with my sister, and I am winning!"

GENESIS 30:8

Leah and Rachel were sisters, married to the same man. Now there's a difficult situation! Add to that the facts that Leah's father had tricked Jacob into marrying her, that she was ugly, that Jacob hated her, and that Jacob had been waiting seven long years to marry Rachel, who was beautiful, and whom he loved to distraction—and you've got a seedbed of strife!

Then watch the battle of the sisters begin as Leah puts her hopes for her husband's heart in giving him children; see her reduced by Rachel, the favorite wife, to bartering for her own husband for the night! And watch the sisters use their maids as baby machines! What a distasteful story it all is!

Yet through it all, I hear God say he cares about the woman who was hated. "But because Leah was unloved, the Lord let her have a child" (Genesis 29:31).

God is still concerned about women who are locked into bad marriages, who must share a house with a man who loves another woman but, being a victim of his culture and his day, does not leave.

God cared about Leah, and he cared about Rachel, too. He knew that Rachel had been tricked by her own father out of the man she loved and made to wait—perhaps past childbearing years. He knew that, for Rachel, beauty was no substitute for babies. "Then God remembered Rachel's plight and answered her prayers by giving her a child" (Genesis 30:22).

If you are ever tempted to wonder if God loves troubled women, remember Leah and Rachel!

My Little Artist

I lived in a country district where the spiritual ground was parched and the earth, scorched. Could the rain of revival ever come? My faith was so small! I, alone, could paint only a tiny cloud.

Then I invited three neighbors into my home to study the Bible. After painting another cloud together, we felt a few raindrops; a year later, more than eighty were meeting together!

Elijah . . . fell to the ground and prayed. Then he said to his servant, "Go and look out toward the sea." . . . Finally the seventh time, his servant told him, "I saw a little cloud about the size of a hand rising from the sea." . . . The sky was soon black with clouds. A heavy wind brought a terrific rainstorm.

1 KINGS 18:42-45

Paint a cloud for Me, My child.
Stroke the canvas with the brush of prayer.
Disregard the strength and brightness of the sun;
Know the One that lives above
Shines brighter there.
Paint on.

Paint a shower for Me, My child,
That will take more time and trouble than you've known.
Work at it, night and day;
The earth is thirsty and the seed is sown.
Paint hard.

Paint a storm for Me, My child,
For many hours and days maybe,
Till lightning strikes the earth
And heaven weeps to see
My little artist
Paint a storm for Me!

Shut-Ins

Yes, everything else is worthless when compared with the priceless gain of knowing Christ Jesus my Lord. I have discarded everything else, counting it all as garbage, so that I may have Christ.

PHILIPPIANS 3:8

When Paul visited a town, he didn't bother checking into a hotel. He simply went to the local jail, knowing it would not be long till he ended up inside it! The apostle's many sojourns in such places brought us the precious Prison Epistles—so called because Paul wrote them from his places of confinement. The letter to the Philippians is one example.

Why should we study such letters? Because people are in prison today. Perhaps you are living in a self-imposed prison. You've been hurt in a deep and close relationship, and you are shut out of the familiar family circle because of it. Or maybe you are old and lonely, and nobody cares for your soul; you are a shut-in. Or then again, you may have just been ousted from your "safe" job and have, in fact, been "shut down." Or perhaps you are battling with an ornery junior high child and have been told by your own flesh and blood to "shut up"!

Paul was old, shut *out* of his family because of his faith, shut *up* (for the moment) by his enemies who were going to shut *down* his ministry, and shut *in,* literally, into a jail cell at Philippi.

It was from this place that Paul's letter of joy was penned. It has a marvelous message for you!

Partnership

Every time I think of you, I give thanks to my God.

PHILIPPIANS 1:3

There is joy in spiritual partnership. There is definitely something special about sharing a common desire with another human being—when we strive for the same ends, fight for the same army, march to the same drum!

Such partnership in the Christian realm transcends all barriers. Augustine's dictum was that the "only thing that really unites men is a common desire for the same ends." Christ provides that unifying element for believers. After all, what did Paul, the Greek Philippian jailer, a slave girl, and a rich Gentile lady have in common? They had Christ! There is true *koinonia*—communion in spiritual life and business.

In another Scripture, Paul talks of Titus as his "partner who works with me to help you" (2 Corinthians 8:23) in the things of the Lord. This partnership deals with past prejudice, present dilemmas, even future problems—for on another occasion, Paul appeals to his wealthy friend Philemon to forgive and receive an errant slave. "So if you consider me your partner, give him the same welcome you would give me" (Philemon 17).

God has often gifted me with the most unlikely partners in ministry. I have served together with the leader of a street gang, a Chinese man, and an extremely wealthy woman! Christian partnership ignores distance as well as social, religious, and political barriers. Paul was separated from his beloved Philippians, but he walked over the bridge of Christian partnership into their hearts, minds, and prayers!

What do you consider a barrier to friendship or fellowship with somebody else? In Christ there is reconciliation, for "you are one in Christ Jesus" (Galatians 3:28).

You Didn't Save Them; You Don't Have to Keep Them.

Paul was confident of the "partnership" the Philippians would have in spreading the Good News "from the time you first heard it until now" (Philippians 1:5). He knew he could depend upon their hearts' involvement in his ministry. The basis of his confidence, however, was not in the men and women themselves but in the one who had begun the good work of regeneration in their lives, whom he could trust to continue until the "day when Christ Jesus comes back again."

And I am sure that God, who began the good work within you, will continue his work until it is finally finished on that day when Christ Jesus comes back again.

PHILIPPIANS 1:6

F. B. Meyer points out that tourists can see unfinished temples and half-finished monuments, abandoned before completion, at Baalbeck. Yet nowhere in the universe do we find unfinished worlds and half-finished stars!

At the Art Institute in Chicago you can view uncompleted paintings. Yet we never see a half-finished sunset! God *always* finishes his sunsets! In fact, unlike us, he always finishes everything he starts! There is great joy in knowing that!

When I used to worry about a youngster's making it off drugs and getting back into the mainstream of society, my husband, Stuart, would point to this verse and say quietly, "You didn't save them; you don't have to keep them!" In no way did this diminish my responsibility toward those teenagers in need, but it surely lifted the stifling clothes of concern from my spirit and replaced them with the light cloak of confidence!

We can have confidence in our charges *because* we have confidence in his continuing work in our charges! Now *that's* joy!

Forever Relationships

You have a very special place in my heart.
PHILIPPIANS 1:7

Do you have joy in people? Do they have joy in you? Who in your life needs your delight? Lloyd Ogilvie says we must "delight in the person to whom we want to relate significantly." He suggests that we need to take an honest inventory of the delight people get from us! Someone needs you to delight in them, to have them "in your heart."

Listen to Paul's rich language of delighted love: "God knows how much I love you and long for you with the tender compassion of Christ Jesus" (Philippians 1:8). I think I understand what he is saying.

Shortly after Stuart and I were married, we were sitting in our new living room after what had not been the best dinner Stuart had ever tasted. Perhaps it should have been he, instead of I, who was experiencing heart pangs. But be that as it may, sitting there in the cozy quietude of our home, I began to cry.

"Whatever is wrong?" inquired the new bridegroom.

"I want my mother," sobbed the bride. I can't describe the sensation better than to borrow Paul's words. At that moment I yearned with a homesick affection for my mom! I had her in my heart, though not in my living room!

Do you have a heart for your mother, your husband, your giggling band of junior high choir girls? Do you know how much they need you to delight in them? Do you have them in your heart, and do they know it? Such Holy Spirit affection builds forever relationships! What joy!

The Things That Really Matter

I pray that your love for each other will overflow more and more, and that you will keep on growing in your knowledge and understanding.

PHILIPPIANS 1:9

What is love? A sticky, sentimental, gooey feeling too big for words? Is love liking a lot, or a warm puppy, or "never having to say you're sorry"?

According to Paul, abounding love incorporates the qualities of knowledge and understanding. What does that mean? Paul says our love for fellow believers will develop when we get a mental grasp of spiritual truth—when we get to know God in an intimate way that is made possible through the disclosure of himself in his Word. This intimate knowledge of God will lead to a depth of insight that will help us be tactful and perceptive in our dealings with people.

We will be able to make good decisions! Some people seem to go through life lurching from one bad decision to the next. God promises us that we will have a sense of the things that really matter—a sense of discernment of what is vital in our love relationships.

For example, what mother of teenage girls does not experience a running battle over clothes? Growing in our knowledge of God helps us to have a sense of the things that *really* matter. We stop majoring on the minors, nit-picking, and wearing ourselves out over a pair of jeans! At the age of thirteen, my daughter wanted to go to church in jeans! I was horrified. My wise husband asked me if I wasn't thrilled that she wanted to go to church!

I grew in knowledge and understanding! I long to grow in these qualities as Paul prayed all Christians would—"more and more."

Chains of Blessing

> **And I want you to know, dear friends, that everything that has happened to me here has helped to spread the Good News.**
>
> PHILIPPIANS 1:12

Paul said the things that happened to him served to advance the gospel. He tells us that even people in the palace guard, and in all other places, had heard of Christ because he had been made a prisoner! Would men in the palace guard have been so soon converted otherwise? Paul thought not and rejoiced! Read what our joyful prisoner wrote at another time to Timothy, his son in the faith:

> And because I preach this Good News, I am suffering and have been chained like a criminal. But the word of God cannot be chained. I am willing to endure anything if it will bring salvation and eternal glory in Christ Jesus to those he has chosen. (2 Timothy 2:9-10)

You could have said Paul regarded the cruel metal manacles as chains of blessing. Just imagine how consistent the apostle needed to be in his lifestyle. If he failed to be Christlike, the guards would make it known.

To whom are you chained? The people who are part of our lives are bound to us for a reason. Do they find themselves bound to Christ because they are bound to us? Would they consider their bonds chains of blessing and delight?

If each of us can only start to say, "everything that has happened to me here has helped to spread the Good News," we will get a whole new perspective on people. And we hope people will get a whole new perspective on Christ!

To Be or Not to Be

For to me, living is for Christ, and dying is even better.

PHILIPPIANS 1:21

Hamlet, the prince of Denmark, packed around the battlements lamenting, "To be or not to be; that is the question." Hamlet believed that if he went on living, it would be grim, but if he died, it would be worse!

Paul the apostle walked around his cell, faced with an identical dilemma: "To be or not to be." His attitude, however, was as different from Hamlet's as chalk is from cheese. "I long to go and be with Christ" (Philippians 1:23), he said, using a military term meaning "to strike the tent." The tent of his body was being dismantled. He had certainly lost a peg or two in his travels! As he contemplated moving camp and setting up his "new tent" in heaven's land, he could be pardoned for ruminating that this would be "far better."

However, he was acutely aware that he had a duty of obligation toward all his spiritual children, not the least of whom were his beloved Philippians. "But it is far better for you that I live," he agreed, as if caught in an eternal debate. "If I die," said Paul, "it will be marvelous; if I go on living, it will be great!" You can't do much to a person who lives by *that* philosophy.

Are you like Hamlet or Paul? Can you say, "For me, living is for Christ," or would you have to say, "For me, to live is misery, anger, hopelessness, depression"? Can you say, "And dying is even better" (Philippians 1:21)? Do you have a high view of heaven?

The Christian has Paul's philosophy of joy—it is the legacy of God's children.

The Gift of Suffering

For you have been given not only the privilege of trusting in Christ but also the privilege of suffering for him.

PHILIPPIANS 1:29

When we think of gifts, we tend to think of good gifts. And when we think of a giving God who is good, it is almost impossible not to think of his giving good gifts to his children. After all, didn't Jesus say, "You fathers—if your children ask for a fish, do you give them a snake instead?" (Luke 11:11).

Yet, Paul tells us in Philippians about the gift (the *privilege*) of suffering. The good gift of suffering for his sake is a gift most of us would rather send back with the heavenly postman when he comes knocking at our door! We pray too blithely, "Jesus, what can I do for you?" One of these days he may well answer, "Suffer for me."

An African man had been away from his village when rebels came and slaughtered or jailed everybody else. Returning, the man, a strong Christian, ran to the jail. As he drew near, he heard the sound of his brothers singing praises and rejoicing that they were counted worthy to suffer for his sake. "Let me in," pled the "free" man, "I want the joy and privilege of suffering for him too."

That man regarded Philippians 1:29 very seriously indeed. He believed that not only was he blessed with the gift of eternal life through believing, but he should also gladly accept the gift of persecution on his Lord's behalf when the occasion arose.

Gratitude

There is consolation in being singled out. There is encouragement in being chosen.

I can remember standing shyly at the side of a dance floor at an early "gawky" stage of my adolescence, watching my beautiful older sister being whirled around the room by boy after boy. I stood there all night, hoping just one boy, however spotty or awkward, would choose me! No one did, and I felt awful.

Is there any encouragement from belonging to Christ? Any comfort from his love? Any fellowship together in the Spirit? Are your hearts tender and sympathetic?

PHILIPPIANS 2:1

I remember my heart filling with a great fear that no one would ever ask me to marry him. After all, if I was not worth a five-minute dance, would I be worth a lifetime's company?

Can you then imagine the encouragement and consolation I felt when asked to belong? "Why me, Lord?" I inquired in gratitude when Stuart walked into my life!

How much joy goes with being united to someone you love! Love brings such comfort. What tender cheer is given when you can meet a beloved one's innermost wish! What fellowship with another's spirit, what tenderness and affectionate sympathy blossoms like a flower when you are married to someone special!

And what of unity with Christ? What can I say? When I stood at the edge of the dance floor of my life, Jesus chose me for his partner! He had all the world to choose from, and he chose me! What eternal consolation, comfort of love—what surpassing compassion—what joy!

A Voluntary Humility

Don't be selfish; don't live to make a good impression on others. Be humble, thinking of others as better than yourself.

PHILIPPIANS 2:3

Being one in spirit and person means minimal strife in the church, even when we are very different. "Do nothing out of selfish ambition or vain conceit" (NIV), exhorts Paul.

When any hint of self-seeking or unworthy ambition motivates our actions, look out! If vainglory, which is simply a cheap desire to boast, is the best that we can manage, we shouldn't join a church. We'd split it!

In pressing toward our goals, to what extent do we use people as rungs on our climb? What happens to the people in our lives, to our Christian service, to our effectiveness as a believer?

Do we really consider others "better" than ourselves? Do we look to the interests of others before our own (see Philippians 2:4)?

Why do our churches attract so much criticism? Is it not because we spend all our time fighting each other rather than fighting the devil? Why is there so much strife in the church choir? "When the devil fell out of heaven, he fell into the choir," responds a cynic! Must we be prima donnas?

You know you can achieve almost anything you want if you are willing to forfeit the credit! For some of us, that will require a radical change of attitude. Voluntary humility is the hardest thing on earth to achieve. For the Christian, it *must be* if we are to be like him.

A Biblical Humility

Your attitude should be the same that Christ Jesus had.

PHILIPPIANS 2:5

Humility is a view of yourself learned at the feet of your Savior. Humility is born from a sense of dependence, not a false depreciation of yourself. Biblical humility gives knowledge of *derived* worth. "I am worth something *because* of him," we can say. I am worth dying for; I was worth creating, saving, sanctifying, glorifying. But none of this is apart from him. When we say we are worth *anything* apart from him, we are in trouble!

Humility was frowned upon in the ancient world. If you were humble, you were considered a cringing object and were despised. Jesus Christ taught us the virtue of humility, and Jesus Christ was the supreme example. Jesus was meek and humble in spirit, and Paul says, "Your attitude should be the same that Christ Jesus had" (Philippians 2:5).

It is good to check up on ourselves once in a while. We need to ask ourselves, What can I do today that will elevate the interests of the people around me above my own? We can get so preoccupied with the cultivation of our own spiritual life that we can miss the noble traits of others.

We must search for and recognize the good qualities in fellow believers and emulate them in our own life. If we would be like Jesus, we must humble ourselves.

Pride Pretends

So humble yourselves under the mighty power of God, and in his good time he will honor you.

1 PETER 5:6

If we do not humble ourselves, God will surely humble us! Quite frankly, I would rather do it myself than leave it to him!

Years ago I was invited to sit with my husband on a platform at a big Christian gathering. I was proud to be asked! I *wanted* to sit up there in front of everyone! Being conscious this attitude was wrong did not help me redress it. I *tried* to feel humble, but nothing changed.

Oh, dear, I thought. *God is going to have to deal with this*. He did! The time for the offering came. I had no money with me, but being out of touch (pride *always* separates), I pretended and put my empty hand into the bucket. To my horror, there was nothing in the bucket in the first place. The boy taking the collection gazed into the empty vessel and then suspiciously at me!

Blushing, I pretended I had dropped my money on the floor (pride *always* pretends). To my horror, the boy got down on his hands and knees to look for it! I followed suit, and there we were, groveling around under the chairs in full view of the entire congregation. At last (it seemed like an eternity), he took his bucket and passed by.

My poor husband had been wondering what on earth was happening. I can tell you having to confess my faults to him *and* the boy had the necessary humbling effect on me! Yes, over the years I had learned to humble myself or God would surely do it for me. "I hate pride," said the Lord (Proverbs 8:13).

In His Steps

I have given you an example to follow. Do as I have done to you.

JOHN 13:15

Jesus gave us many examples that we should do as he had done. He washed the disciples' feet; he was king to little children; he did not boast; and he lived humbly and simply.

Peter told us that we were called to suffering because "Christ, who suffered for you, is your example. Follow in his steps" (1 Peter 2:21). "But how can my little aching feet follow in his majestic, godlike steps?" you may ask. Don't you know that if God calls us to *anything,* he provides the enabling?

The first snow had fallen in Wisconsin. It was our first winter in the United States and our first experience of snow fun. Our children, twelve, ten, and eight years of age, dragged their father up a big hill and asked him what they should do. Stuart set off running with giant strides and called to the children, "Follow me."

Well, they all tried, but not one of them succeeded in putting his or her feet in Dad's footprints. How could little children ever match his steps? Then Dad climbed the hill again, and, putting David's feet on his own, grasped him under the armpits and set off again. "I'm doing it! Look, I'm doing it!" shrieked David, resting on his father's arms. He was, yet he wasn't.

There's only one way we are ever going to follow his example, whether it be to suffer, to serve, or to live a godly life. That is to rest in our Father's arms and allow him to enable us. Don't forget his promise: "God, who calls you, is faithful; he will do this" (1 Thessalonians 5:24).

Letting It Go

Though he was God, he did not demand and cling to his rights as God.

PHILIPPIANS 2:6

Jesus did not cling to his equality with God. Christ had his privileged position and could have asserted his right to seize the glory and honor of the acknowledgment of his office, but "he made himself nothing" (Philippians 2:7). He didn't grasp, clutch, or hold on to what was rightfully his; he let it go! He laid aside his glory, but not his deity.

Bishop H. C. G. Moule said, "He rather made himself void by his own act." Lloyd Ogilvie added, "He emptied himself utterly of divine aloofness and poured himself into our humanity." By doing this, however, he didn't hurt or destroy his absolute fitness to guide and bless us whom he came to save.

Adam, the son of God, attempted robbery by asserting himself, desiring to be like God. The second Adam, Christ, the Eternal Son of God, faced with the same temptation, renounced what was his by right and chose the way of obedient suffering as the pathway to lordship. To cling or not to cling—that is the question!

Release my grasp, Lord.
Tired I am with clutching
My plans and dreams, ambitions that I hold.
Release my grasp and hold my
Hand, Lord Jesus,
Lest things I grasp grow tainted with the mold
Of selfishness—of tinsel triviality,
A self-destructive guarding of my ways.
Release my grasp and set my life in order
To grasp Your plan and purpose for my days!

Obedience

And in human form he obediently humbled himself even further by dying a criminal's death on a cross.

PHILIPPIANS 2:8

Obedience: for Christ, a choice; for us, a necessity. Thomas Torrance says, "Don't try and sneak around Golgotha." We don't like to face suffering—to stare full in the face of dying people, to attend funerals, to talk to handicapped children. But there is one Man of Suffering we must face—the Christ of Golgotha. We must face the Christ and his sufferings and our own unwillingness to admit that we needed something that drastic to save us from our sin and self-centeredness. And when we stand there, at the foot of the cross, we will be reminded that we are seeing the supreme eternal act of obedience.

For Christ, the Cross was a choice. He didn't need to die; he chose to because it was the only way. But for you and me, obedience is a necessity. We, too, must die; we, too, must choose the path of suffering. Every time we are unselfish, it hurts. Every day we lay down our time, our money, our involvement for a hurting world, and we suffer a little bit. Serving God costs us something because we naturally want to serve only ourselves. That doesn't cost us anything at all! It doesn't hurt me to pamper and coddle myself and give in to my every whim and desire. It only hurts to deny myself in the cause of Christ.

Oswald Chambers says in his classic devotional *My Utmost for His Highest*, "Jesus Christ has no tenderness whatever toward anything that is ultimately going to ruin a man in the service of God." Disobedience will ruin people; obedience will make them. For Christ, obedience was a choice; for you and me, it is a necessity.

AMEN

> **Because of this, God raised him up to the heights of heaven and gave him a name that is above every other name, so that at the name of Jesus every knee will bow, in heaven and on earth and under the earth, and every tongue will confess that Jesus Christ is Lord, to the glory of God the Father.**
>
> PHILIPPIANS 2:9-11

You have just read the Father's "Amen" to the Son's "It is finished!" (John 19:30). In other words, the Father said, "I care not what you think of my Son. This is what I think of him!" The Father installed Jesus Christ in the place that properly belongs to God himself.

Does this mean there are two thrones in heaven? What mystery is this? Didn't Jesus say, "I will invite everyone who is victorious to sit with me on my throne, just as I was victorious and sat with my Father on his throne" (Revelation 3:21)? We need only understand there is no competition in the Godhead. Christ as Lord gathers (see Ephesians 1:10) that God may be all in all (see 1 Corinthians 15:28).

It is God's intent that angels, men, women, devils, and all creatures in heaven and earth and under the earth—in other words, all intelligent beings—will acknowledge that "Jesus Christ is Lord, to the glory of God the Father."

Have you bowed your knees to Jesus Christ yet? It's better to bow them now, when you have a choice, than on that great and terrible day, when all will have to. Better now because you want to than then because you must! You too can add your "Amen" to the Son's "It is finished!" Do it now!

Finally

And I have confidence from the Lord that I myself will come to see you soon.

PHILIPPIANS 2:24

It seems that Paul was winding up his letter at this point—in fact, this could have been his last line. But it wasn't. He continued for another two and a half chapters before he finally ended this letter.

And how glad I am about that, or we might have missed out on the apostle's autobiography—his Jewish heritage, his devotion to the Torah, and his life as a Pharisee. The rabbis of Paul's day held that if you lived strictly and completely according to their law, you were blameless! Paul claims he qualified: "I am a real Jew if there ever was one! . . . I obeyed the Jewish law so carefully that I was never accused of any fault" (Philippians 3:5-6). Paul had fervently believed that he was justified by observing to the letter the strictness of the religious law. He put his faith in it.

But it's the object of your faith that matters, not how much faith you have. You can have an awful lot of faith in very thin ice and still get very wet, or you can have just a little faith in very thick ice and stay very dry! Are you like Paul, putting your faith in a religious heritage—churchgoing, keeping the Christian rules (at least some of them), or even perhaps putting your faith in your faith? Someday you will only be able to rejoice in the Lord when he is the object of your faith and you are not trusting in your own religious activities. Like Paul, you will need to:

> become one with him. I no longer count on my own goodness or my ability to obey God's law, but I trust Christ to save me. For God's way of making us right with himself depends on faith. (Philippians 3:9)

PROFIT OR LOSS?

He made himself nothing; he took the humble position of a slave and appeared in human form.

PHILIPPIANS 2:7

Paul said the personal knowledge of Christ involved discarding everything else (see Philippians 3:8). Jesus asked, "And how do you benefit if you gain the whole world but lose your own soul in the process?" (Mark 8:36). Paul counted up all the things he lost, tied them all in a parcel, and left them at Calvary. He turned his back on them and never bothered to look at that bundle of self-righteousness again.

The problem some of us have is continually untying the bundle to have a longing look at the things we have left behind! We are like Lot's wife, gazing over our shoulders at the old life and wishing we could take some of it along with us.

For Paul, it was different. He carefully counted the things in the bundle and declared them "as garbage, so that I may have Christ . . . [and] know Christ and experience the mighty power that raised him from the dead" (Philippians 3: 8, 10).

Paul didn't want to use enticing words of human wisdom anymore, but longed that his preaching would be through the power of the Holy Spirit (see 1 Corinthians 2:4). For Paul, it was no longer to be a case of a powerful personality, dramatic rhetoric, or lisping lyric, but of the dynamics of God's blowing open people's hearts and minds that they should be changed.

For Paul, the loss of all things eventually included life itself. But to this man, martyrdom was but a door to life eternal!

The Big, Dark House

All Scripture is inspired by God and is useful to teach us what is true and to make us realize what is wrong in our lives. It straightens us out and teaches us to do what is right.

2 TIMOTHY 3:16

"The Old Testament is like a big, dark house. I'm afraid to go inside," a teenager told me. What a joy to take her hand, step inside the Scriptures, and see the Holy Spirit switch the light on, banishing her grim forebodings!

Do you feel like she did about the Old Testament? When I first started to read the Bible, I made an elementary mistake. I began at Genesis, faltered in Exodus, and died in Leviticus! Yet the Bible says, "All Scripture is inspired by God"! "All" means the Old Testament as well as the New.

God breathed into the spirits of holy men of old, inspiring them with his thoughts. The men thus were moved to write down God's thoughts. The New Testament explains the Old. As the little couplet goes,

The new is in the old concealed
The old is in the new revealed.

Jesus was always quoting the Old Testament Scriptures. He told the Jews who persecuted him, "You search the Scriptures because you believe they give you eternal life. But the Scriptures point to me!" (John 5:39). After his resurrection, he rebuked the two disciples on the road to Emmaus, saying, "'You are such foolish people! You find it so hard to believe all that the prophets wrote in the Scriptures.' . . . Then Jesus quoted passages from the writings of Moses and all the prophets, explaining what all the Scriptures said about himself" (Luke 24:25, 27).

The Old Testament hasn't been done away with, now that the New is come. It is Christ's home. He lives in all Scripture, walking its grand corridors, hoping to meet us there.

The Red Carpet

The prize for which God, through Christ Jesus, is calling us up to heaven.

PHILIPPIANS 3:14

Half the time we quit before the race is through. One of the reasons is the pace. Perhaps we are out of shape, or we compare ourselves to the better runner who passes us easily, and we grow discouraged. Some of us quit because we want little prizes along the way and are not content to finish the race before we get the big reward.

A missionary couple returned from a lifetime of service in an extremely hard situation. They were glad to be finished but not a little apprehensive as to what they would find in their home country. The president of the United States happened to be on their boat, which made for great excitement, and they joined in all the fun and enjoyment of seeing the red carpet rolled out at the harbor. What a reception he received.

When it was over, the couple looked around for family and friends, for representatives of their mission board, but there had been a mix-up in the communications, and no one was there to roll out the red carpet for them! "What a homecoming!" sobbed the wife.

Bewildered, they prayed together and, in the words of the husband, "It was just as if God leaned out of heaven and said, 'But you're not home yet! Wait a bit, it will be your turn soon!'"

You're not home yet—
Keep running;
You're not home yet—
Be strong;
You're not home yet—
Be encouraged;
Jesus will receive you
Ere long!

Model Models

Dear friends, pattern your lives after mine, and learn from those who follow our example.

PHILIPPIANS 3:17

After I gave the commencement address for a modeling school, I watched the girls walk across the platform to receive their graduation certificates. They were perfectly poised and coifed with just the right amount of cleverly applied makeup in just the right places! They were, I mused, model models. Lastly, their popular teacher stood up to receive a standing ovation from the girls. It was then that I understood why the girls looked as they did. They were obviously her followers. She was perfectly poised and coifed with just the right amount of cleverly applied makeup in just the right places!

That is really what following, or being a disciple, is all about. Paul told the young Christians in the church at Philippi to watch how he lived the Christian life and do the same. He knew how important it was for those eager young believers to have a model.

This does not mean we should proudly set ourselves apart, put ourselves on pedestals or pretend we are something special. Always remember that even the great apostle Paul did not count himself to have arrived at perfection (see Philippians 3:13). We are to be models of growth, not models of perfection. That is the key!

Paul draws attention to other unknown, godly people and says, "learn from those who follow our example." Could Paul point us out as a model for younger Christians? Could you and I ask others to join in following our example?

AGAIN!

Always be full of joy in the Lord. I say it again—rejoice!

PHILIPPIANS 4:4

Paul intended that the Philippians repeat the experience of joy over and over. To "always . . . rejoice" appears to be a command. Notice Paul didn't command the Christians to rejoice in their present problems but "in the Lord."

I asked a young missionary the secret of her faithfulness. "The joy of the Lord is my strength," she replied.

I've discovered when I can't praise him for what he allows, I can still praise him for who he is in what he has allowed! What is more, that young missionary had learned to repeat the exercise over and over again in the face of horrendous odds.

For all I'm not;
The times I've failed!
For fleshly effort;
Broken dreams,
I'm tired with trying
Or so it seems!

For who You are;
Not what I am;
For how You choose
The Word to bring
Into my path to comfort me—
Your praise I'll sing.

For who You are
I'll praise Your name.
Your power and peace are just the same
As in Paul's day; so I'll
Rejoice—
Always!

Sweet Reasonableness

> **Let everyone see that you are considerate in all you do. Remember, the Lord is coming soon.**
>
> PHILIPPIANS 4:5

Are you a considerate person? Paul says our sweet reasonableness—the mercy and forbearance that we must exercise if we profess the name of Jesus—should be evident to all. Other versions render the word "considerate" as "gentleness." A considerate, gentle spirit is to be recognized by "everyone." We are, in fact, to have a good reputation for moderation and clemency.

Gentleness is not my thing. I have a strong, bossy personality, and learned early in life that it was going to take Christ's sweet, reasonable spirit to soften my harsh treatment of people.

Paul reminds the Philippians that "the Lord is coming soon." He could hear and see everything they were doing and might even come again in the midst of a bout of temper or some unmerciful or unfair treatment they may be meting out.

When I was a young mother, shut away for long periods of time with my little children, I often resorted to this verse. It was hard for me to be sweetly reasonable in the face of three small, but determinedly willful, children, who apparently were defying my attempts to bring them up as I knew I should! When I shut the windows before I bawled them out, the Lord reminded me I had shut him in with us. He was on hand to hear my rantings, even if no one else could! God can make the harshest people gentle. I know; he's been doing it for me all my life!

Gentle me, Lord.
Speak hardly to my harshness;
Humble it into submission.
Gentle me, Lord;
Make me like You!

A Graduated Worrier

Don't worry about anything.

PHILIPPIANS 4:6

Now there's a mouthful! "Don't worry about anything," Paul says blithely, as if it's as easy as falling off a log.

When I was a little girl, I worried my shoes would shrink. After all, I had heard my teacher say my sandals were getting too small. When I was a teenager, I worried that I wouldn't get a date. When I got engaged, I worried I might be in a car wreck the eve of my wedding. When I had my first baby, I worried he would fall into the washing machine and drown! When my children became teenagers, I worried they wouldn't get a date (or get a bad one), or they might be in a car wreck on the eve of their wedding, or their children might fall into the washing machine and drown!

There's no end to the possibilities for worry. You'll never run out of things to worry about, that's for sure! Being a graduated worrier, I have had to learn some hard lessons about what worry does to me—and my family! Worry does not empty tomorrow of its problems; it simply empties today of its strength.

But more important, worry betrays a lack of trust in God's care and is really an unconscious blasphemy of him. That's what really helped me to realize that lack of trust in God, the seedbed of worry, is *sin!* Now I can do something about that. I can repent of it and be determined to sin no more! My God delights to lend his strength to such resolve. "Trust me," he says. "Don't worry about anything."

The Best Medicine

Pray about everything. Tell God what you need.

PHILIPPIANS 4:6

Have you ever suspected that "the reason you don't have what you want is that you don't ask God for it" (James 4:2)? Perhaps you never really let your requests be made known to God. Maybe you have a high concept of God's size and cannot really believe he would be interested or bothered with such infinitesimal requests as you may bring.

The Bible tells us over and over again that our heavenly Father loves to hear his children's voices; so come and pray! When you do, make sure you include the elements of prayer mentioned here.

First, pray for yourself. Talk about the things that are worrying you. It's necessary, not because you need to tell God something he doesn't know, but to talk it out with him! When you have talked about your troubles, try asking God specifically to intervene. This is called *petition*. If it helps, make a list of the things you would like God to do for you. Writing it down may help you clarify issues.

Second, make sure your prayers and petitions are presented with thanksgiving. Thank him for hearing your prayers; thank him for his watchful care and his working on your behalf (though you might not always see the results). Thank him for all you are learning of him because of your prayer time. The recalling of God's goodness overcomes our concern with our own immediate problems.

Finally, make sure you praise him. Try finishing every prayer time with praise. It's the best medicine!

God's Garrison

If you do this, you will experience God's peace, which is far more wonderful than the human mind can understand. His peace will guard your hearts and minds as you live in Christ Jesus.

PHILIPPIANS 4:7

Prayer to the God of peace brings peace of mind. And the peace of God will keep your heart and mind safe from the wounds of worry. The word *guard* is a military term denoting a garrison of soldiers. God's peace will stand guard around the heart of the believer, watching out for and repelling the warriors of worry that fight against the soul.

Notice that both the heart and mind need to be kept. The heart *feels* worry, the mind *feeds* it! If inner tranquility is to be enjoyed, certain decisions have to be made. Our thinking will decide the conditions of our heart and whether the Prince of Peace will tarry there. If a person cherishes unholy thoughts, he or she will become unholy.

"Thoughts," according to F. B. Meyer, "are the looms . . . weaving the garment in which the soul shall be arrayed." John Bunyan describes Ignorance in his *Pilgrim's Progress* as being stupid in his disregard for the importance of his thoughts. "My heart is as good as any man's heart," he said. Then he added, "As to my thoughts, I take no notice of them!"

Ignorance, aptly named, was, alas, like too many of us. He put no guard at the gate of his thoughts which were, as a result, open to any intruders from heaven or from hell. According to Paul, God would set a garrison of soldiers around our mind. Only then will the peace be kept.

God's Gatekeepers

Fix your thoughts on what is true and honorable and right. Think about things that are pure and lovely and admirable. Think about things that are excellent and worthy of praise.

PHILIPPIANS 4:8

Paul names six gatekeepers—thoughts that are true, honorable, right, pure, lovely, and admirable—that should stand in the gateway of our thinking. These are moral absolutes to which I am expected to adhere as a Christian and which I can use to test the information I receive.

First, as our mind is fed information, we should ask ourselves, Is it true?

Then we should inquire, Is it honorable? Does the thing I hear have an honorable ring to it? Is the action I am being asked to take honorable?

Then we need to determine, Is it right, just, and fair?

Next, we can inquire, Is it pure?

When I read, I can test magazines with this question: Is it lovely? We can ask ourselves, Will this data I am feeding my mind result in godly love or produce beautiful actions?

What's more, we have every right to know, Is it admirable? Moffatt renders "good report" as "high-toned." I always remember a friend's comment about another friend. "It's no good telling her," she said with grudging respect. "She won't listen to gossip." The woman in question was undoubtedly a "high-toned" Christian lady.

If we would all determine to allow only that which calls down the approval of God into our thought patterns, then we would be well on the way to experiencing continual peace of mind. So, if you value the approval of God, Paul concludes, "Think about things that are excellent and worthy of praise."

THE POSITIVES OF LIFE

I know how to live on almost nothing or with everything. I have learned the secret of living in every situation, whether it is with a full stomach or empty, with plenty or little. For I can do everything with the help of Christ who gives me the strength I need.

PHILIPPIANS 4:12-13

Paul enjoyed the peace of God because the God of Peace ruled his thinking and his doing. He knew what it was to be at peace with poverty and to be at peace with plenty. He had learned the secret of being content in any and every situation. Whether well fed or hungry, persecuted or popular, rich or poor, he handled it all to the glory of God "with the help of Christ who gives me the strength I need."

Sometimes it takes just as much strength to handle the positives of life as it does the negatives. Paul was able to be rich yet humble, enjoyed being well fed yet not gluttonous, and handled adulation yet did not allow himself to become an idol. God had wonderfully met his needs when he had "almost nothing" or "everything," and that was why he had no hesitation in assuring the Philippians the same God would supply all of their needs (see Philippians 4:19)!

Epaphroditus had brought Paul a sacrificial gift from his dear friends, and Paul's cup was full. He had not a doubt in his mind that they would be richer spiritually, though poorer materially. After all, hadn't he proved that the way to life was death, and the way to glory, giving? His benediction followed, "May the grace of the Lord Jesus Christ be with your spirit," he prayed (Philippians 4:23). It was; it would be; and Paul rejoiced!

Heaven

Do you believe in heaven? What do you think it is like? Do you imagine yourself sitting on a pink, damp cloud, playing a harp?

Then I saw a new heaven and a new earth, for the old heaven and the old earth had disappeared.

REVELATION 21:1

Jesus said, "I am going to prepare a *place* for you" (John 14:2, italics mine). Heaven, first of all, is a prepared place. But what sort of a place is it?

Heaven is a *pretty* place. Revelation 22:2 tells us fruit never fades there. I'm always sad when I see the plants fade in my garden. I will never see them fade in heaven.

Heaven is a *permanent* place. The Builder and Maker is God, and Christ is the cornerstone (see Ephesians 2:20). Heaven is forever because God is forever. It is a permanent place, filled with permanent people.

No one will ever die in this *painless* place—no one is ever sick (see Revelation 21:4)! Can you imagine a place where there is no more suffering? Our sorry world needs to hear about a place like that!

Lastly, it is a *perfect* place. The perfect person, the Lord Jesus Christ, lives there, and no sin will be allowed to enter heaven (see Revelation 21:8). If sin entered heaven, it wouldn't be heaven anymore!

"We haven't any idea where you are going, so how can we know the way?" Thomas asked (John 14:5).

Jesus answered him: "I am the way, the truth, and the life. No one can come to the Father except through me" (John 14:6).

Do you want to go to heaven? Ask Jesus about it. Ask him to forgive your sin. If you do, heaven will come down and fill your soul!

The Lord, My River

> **And the angel showed me a pure river with the water of life, clear as crystal, flowing from the throne of God and of the Lamb.**
>
> REVELATION 22:1

The Lord is my river! The word *river* conjures up many biblical pictures, not the least of which is the river of the sanctuary. Ezekiel's vision is of the river of life, ever deepening and widening, and "everything that touches the water of this river will live" (Ezekiel 47:9).

What's more, wherever the river flows, there will be laughter. "A river brings joy to the city of our God" (Psalm 46:4). "You . . .[let] them drink from your rivers of delight" (Psalm 36:8).

The book of Revelation pictures the river of life, flowing out from the throne. It tells us trees are growing on each side. The leaves of these trees have healing properties (see Revelation 22:1-2). Trees are constantly featured metaphorically in Scripture. Isaiah pictures all the trees of the field clapping their hands (see Isaiah 55:12). The rustle of rejoicing will be a feature of the Lord's trees because his river is a river of jubilation.

Oh, to be picked up in the Planter's hands and planted on the banks of that river. There I stand, a sapling of the Lord's, carefully planted beside the refreshing waters of life! The tree planted thus is never a wild tree. It is cultivated and cared for.

God's river never dries up. Deep and wide, clear and clean, God's river runs past my door. I can walk to it, kneel down, and quench my thirst. I can decide to be a tree and let him plant me!

The Worry Tree

They are lik
shrubs in the
no hope for t.
They will live
ren wilderness, ... the
salty flats where no one lives. But blessed are those who trust in the Lord and have made the Lord their hope and confidence. They are like trees planted along a riverbank, with roots that reach deep into the water. Such trees are not bothered by the heat or worried by long months of drought. Their leaves stay green, and they go right on producing delicious fruit.

JEREMIAH 17:6-8

I love the picture of an anxious tree, wringing its twigs in frenzy! The Lord's tree, planted by the river of life, is not a worry tree—even in a year of drought!

We had a staff retreat for our women's work. About fifty dedicated ladies—or trees—attended. There were oaks and firs, rosebushes and holly, all sorts and sizes. But they all had one thing in common—their roots drank of the river.

Around the campfire at night, the ladies began to talk. I had thought I knew them well, but I had had no idea what a year of drought it had been for so many of my dear friends. One after another talked of the dry places of disease, of alcohol, of unemployment, of battering and abuse, of widowhood. One had a father who had committed suicide. Another had seen her daughter through an unwanted pregnancy. One faced divorce, another estrangement. It had indeed been a year of drought.

Yet, through it all, their leaves had been green—wet perhaps with tears of testing, but green! Those precious friends had not been anxious in the year of drought, and they had never failed to bear fruit. I couldn't help thinking of Jeremiah.

They would be all right—after all, their roots were in the river!

E LION GOT HIM

Like roaring lions attacking their prey, they come at me with open mouths.

PSALM 22:13

The Greek poet Homer said, "All kings are shepherds of the people." Shepherds and kings went together in the minds of the ancients.

The writers of Scripture use the shepherd picture constantly. God is shown to be Shepherd King of Israel. The writer of Psalm 80 prays, "Please listen, O Shepherd of Israel, you who lead Israel like a flock" (Psalm 80:1).

Three psalms among the favored in the book of praises form a shepherd trilogy: Psalm 22, Psalm 23, and Psalm 24. The first, Psalm 22, graphically portrays the shepherd's cross. Jesus Christ told us he was the Good Shepherd who had come to give his life for the sheep (see John 10:11).

In David's time, the shepherd would count his animals into the fold, then lay himself down across the opening, becoming the "gate." If any wild animal would have lamb for dinner, he would have to deal with the shepherd. Therefore, Jesus is the gate by which if anyone enters in, he or she shall be saved (see John 10:7).

We all know the gospel story. The Good Shepherd came to "seek and save those . . . who are lost" (Luke 19:10). He gathered his flock, lay down in the gate, and the lion got him! You can read in Psalm 22 about the fight that ensued. The Shepherd fought alone, feeling forsaken by his God. Jesus didn't have enough strength to finish the psalm when he was being crucified; the lion was very terrible. The psalmist finished it for him: "For he has not ignored the suffering of the needy. He has not turned and walked away. He has listened to their cries for help" (Psalm 22:24).

The lion got him, but on Easter morning, he got the lion!

Hind of the Morning

Rescue me from a violent death; spare my precious life from these dogs. Snatch me from the lions' jaws.

PSALM 22:20-21

When David wrote Psalm 22, he set his poem song to a tune called "The Doe of the Dawn." We don't know if the psalmist was simply thinking of a tune by this name, or if he was writing about his Savior, who would be like a vulnerable doe, run down by dogs (Psalm 22:16), or torn to shreds by the lions (Psalm 22:13). The picture is poignant and powerful.

Hind of the Morning—
Jesus, my Saviour—
Facing the lion that raged
round the cross.
Nowhere to run to,
and nowhere to shelter.
No time to reflect on life's
bitter loss.

Hind of the Morning
forsaken by brothers.
Family stand helpless,
diplomacy fails.
Hind of the Morning,
waiting the death bits.
Pinned into place
by a hammer and nails!

But look at the lion now—
wounded and beaten,
Frightfully, powerfully—
brought to his knees.
Hind of the Morning,
decked in white raiment.
Raised by Your Maker to do as You please!

A Special Yoke

Don't let the excitement of youth cause you to forget your Creator. Honor him in your youth.

ECCLESIASTES 12:1

"May I come to see you?" I asked my newly married daughter.

"Great, Mom! Come on!" she replied.

Arriving late on the day of rest, I noticed how exhausted my daughter and son-in-law looked. They chatted about their total involvement as team leaders of the youth group at their church. They were happily over their heads with a commitment to youth in the name of Jesus Christ.

The next morning I awoke very early to see them going out the door to take rented vehicles back to the depot. I lay snuggled on the pullout bed in the living room, glad I didn't need to get up with them. I dreamed of my own youth, remembering the frantic pace of involvement with kids off the back streets of Liverpool, and I was glad I was able to dream about it and not have to be up and about, going the extra mile and a half that youth demands, before putting in a hard day's work.

"It is good for the young to submit to the yoke of his discipline," the Master said (Lamentations 3:27). Young life needs young life to work with it. What joy to be able to give Jesus Christ the best years of our life.

I lay still, praising God for our children. They would find strength, because I knew it was a special yoke they bore, one that Jesus shared.

The Great Shepherd

The great Shepherd was brought again from the dead to care for and to perfect the sheep. The Good Shepherd satisfies his flock, making them "rest in green meadows" (Psalm 23:2).

A sheep never lies down unless its stomach is full. God wants to look down from heaven and see contented sheep lying on the grass and saying, "O Shepherd, I can't eat one more thing!"

And now, may the God of peace, who brought again from the dead our Lord Jesus, equip you with all you need for doing his will. May he produce in you, through the power of Jesus Christ, all that is pleasing to him. Jesus is the great Shepherd of the sheep by an everlasting covenant, signed with his blood.

HEBREWS 13:20-21

People are spiritually hungry and thirsty. They try to fill an inner appetite with physical, social, or intellectual food, but the hunger remains. If we ask Jesus, he will feed us until we want no more.

The "peaceful streams" (Psalm 23:2) are a beautiful picture of prayer. It's important that we "keep on praying" (1 Thessalonians 5:17), and so it follows that some praying will have to be accomplished in the marketplace. It's hard to pray in the midst of movement and noise, but we know the Shepherd will lead us to quiet places. There are times the Shepherd says to us, "And this righteousness will bring peace. Quietness and confidence will fill the land forever. My people will live in safety, quietly at home. They will be at rest" (Isaiah 32:17-18).

Are you following the Shepherd from afar? Perhaps you need to catch up and listen to his voice. He wants you to know, "Only in returning to me and waiting for me will you be saved. In quietness and confidence is your strength" (Isaiah 30:15).

God's Grass

He lets me rest in green meadows.

PSALM 23:2

Why does the grass on the other side of the fence always look greener than God's grass?

"I don't love my husband anymore," a young wife confided in me. "Everyone else's husband looks more desirable than mine!" This woman left her husband and enticed a young father away from his children. After a short time, she grew restless again. "Older men look more appetizing than younger men," she said wistfully.

When I was a student, I couldn't decide what courses to take. Everyone else's major looked so much more interesting than mine. When I got married, other men seemed to have better jobs than my husband had. When I had children, other houses looked more useful for rearing a family.

The grass on the other side of the fence may look greener, but it doesn't satisfy like God's grass! The Good Shepherd led his sheep to the good grass. The green pasture, or God's grass, is obedience. Feed on it, and you will find rest for your soul. Like a happy lamb, you will lie down and find comfort in doing the Shepherd's will. Through the years I have come to realize that when I follow the Shepherd and feed on his will for my life, I find all I ever needed, all I ever wanted, and all I ever imagined could be mine.

Trot On

He renews my strength. He guides me along right paths, bringing honor to his name.

PSALM 23:3

The great Shepherd not only satisfies his sheep, he sanctifies them—sets them apart for himself.

He owns the flock. A hired person does not own the sheep—if he sees the wolf coming, he will leave them (see John 10:12). But not Jesus!

Sheep that know their Shepherd have a restored soul. They feel complete. They know they matter. They have a marvelous inner sense of belonging. Someone is guiding them as they cross the road and open the fold's gate on a dark night.

Being sanctified means walking close to the Shepherd and making sure you're on the right path! Being sanctified means deciding your little hooves are not going to trot into trouble! For his sake, you want to stay on the right track!

Trot not into trouble.
Trot on!
Trot not into fields
That lambs should shun.
Trot not into night
But in the day.
Follow the Shepherd
In the way.
Trot on!

Trot not into other fancier paths.
Trot on.
Trot not into dens
Of doubt that sleep should shun.
Trot not into greener
Fields that beckon thee.
Stay rather 'mongst the rocks
But stay by Him who
Tells thee to
Trot on!

The Greenest Grass

Even when I walk through the dark valley of death, I will not be afraid, for you are close beside me. Your rod and your staff protect and comfort me.

PSALM 23:4

The great Shepherd supports the sheep when they are frightened, but he knows the greenest grass is found in the valleys. Do you believe that? What dark valley are you traveling through just now?

Not long ago my husband went away on business for five weeks. All the children are grown now, so I was alone. This time, because the dog had died a few years earlier, there was not another living, breathing soul in the house with me! I am not usually nervous, but I found myself wondering why I had never before noticed the veritable symphony of creaks and groans in the timbers of the house! It may seem a small valley to you, but it became a very big one for me.

I began to devise ways of staying out as late as I could after work, rather than coming home to face that empty house. One day when I had had enough of my churning stomach, I simply put my hand in my Shepherd's and said, "Help me walk through this valley with you."

"Stop running," he replied. "You have been sprinting along, intent on getting out of this situation as quickly as you can! Walk slowly and take a long look around. See, here is some green, green grass."

Verse after verse of Scripture flooded my mind, bringing peace and calm and a sensible acceptance of the situation. I ate my fill and was satisfied. Yes, the greenest grass is *always* found in the valleys.

PICNICS

You prepare a feast for me in the presence of my enemies. You welcome me as a guest, anointing my head with oil.

PSALM 23:5

The great Shepherd not only satisfies and sanctifies his flock, supporting them in their valleys of fear; he supplies them with picnics along the way! He gives us time for enjoyment of others, for release from the strain of circumstance, for fun!

There is nothing that calms an English lady more than putting the kettle on. I believe every crisis needs a pot of tea—a time to sit and regroup; a kind friend to share the pause, to reach across the table of trouble, take our hand and say, "Eat a little something. You'll feel better." When fears fight us, trying to put us to flight, Jesus puts the kettle on!

Our great Shepherd lays a table for us in the very presence of our enemies. I have a picture of his covering a table in the dark valley with a white cloth, finding a leaf for a plate, and picking some lovely green blades of grass for his jumpy lamb! By the time the lamb has eaten his fill, he will have had his head anointed with the oil of gladness, and his cup of joy will overflow. He will be up and away to gambol about the valley, sure his Shepherd is big enough to keep the lions and bears away from him.

Do you need a picnic right now? Jesus is waiting for you to say yes.

What More Could a Loved Lamb Need?

Surely your goodness and unfailing love will pursue me all the days of my life, and I will live in the house of the Lord forever.

PSALM 23:6

"These days, houses aren't built to last forever," complained a homeowner friend as he looked at some poor workmanship.

"I know of one that is," I ventured timidly.

"Really? Who is the builder?" my neighbor replied, looking interested.

"God," I whispered.

"Who?" he asked, shooting me the strangest of looks.

I was able to share, somewhat clumsily I'm afraid, that those who follow the Shepherd have been promised a dwelling in heaven, "a home in heaven . . . made for us by God himself and not by human hands" (2 Corinthians 5:1). What's more, the Shepherd has told us it is to be a forever fold, having a firm foundation whose Builder and Maker is God!

By this time my friend had forgotten his repair job, obviously thinking it was I who was falling apart! I grinned at him and changed the subject. Much later I heard his wife had died. I knew she followed the Shepherd, and I was glad her husband asked Stuart to do the funeral.

Can you imagine my joy when the soloist chose to sing Psalm 23? Psalm 23 is used so often to bring comfort to the bereaved, people forget that it is a psalm primarily for the living! It speaks of a relationship with the great Shepherd.

When the time comes to follow him into the heavenly fold, the journey will be made that much easier for those who are used to following him. We know if the Shepherd has cared for us down here, he will surely care for us up there. What more could a loved lamb need?

THE SHEPHERD'S CROWN

Open up, ancient gates! Open up, ancient doors, and let the King of glory enter.

PSALM 24:7

Psalm 24 speaks of the King of Glory, our heavenly Shepherd, entering heaven in triumph. He shall come to judge the living and the dead (see 2 Timothy 4:1). When he does appear, he will have crowns of glory in his hand for the shepherds of his flock (see 1 Peter 5:4). Hebrews tells us:

> And now, may the God of peace, who brought again from the dead our Lord Jesus, equip you with all you need for doing his will. May he produce in you, through the power of Jesus Christ, all that is pleasing to him. Jesus is the great Shepherd of the sheep by an everlasting covenant, signed with his blood. To him be glory forever and ever. Amen. (Hebrews 13:20-21)

Those of us who have the priceless privilege of caring for the flock can know he will help us to do that. He is the great Shepherd who has equipped us with great gifts. He does not ask us to chase after wayward sheep without a rod and a staff. He shows us how to prod people's consciences and rescue them from the folly of their own bad choices. Not only is he my model, he is my might. What greater joy than to have the crown of well doing placed upon my head and see his smile?

I never thought of myself as a leader. It was only as I followed that I led. Unless we learn to follow, we shall never learn to lead. As I began to take opportunities and responsibilities in my church, I found myself with a flock that needed care. The sobering fact is I must answer for that privilege to God, who is determined to hold me to account!

Delightful Desires

> **But they delight in doing everything the Lord wants; day and night they think about his law.**
>
> PSALM 1:2

Some people believe you are at the mercy of your feelings. I don't believe that! I believe you are at the mercy of the Lord, and when you know that, he will give you the very feelings of your heart.

Are you looking for happiness? The man or woman who looks for delight in all the wrong places needs to be told where true happiness lies. According to Psalm 1, the truly happy person delights to think about or meditate on the truth of God.

Delighting in his Word brings a deeper delight, a delight in the Lord himself. The Word, after all, speaks of him. How can you ever get to know God apart from his self-revelation? For many, reading the Bible is a drudgery—a drag. But when you are weary of the words of cynical people, try delighting in his words and see the difference it will make in your life.

Psalm 37:4 tells us: "Take delight in the Lord, and he will give you your heart's desires." When our delight is in the Word of the Lord and in the Lord of the Word, it follows quite naturally we will delight to do his will. Speaking prophetically of Jesus, the psalmist wrote, "I take joy in doing your will, my God, for your law is written on my heart" (Psalm 40:8). Jesus would have us say the same.

The Nowhere Woman

But this is not true of the wicked. They are like worthless chaff, scattered by the wind.

PSALM 1:4

Do you get your advice from people who don't care about God? Do you listen to the opinion makers of the day—film stars, models, important women in top jobs, glossy-magazine editors? Do you do things you'd rather not do, go places you'd rather not go, and say things you'd rather not say to be accepted among your nowhere friends? Do you stay silent when your peers make a mockery of everything sacred?

Do you feel you are a nowhere man or a nowhere woman? Do you know you are going nowhere in life and, in death, somewhere that's like nowhere forever?

Nowhere men and women follow the advice of the wicked, stand around with sinners, and join in with scoffers (see Psalm 1:1). The psalm tells us nowhere people are "worthless chaff"—used throughout Scripture as a symbol of the weak and worthless. In the Middle East, grain is thrown up in the air in an open space to allow the wind to winnow out the residue. But when the fan or shovel of God's power throws nowhere people up to the wind of his judgment, they will not be found again. The moment a nowhere person decides to go somewhere with God, she will be taken by the hand and led home!

I'm getting nowhere, Lord
—that's bad.
Help me see
You died for me,
to take me somewhere, Lord.
—that's good.
Jesus, take me home!

The Somewhere Woman

Oh, the joys of those who do not follow the advice of the wicked, or stand around with sinners, or join in with scoffers. But they delight in doing everything the LORD wants; day and night they think about his law.

PSALM 1:1-2

The somewhere woman is a happy woman! She knows exactly where she's going and how she's going to get there.

She has been given a map—the law of the Lord, the Bible. She thinks about and studies and meditates on this map until she is thoroughly familiar with the road she is to take. The words *think about* mean to mull over until you have absorbed the meaning.

I get a picture of an intent traveler, poring over a map, trying to choose the best road, seeking to avoid needless hazards, carefully calculating the time of departure and arrival so she will be going at exactly the right speed! She will be able to see the hazards, the rest areas, and the bad corners. She will have instructions about her speed and behavior as she drives her car along. Only a stupid person would go on a long journey, through unfamiliar territory, without a map.

Yet many Christian people travel the roads of life, depending on some sixth sense, on trial and error, to get them to their destination. It is as silly for a Christian to set out upon the journey of life without the Bible to guide them as it is for a traveler to set off without a map.

Sometimes you'll need to read your map at night. After all, we drive in the dark as well as the sunlight.

The somewhere woman always takes her map along—just in case she finds herself getting nowhere!

Even at Midnight

Your decrees please me; they give me wise advice.

PSALM 119:24

"I don't have anyone to talk to," complained a middle-aged woman. "My husband watches football all the time, and my daughter has a pair of these newfangled earphones so she can listen to her music without disturbing us all the time. I have many problems. I need to talk to somebody. That's why I came to you."

I asked her if she had ever turned to the Bible and let it be her counselor.

"Oh, I'm not good at understanding the Bible," she said. "I tried reading it once, but I didn't like it, so I gave up."

Opening the Word of God, I began to show her verses that matched her need. I turned to Psalm 119:103 and showed her the words: "How sweet are your words to my taste; they are sweeter than honey."

"That was a sweet time," she said after an hour's "discovery" session. She smiled and left with a small pamphlet to help her get started reading her Bible for herself.

After she had left, I found myself reflecting on all the times his Word has been my counselor and friend. Reading through Psalm 119 again, I borrowed the words and rejoiced: "I will quietly keep my mind on your decrees" (119:95); "Your decrees are my treasure; they are truly my heart's delight" (119:111); "I am overwhelmed continually with a desire for your laws" (119:20); "At midnight I rise to thank you for your just laws" (119:62).

The Ring of Truth

I know, O Lord, that your decisions are fair.

PSALM 119:75

Our Bible is unique. It claims to be inspired by God (see 2 Timothy 3:16). Jesus endorsed it, saying, "People need more than bread for their life; they must feed on every word of God" (Matthew 4:4).

Its writers wrote history before the events they wrote about had ever happened. We call that prophecy.

Its stories ring true. They tell us about real people who struggled as we struggle and hurt as we hurt. It introduces us to people who lived and died, had children or couldn't, doubted God or displayed great faith in him.

But the Bible not only declares the events in God's plan for time and rings true, it also works in our life when we put its wise advice into action, claim its promises, or heed its warnings.

For eighteen years my life was a bed of roses. Then I felt the thorns. I landed in a hospital where a fellow patient caused me to come face-to-face with the Christian gospel. I came to faith in Christ and knew the trust of the psalmist's words in 119:67, "I used to wander off until you disciplined me; but now I closely follow your word," and in 119:75, "you disciplined me because I needed it." I would say *Amen* to that.

Since that day I have seen other affliction, and I now fully understand that sentiment of 119:92, "If your law hadn't sustained me with joy, I would have died in my misery." My sheer delight in his law in those times of affliction has sustained me.

A Lamp and a Light

Your word is a lamp for my feet and a light for my path.

PSALM 119:105

The Bible describes itself in many ways. It uses familiar objects to clarify its meaning. The Bible is a lamp to our feet and a light to our way. "As your words are taught, they give light; even the simple can understand them" (Psalm 119:130).

Sometimes we need to have some clarification from heaven about a future course of action. I was wondering if I should put time aside many months ahead and take a theological course in a study center. It would mean dropping out of many responsibilities and refusing ministry opportunities. Over and over again, God confirmed that I should take that course. The final confirmation came when I specifically asked God for guidance, and that very day read 2 Timothy 2:15: "Work hard so God can approve you. Be a good worker, one who does not need to be ashamed and who correctly explains the word of truth"!

Before my father died, he made it known that he wished to be cremated. A relative was most concerned. "What will happen if he doesn't have a body to be resurrected?" she wanted to know. The family looked to me for an answer. I needed immediate biblical insight and found it in 2 Corinthians 5:1: "For we know that when this earthly tent we live in is taken down [King James Version says "dissolved"] . . . we will have a home in heaven, an eternal body made for us by God himself and not by human hands."

Living Letters

But the only letter of recommendation we need is you yourselves! Your lives are a letter written in our hearts, and everyone can read it and recognize our good work among you.

2 CORINTHIANS 3:2

God reveals himself in many ways—not least, through people. Paul reminded the Corinthian believers that their lives were like open letters. We are the only Bible many people read! What a challenge!

I remember a young German student giving his testimony in front of a crowd of friends at a youth meeting. He stood there shyly. He was extremely tall, and his legs seemed especially long in his short *lederhosen*—the leather trousers typical of his country. "I want to be zee Bible—on two legs," he began haltingly! It was very impressive!

You and I are the Bible on two legs, whether we want to be or not. We are living letters, known and read by all people. This, of course, gives us a great opportunity.

A young husband was trying to adjust to his wife's newfound faith in Christ. Seeing her reading her Bible, as she did every night before she came to bed, he said, "You'll never get me into the Bible." She nodded. She knew that he was angry and confused. *O God, if he won't read the Bible, let him read me,* she prayed silently. A few days later she came across 2 Corinthians 3:2 and was encouraged. Months later, liking what he had read, despite himself, the young husband committed his life to Christ.

What did your husband read this morning before he went to work? A happy psalm or a chapter of Lamentations?

Taking God at His Word

And this is what God has testified: He has given us eternal life, and this life is in his Son. So whoever has God's Son has life; whoever does not have his Son does not have life.

1 JOHN 5:11-12

If eternal life is the life of the Eternal One, it follows that we have eternal life now if we have him. Have you asked Christ into your heart?

First John 5:13 says, "I write this to you who believe in the Son of God, so that you may know you have eternal life." We can *know that we have,* not *hope that we may receive.* Lots of people think they have to wait till they get to heaven to see if they can stay there. But you can know that you have eternal life now! Thank him for that.

Our daughter used to ask Christ into her life every single night as she said her prayers. In vain, I tried to tell her she didn't need to go on asking. He had promised to come in the first time, and she could trust him to do what he said. One day I sent her to answer the doorbell. It was her friend. "Ask her in, Judy," I said, and she did. Ten minutes later I asked my daughter, "Why don't you ask your friend in to play with you?"

"She's in already, silly," replied my little girl! I reminded her that Jesus was the same. She got the point.

"If you . . . open the door, I will come in," Jesus said in Revelation 3:20. What is more, Christ has told us that he comes in to stay. He shuts the door behind him, and no one can open it. Jesus Christ does not change his mind about eternal things.

SAYING SORRY

"No," Peter protested, "you will never wash my feet!"

JOHN 13:8

When I first came to America, I was invited to a "shower." The only shower I was familiar with was the one sticking out of the wall in the bathroom. As I hesitated, struggling with comprehension, the lady who had invited me said, "Don't be shy. Do come; there will be about eleven of us there!" I'd heard about these way-out Americans! But when I learned the nature of the event, I breathed freely again!

In Jesus' day, people didn't have showers, but they did have the Oriental bath, communal affairs where people could wash themselves from head to toe. After their ablutions, however, they dirtied their sandaled feet getting home through the dust and dirt of the city streets.

When Jesus took a towel and washed his disciples' feet, Peter objected. Jesus objected to his objections! "But if I don't wash you, you won't belong to me," he told him (in the rest of John 13:8).

Peter replied, "Then wash my hands and head as well, Lord, not just my feet!" (John 13:9).

Jesus answered him, "A person who has bathed all over does not need to wash, except for the feet, to be entirely clean" (John 13:10). When we come to Christ, he forgives us and cleanses us from all our sin. But our feet tread the paths of our world. They get contaminated as we walk in ways that displease him, and we need to be cleansed. He kneels before us when we should kneel before him! He knows we have walked in dusty places. When we let him wash our feet, we are saying we are sorry.

Grace Never Throws Stones

All right, stone her. But let those who have never sinned throw the first stones!

JOHN 8:7

The Pharisees who brought the woman caught in adultery didn't care about her. They were simply using her for their own ends—mainly to trap Jesus into trouble. Their law said adulterers should be stoned to death, and the woman was undoubtedly guilty. They knew that Jesus was familiar with that law, and they hoped he would pass judgment and get himself in trouble with the authorities.

After a quiet moment, Jesus looked at the Pharisees and said, "Those who have never sinned throw the first stones." At this, Jesus' enemies were shamed; truth always gives error a red face. The oldest men, who possessed perhaps the tenderest consciences, left first, leaving the youngest and fieriest men behind. But in the end, all of them filed out. They knew very well that they too were guilty of some sin—perhaps not adultery, but certainly some part of the law.

It's easy to throw stones, isn't it? We would never commit adultery, we say proudly, forgetting that the pride with which we speak is a sin that God abhors! The more mature we become in Christ, the fewer stones we should cast. Anyway, casting stones is a risky business. Someone may pick one up and throw it back! Have you ever criticized someone to his face, only to have him point out some blind spot in your own life?

Instead, we, who deserve to be stoned by God for our sin, know we can escape such fair judgment because of his grace. Grace never throws stones.

The Unforgivable Sin?

Didn't even one of them condemn you? . . . Neither do I. Go and sin no more.

JOHN 8:10-11

Is the sin of adultery unforgivable? No. Face-to-face with God in Jesus Christ, the woman who had been discovered "in the very act" (John 8:4) heard herself forgiven. If the sin is forgiven by God, I must learn to forgive it, too. We are too swift with our stones. Mercy and grace take them from our hands and lay them down where they belong, at Jesus' feet.

I caught her in the act!
She lied to me.
I rushed her to my friends. They shouted, "Guilty!"
I stooped down to the ground to pick up stones
of condemnation.
Then saw the writing in the dust—my Saviour's
proclamation:
Without sin? Throw!
Without sin? Go!
Before I cast My stones at thee
I've caught you in that act—
You've lied to Me!
And in the courts of heaven they shouted, "Guilty!"

He caught me in the act of all that's sinful
And ushered me up to the spires of heaven.
The angels stooped to pick up stones of righteous
indignation.
Then saw the blood drops in the dust that spelled
justification:
"Go—sin no more.
These stones you store
Within your heart, leave here with Me.
Judge not, lest ye be judged!"
And in the courts of heaven they shouted, "Glory!"

Trusting God

I trust in God, so why should I be afraid?

PSALM 56:11

Are you good at taking risks? Are you frightened to trust God in case you are let down?

An evangelist decided to use a very dramatic method to teach his audience about faith. He wanted to show them that it is absolutely safe to depend only on God. He cleverly cut a hanging rope to within two or three strands, believing it would break as soon as he put his full weight on it. This would prove temporal objects shouldn't be trusted.

When the time came, the evangelist took a running leap across the platform, caught the end of the rope, and swung out over the people. Amazingly, the strands held, and his momentum carried him over everyone's head and through a glass window at the back of the church, depositing him in the narthex! Shocked and bruised, but retaining his creative ability, he picked himself up, returned to the amazed congregation, and used the illustration in a much more powerful way than he had first intended. Mopping the blood from his brow, he explained. "When we trust ourselves to God, expecting the rope to break, we are thoroughly shocked to find ourselves carried, in spite of our lack of faith, to worlds unknown!" Are you expecting the rope to break?

Graveclothes

Then Jesus shouted, "Lazarus, come out!" And Lazarus came out, bound in graveclothes, his face wrapped in a headcloth. Jesus told them, "Unwrap him and let him go!"

JOHN 11:43-44

Lazarus found himself unable to see or to move hand or foot. Straining to hear sounds he couldn't fathom, he realized the incredible fact of his resurrection. He was back on earth, imprisoned in his graveclothes, after having been a free spirit in heaven's land.

Jesus, looking on him and loving him, loosed him. Eager hands unwrapped the stifling cloth from his face, his body, his arms, his legs. Lazarus walked home, and God was glorified. Poor Lazarus—healed to die a second time!

The graveclothes lay in a heap in the street, an incredulous crowd fingering them, gawking at the mute evidence of the might of God. "Only God can raise the dead," whispered someone. God, meanwhile, had walked away, probably to Mary and Martha's home, perhaps to talk with Lazarus of loved ones that Lazarus had seen a while ago.

When Jesus rose again, he left his graveclothes behind, too. Graveclothes have no business on the living. Graveclothes belong to the grave.

What are your graveclothes? What did you bring into your Christian life that should have been left behind? What binds your mouth, your hands, your feet? Listen to Life himself. He is saying to friends, family, and disciples, "Unwrap him and let him go!" Why do you keep your graveclothes? They are poor dress for a living person!

Know Power

> **You know these things—now do them! That is the path of blessing.**
>
> JOHN 13:17

People who leave their graveclothes behind them act, speak, and walk quite differently.

A young teacher accepted Christ. Dead to God, he was called by Christ out of the tomb of his troubles and loosed from his graveclothes. "Whenever teachers are on playground duty in my school," he told me, "the rest of us rip them to shreds behind their backs. Since I've found Jesus Christ, I can't find it in my heart to do that anymore!"

Another woman, who worked in a factory, held her own with the coarsest of men, her language turning the air around her a royal blue. The day after she walked forward at a Billy Graham crusade, a man sidled up and made a snide remark. She stood there, listening in silence. "What's up with you?" the man asked in amazement. "Last night I lost half my vocabulary," she said simply. Her graveclothes lay at the foot of the cross, where they belonged.

But how do you find the power to live without the old, familiar graveclothes that have been so much a part of your old life? Sometimes, as in Lazarus's case, you need a helping hand. At other times God frees your hands to remove them yourself. He tells you to put off the rags of the old life. We are to remove lying, stealing, laziness, bad language, bitterness, and clamor (see Ephesians 4:26-31).

"Know power" works. "You know these things—now do them!" said Jesus.

THE STORM

Though the rain comes in torrents and the flood-waters rise and the winds beat against that house, it won't collapse, because it is built on rock.

MATTHEW 7:25

We live in a society where the concept of Christian marriage—of marriage itself—is under incredible attack. The problem could well be described as a rising flood of divorce statistics. You feel that you are indeed going against the stream of general opinion if you hold to a marriage ethic as taught in the Scriptures.

Some friends of mine were introduced at a neighborhood party as the only couple in the room still on their first marriage. "How cute," commented one of their new friends! It's now "cute" to be married more than five years!

Hundreds of people busily construct their homes on the sand of secularism and allow themselves and their marriages to be engulfed in the mainstream of public opinion. When their tottering house collapses around their ears, they make little effort to save it. The Bible says that fools build their houses on the sand.

The world may consider it wise to opt out of a marriage at the slightest hint of a storm, but that is being worldly wise. When we build our individual lives and our marriages upon the rock, they will not be shaken by the floods of opposition. God's wisdom teaches us that there is another way. Notice the text says the floods came and the winds blew; it doesn't say *if*.

The Way to Kill a Snake

From now on, you and the woman will be enemies, and your offspring and her offspring will be enemies. He will crush your head, and you will strike his heel.

GENESIS 3:15

I was sitting at the airport, people watching. *Where are all the people going?* I wondered. Were some perhaps hurrying home to disappointment? Had others expended huge effort in the life of a child with no appropriate return? Had some been rejected, abandoned, discarded?

The sad faces of many reminded me of bruised reeds. Some of these "reeds" were undoubtedly bruised by sickness or by emotional batterings that had left their whole personality red, raw, and inflamed. Among this thronging crowd, there would be the important people—the ones who had made the headlines. *What must it be like to be the parents of a murderer?* I mused. *Or what about the familiar athlete too old to run anymore, or the model past her best?*

I wanted to stand on my chair and tell them about Jesus. Because he had been bruised, he understood pain; but greater still, his Father had promised that bruised reeds would never be broken. As a Christian, I had the answer for one crushed by the sense of her own inadequacy, or even literally battered by a drunk partner. "Jesus can take the pain out of the pounding you've taken," I explained to a fellow traveler a little later as we boarded the plane to our destination.

Satan would like to destroy us all, but he is the only one who is bruised beyond repair. The Bible says he struck Christ's heel on the cross, but Christ crushed his head—that's the way you kill a snake!

Nature

God has revealed himself in many ways. For example, he has shown himself to us in nature. For "from the time the world was created, people have seen the earth and sky and all that God made. They can clearly see his invisible qualities—his eternal power and divine nature. So they have no excuse whatsoever for not knowing God" (Romans 1:20). Paul says that as this natural revelation of God's eternal power and Godhead is so obvious, people have "no excuse" if they refuse to come to know him.

Your faithfulness extends to every generation, as enduring as the earth you created. Your laws remain true today, for everything serves your plans.

PSALM 119:90-91

As we were talking to some teenagers on the city streets, one said, "Just show me God and I'll believe." The city lay at the gateway to the beautiful English lake district, and I inquired if he ever took a country walk and appreciated the fabulous scenery.

"I know what you're going to say," he said. "You're gong to tell me God made all of that! Well, I don't believe in God! I believe it all just happened!"

Taking my watch off my wrist, I opened the back of it and showed the kids the intricate workings. They were duly impressed. "It just happened," I said casually. "One day all the little pieces appeared from nowhere and fell into place inside this little gold case. Then it began to move at just the right pace and told the right time!"

"Do you think we're stupid?" exclaimed one of the boys. "That watch had to have had a maker."

"Right," I answered him. "And so did flowers and trees; and so did you and so did I." He got the point. God's attributes are displayed in his world. Nature is the servant that shows us the Master!

Conscience

> **Your commandments give me understanding; no wonder I hate every false way of life. Your word is a lamp for my feet and a light for my path.**
>
> PSALM 119:104-105

A "conscience" is a built-in early warning system, a hidden moral knowledge. A "precept" is our moral obligation as enjoined by God. As we read God's written Word regularly and hide his Word in our heart so we might not sin against him (Psalm 119:11), these precepts will give our conscience support. The understanding we gain from his precepts makes us hate every wrong path. A healthy conscience will not allow us to walk comfortably down a wrong path.

When I was a freshman in college, I received a dubious invitation to a party. The way it was worded left me no doubt about the type of fun that was being planned. All my friends were going to be there, and I didn't want to be left out. Though I was not a Christian, I knew inside the things that would be happening that night were wrong. My built-in early warning system was telling me not to go along, even though it had no precepts to appeal to; and even though I tried to chloroform my conscience, I somehow couldn't rationalize sin by calling it growing up. I declined the invitation. Someone must have been praying!

The writer to the Hebrews spoke of God, who said, "I will put my laws in their hearts . . . and I will write them on their minds" (Hebrews 10:16). God has written a message that is impossible to erase from our heart. We know what is right, and we know what is wrong. We may not want to know it, but we do anyhow.

Tablets of Stone

Come up to me on the mountain. Stay there while I give you the tablets of stone that I have inscribed with my instructions and commands.

Exodus 24:12

God gave Moses a pretty substantial message for us. On tablets of stone were written ten things he wanted us to know so we could set about doing them. These laws were given to the Jewish people to give to the world. They are the foundation of our society, the bedrock of our system of law and order.

They are expanded and explained in the ordinances and judgments—the legal pronouncements and rules of divine administration found in the books of Moses, the Pentateuch. The statutes that Psalm 119 extols are the civil and religious applications of the Mosaic law.

The Bible is a whole book. The Old Testament was the preparation for the Gospels, which contained the manifestation of the living Word of God; the Acts of the Apostles, the propagation of his message; the Epistles, the explanation; and the Revelation, the consummation of all things. The Bible is God's library, yet some don't even bother to join! God in Christ intervened in human history. The Old Testament set the stage for it, and the New Testament described it as it happened.

The Ten Commandments are not ten suggestions; they are the foundation of all the laws of life. They have to do with our relationship to God, to other people, and even to ourselves. Psalm 119 tells us his laws are good (119:68), fair (119:137), and true (119:151). Jesus said, "Heaven and earth will disappear, but my words will remain forever" (Matthew 24:35).

Total Information News

And this is the way to have eternal life—to know you, the only true God, and Jesus Christ, the one you sent to earth.

JOHN 17:3

The knowledge of God is imperative for salvation. You can't go to heaven unless you know God; and the Bible says that God can be known. Obviously, an exhaustive knowledge of God is impossible—that would make us God himself—but we can obtain a knowledge of God totally adequate for our need of eternal salvation.

When we first came to live in the United States, I remember being fascinated by the radio news programs. Switching stations, my attention would be caught by a dramatic announcement: "This is the total information news service," the voice said with great authority! Being starved for news of home, I was excited!

Imagine my disappointment when the total information news broadcast lasted all of three minutes! It was hardly "total," lacking a huge body of newsworthy information and very insular, reporting only news related in some way to America! I learned, subsequently, that this particular news station gave only the headlines hourly and filled in details at regularly scheduled times.

So it is with the good news of salvation. God has given us the headlines—all that we need to know God. Once we grasp that, we can tune in to various "programs" to learn all that we can about the world in which we live, the God who controls it, and the people who inhabit it!

Light Tells Secrets

I am the light of the world.

JOHN 8:12

"Then God said, 'Let there be light,' and there was light" (Genesis 1:3). Light is the color of heaven. Painted in light, heaven's streets reflect the character of God. The radiance of his Presence is lamp and light to his friends in God's living room.

Revelation 22:5 tells us that in heaven there shall be no night. When John looked through the door of heaven, he didn't need to switch the light on to see who was there. He who said, "I am the light," was!

When Saul of Tarsus, "uttering threats" (Acts 9:1), met Jesus, "a brilliant light from heaven suddenly beamed down upon him" (Acts 9:3).

When you deal with heaven, you deal with light. When Jesus Christ said, "I am the light of the world," he was not claiming merely to have received light from the Father, but rather to be the very source of it.

Some people make fun of Christians, asking them if they have "seen the light." A fellow airplane passenger, to whom I had been talking about God, teasingly asked me that question. I replied, "I would rather say I *know* the Light. The Light is a person!"

John 1:9 tells us that Jesus is the "one who is the true light, who gives light to everyone." The Light shines into the darkness of people's comprehension, but, unfortunately, they don't understand it. They don't understand it because they don't want to know; they don't want to know because they love darkness; and they love darkness because they want their actions kept secret! Light reveals secrets. Don't come to him unless you want all your secrets known (see John 3:20).

Lesser Lights

God sent John the Baptist to tell everyone about the light so that everyone might believe because of his testimony.

JOHN 1:6-7

John was a lesser light, sent to draw people's attention to the Light of life, Jesus Christ (see John 1:8). Such a lesser light must not draw attention to itself.

When we go around shining only our own light into people's eyes, we give them a headache and prevent their seeing Jesus! We must not become totally absorbed with our own spiritual shininess! Our job is to do what John did—draw attention to Christ by using our own enlightened personalities and gifts. Having achieved our goal, however, we need to diminish the brightness of our own involvement and let Jesus shine into their lives.

There was a time in my life when I tried to draw attention to myself. I told people (humbly, of course) how God had answered my prayers or how wonderful it was that someone had come to know Christ through my testimony.

Janet was a lesser light, knew it, and never tried to compete. She led me to Jesus because of her bright, clean life. It shone across a hospital ward, waking me out of a dark sleep of selfishness. Once she saw I was alerted and attracted by her brightness, she dimmed her light to allow me to look into Christ's face, causing me to fall in love with him. We must strive to do the same.

No Part Dark

God is light and there is no darkness in him at all.

1 JOHN 1:5

During a storm, a window in a lighthouse on a Scottish peninsula was broken. The lighthouse keeper, being a lazy sort of man, boarded up the hole, determining to fix it the next day. That night, a ship was blown off course and came upon the peninsula from the dark side of the lighthouse. With no light to warn of danger, the ship foundered upon the rocks.

The lighthouse keeper was devastated. He hadn't thought the one dark part mattered. But it always matters! We never know when a ship will come on the blind side and get into trouble.

When I first became a Christian, I had a bad habit of swearing whenever I was frustrated. As I began to grow in the Christian faith, I struggled to clean up my act. I worked hard on other "dark" places in my life, leaving the swearing issue until later. I really didn't think it mattered that much.

After witnessing to a friend, I caught my hand on a nail and swore. The look on her face told me that everything I had been trying to tell her was negated at that point. Praying about it later, I came upon this verse and realized that because he is the Light of the World, I can be his lighthouse. What joy, but what responsibility! My one dark part had caused my friend to founder on the rocks.

The Lampstand of Love

You are the light of the world.

MATTHEW 5:14

When Jesus said, "You are the light of the world," he meant just that. He didn't say, "Would you like to be the light of the world?" or "I would be so pleased if you got around to being the light of the world before you die." He said, "You *are* the light of the world." If Jesus, the Light, lives within, he lives to shine without. He wants us to shine first into the dark world; second, into the lives of other Christians; and third, into our homes.

We must let our light shine into the world. Jesus told us that we are to be as bright as "a city on a mountain, glowing in the night for all to see" (Matthew 5:14). Such a light cannot be hidden, and neither can the light of the world. The surrounding darkness will only enhance its shining.

We must also shine in the church. "But if we are living in the light of God's presence . . . then we have fellowship with each other" (1 John 1:7). As we let the light search our heart and as we obey its revelations, we will keep our relationships light and right.

We must be light in our home. "Don't hide your light under a basket! Instead, put it on a stand and let it shine for all," said Jesus (Matthew 5:15). We shine when we are the best mothers for Jesus we can be. We shine when we say we're sorry. We shine when we are fair and firm with our rules, following through with godly discipline. We shine when we are submissive to our husband and responsive to our parents. We shine most of all when we live our life on the lampstand of love.

How Many Marys?

Gabriel appeared to her and said, "Greetings, favored woman! The Lord is with you!"

LUKE 1:28

"Congratulations, you're a woman," said Gabriel to Mary. Only a woman could bear God's Son.

When some messenger of God asks us for our womanhood, what will we say? Will we rejoice?

How many Marys, Lord, were there?
How many times did You try?
How often did Gabriel venture
Through the myriad stars of the sky?
How many minuscule humans?
How many a devout little maid
Heard Your request for a body
And answered You thus so afraid?
"My love, Lord, You have it. My will, Lord, 'tis Thine.
I, to mighty Jehovah, my worship assign.
But my body, my body, my body,
'tis mine."

How many Marys, Lord, were there,
Till Gabriel found her at prayer?
How many angels in glory,
Were wondrously envious of her?
And how did it feel, Lord, to see her,
And watch at Your feet as she fell?
As she yielded her soul and her spirit
And gave You a body as well?
"My love, Lord, You have it.
My will, Lord, 'tis Thine.
I, to mighty Jehovah, my worship assign.
And my body, my body, my body,
*'tis Thine!"**

*taken from *A Time for Giving,* by Jill Briscoe (Ideals Publishing Co.)

Grave Risks

> **"Greetings, favored woman! The Lord is with you!" . . . "Don't be frightened, Mary," the angel told her, "for God has decided to bless you!"**
>
> LUKE 1:28, 30

Did it ever seem strange to you that Mary was "confused and disturbed" (Luke 1:29) at the angel's words? After all, the great being had been careful to tell her she was "favored" and that the Lord was with her. Surely she should rather have been greatly comforted than disturbed.

The angel had to tell her not to be frightened. He then reiterated that she had found favor with God! Maybe it was this very statement that really worried her. Perhaps she was thinking, *If God favors me, then he might ask me to do something special for him!*

She was right, of course. God does choose favored people to do special things for him! I remember thinking, *If God chooses only his best to suffer for him, I don't know whether I want to be one of his best!* After all, the soldiers who are nearest their commanding officer usually draw fire!

Sometimes the fear of what God may ask of us prevents us from qualifying for service. "If I get too close to God," I reason, "I won't be able to avoid hearing his voice. He might tell me something I don't want to hear!"

Being highly favored carries grave risks. It means God will ask grave things of us, but it also means grave fears will be laid to rest. Great joy will be the end result.

His Favorite Child

Mary was afraid of being God's favored child. I am too. I remember that Jesus was God's favored Son, and I realize the somber privilege of being favored. "This is my beloved Son, and I am fully pleased with him" (Matthew 3:17). "He personally carried away our sins in his own body on the cross" (1 Peter 2:24).

Confused and disturbed, Mary tried to think what the angel could mean.

LUKE 1:29

When I was a little girl, playing team games with my friends, I always wanted to be picked first for the team! I wanted that warm sense of appreciation for my talent and trust in my ability. If I was a favorite player, I thought I had worth! Along with that good feeling, however, went the bangs and bruises. After all, first-picked team members usually get put in the hottest spots! One day I had a talk with the Father about picking me for his team.

"I want to be your favorite child, Father!"

"You do?"

"Yes, I really do; that sounds like fun!"

"My favorite child, like whom?"

"Well, like Jesus."

"Then flatten out your hands upon my cross. Pile foot on foot, that nails may stave them in. Hang high, hang long above the blood-soaked turf, and bear my judgment deep upon your soul for others' sin. Then, go to hell, my child—my favorite child!"

"Oh! That doesn't sound like much fun after all!"

Most of us want privileges without responsibility. Having faith to please God and do his will isn't always fun. But it's the only way to true fulfillment because after the cross, there's the crown!

GRAVE DOUBTS

"You will become pregnant and have a son, and you are to name him Jesus." . . . Mary asked the angel, "But how can I have a baby? I am a virgin."

LUKE 1:31, 34

Mary had grave doubts about the grave risks of being highly favored of God. She must have been tempted to think about other godly men and women who had been specially chosen, too.

There was Daniel, who was described by another great angel as a man "greatly loved" (Daniel 10:11) of his God. Mary remembered that he had ended up in a lions' den!

Then there was David—he had been hounded from pillar to post by the king's army and had lived in the dens of the earth. God seemed to ask such hard things of his favored ones!

How was Mary going to be able to cope with the privilege of it all? She had no problems believing God could do what he had promised he would do. Her fears were rather within herself. Would she be able to do what she had promised? How could she have a baby when she wasn't even married? It seemed impossible—harder than facing Daniel's lions or David's Goliath and Saul's army combined! In other words, Mary had grave doubts concerning her own abilities.

Have you ever doubted your own ability to obey God? Oh, you know what God wants you to do. He has made that abundantly obvious, but just how, you wonder, are you going to accomplish it? God supplies the answer to our grave doubts about the grave risks of obedience. He offers us the promise of his power—the overshadowing of his Holy Spirit.

Obedience Is a Lonely Place

And then the angel left.

LUKE 1:38

Now why ever did he do that? Wouldn't you have thought the angel would have stayed? After telling her what was going to happen to her, the very least he could have done was to stick around and see her through.

Mary must have wondered how she was ever going to manage without him. But the fact of the matter was that the angel departed and left her to face the grave consequences of her submission. Where was the angel when she had to try to explain the situation to Joseph? If only the angel had appeared by her side as she struggled to relate her incredible experience, Joseph might have believed her! She had to explain herself to her parents—and to the strict rulers of the synagogue. Where was the angel then?

Mary discovered that obedience is a lonely place. To say yes to God when an angel is talking to you is one thing, but to go on saying yes when the angel has left is another thing altogether! But God wants to see if we will walk on in the dark. Obedience says, "I'll do it without a flashlight. I'll even do it without an angel. I'll do it for no other reasons than he asked me to do it and I promised I would!"

If we can come to that point, we may have the privilege of having the angel slip back and whisper in our ear, "God has decided to bless you" (Luke 1:30), and that should be enough! What is God asking you to do? Will you do it? More important, will you do it without the angel?

Thank God for Elizabeth

> **Elizabeth gave a glad cry and exclaimed to Mary, "You are blessed by God above all other women, and your child is blessed."**
>
> LUKE 1:42

If obedience is doing without the angel, how am I going to get through? The answer, of course, is faith for the times I don't *feel* like doing the right thing. The first step to faith is saying yes. Mary said yes to the angel. After the angel left her, she followed through. She stuck to her word.

I have noticed that women are quite easily moved to say yes to God at a conference or praise gathering, responding readily and sincerely at such times. But what happens when they walk through their own front doors and are confronted by harassed husbands who've been left to baby-sit lively toddlers while they've been away getting their inspiration? Perhaps they don't understand their wives' delight and dedication.

Mary did a very wise thing. She sought out one person whom she knew would understand and went to her for encouragement and support. Thank God for our Elizabeths—those women who recognize our dilemmas and join us in prayer and praise, who have also known what it means to utter the yes of relinquishment!

When I first became a Christian at the age of eighteen, and my own dear family did not quite understand me, God provided an Elizabeth—a sweet, older lady at my church, who took me under her wing. Remembering her encouragement makes me want to be that sort of help to others.

Pray that God will provide an Elizabeth for you as he did for Mary.

A Question of Divorce

> **As he considered this, he fell asleep, and an angel of the Lord appeared to him in a dream. "Joseph, son of David," the angel said, "do not be afraid to go ahead with your marriage to Mary. For the child within her has been conceived by the Holy Spirit."**
>
> MATTHEW 1:20

The angel had visited Joseph in his sleep and told him not to be afraid to make Mary his wife. But in the cold glare of morning light, Joseph found himself alone. *He* had to do without the angel too!

Saying yes in a dreamlike state is one thing, but saying yes in reality, when your friends are urging another course of action, is another thing.

Joseph was struggling with a marriage problem or, to be more exact, a divorce problem. He had, in the words of Scripture, "decided to break the engagement quietly" (Matthew 1:19). He didn't want to publicly disgrace her, for he was "a just man." He desperately wanted to do the right thing. Many people are caught in such agonizing dilemmas today. "Do I stay in this marriage or not?" they ask. Joseph was asked to commit himself to what appeared to be a "bad marriage."

God asks the same of some of us. He can make bad situations blossom into blessing, as he did for Joseph and Mary. Joseph had to do it without the angel but not without God, and *that's* what made the difference. God is committed to marriage, home, and family, as he demonstrated to us that first Christmas when he sent Jesus to Joseph and Mary at Bethlehem.

Answer Me

In the beginning the Word already existed. He was with God, and he was God. . . . But although the world was made through him, the world didn't recognize him when he came. . . . So the Word became human and lived here on earth among us.

JOHN 1:1, 10, 14

The Word lay in a manger. Just a Word—no long sentence or complicated explanation.

It was pink and warm, with a little puckered mouth that seemed to be smiling at the cows!

A Word, lying in a box of new-mown hay in the shape of a man-child.

"Baby," said the Word. "That's what I am, a baby!"

Then it said,

"Hello, world, it's me, your Creator."

Then it cried—because it was hungry.

The Word played in the streets of Nazareth.

It tumbled down the slopes and romped about the lake. It liked that.

"Boy," it said. "That's what I am—a boy, Jewish, strong, part of a family."

Then the Word grew up and went about doing good.

It said, "Let there be light," and there was!

When it said, "Look at me!"—even blind eyes saw it!

Some followed the Word to quiet places so they could hear what it said.

It said, "I am God's Best Thought, and his Last Word. Listen to me! Answer me!"

The Shepherd's Song

> **The shepherds went back to their fields and flocks, glorifying and praising God for what the angels had told them, and because they had seen the child, just as the angel had said.**
>
> LUKE 2:20

And what of the shepherds? They had a mountaintop experience if ever anyone did. "Suddenly, an angel of the Lord appeared among them, and the radiance of the Lord's glory surrounded them. They were terribly frightened" (Luke 2:9). They were terrified, as Mary and Joseph had been, but were commanded, "Don't be afraid!" (Luke 2:10), because there was some good news to share. The angels told them the Messiah had been born right in their own small city; in fact, within walking distance! Being within walking distance of God requires some action.

It was at this point the angels sang a marvelous hymn of praise and "returned to heaven" (Luke 2:15). The angels left them to decide what they were going to do with the good news they had received. The shepherds talked about it among themselves. They had to decide whether to go and see and whether, having seen for themselves the thing was true, to go and tell (see Luke 2:17). And they had to do it without the angels. They went and then made known to others that Christ the Lord was born.

Will you share the Good News without the angels' help? Do you ever face friends who don't know God? Do you ever long to tell them the Christmas story? Do you stand there praying, "O God, where's the angel?" If only they had seen what you have seen and heard what you have heard. If you tell them anyway, the chances are that those who hear it will be astonished at those things that were told them—even by the shepherds!

Wise Men Still Seek Jesus

The members of the council were amazed when they saw the boldness of Peter and John, for they could see that they were ordinary men who had had no special training. They also recognized them as men who had been with Jesus.

ACTS 4:13

How could these men, who've had no special training, know so much? the members of the council wondered. Here was this rough fisherman, Simon Peter, giving an excellent little sermon to the elders of Israel. He was difficult to discredit because the cripple whom Peter and John had healed was standing right there with them—rather telling evidence to the power of the risen Christ (see Acts 4:14)!

At this point, the Bible tells us, the members of the council "recognized them as men who had been with Jesus"!

Jesus thanked his Father for his little band of "unlearned" disciples: "O Father, Lord of heaven and earth, thank you for hiding the truth from those who think themselves so wise and clever, and for revealing it to the childlike" (Matthew 11:25).

Christ is wisdom, and knowing him makes us wise. Those in this world who think themselves wise are fools in God's sight because they count the knowledge of him irrelevant. It's better to be childlike in your understanding of Christ, than an old person in your mere human knowledge.

When you've been with Jesus for a little while, you begin to discern what is really important. And it's what we learn of him that will make the world marvel. Do you have lots of degrees or a bright mind that you have tuned to the world's pitch? What gifts are these? You may be "forever following new teachings, but . . . never understand the truth" (2 Timothy 3:7), and what a waste of God-given intelligence! Wise people seek Jesus first, then use their gifts to glorify him.

Healing

With healing in his wings.

MALACHI 4:2

The prophet Malachi closes the door of the Old Testament with a stern message concerning the corruption of the priests of Israel, the sins of the people against their families, and their miserliness toward God. He speaks of judgment and retribution upon all the wicked, warning that they will be "burned up . . . consumed like a tree" (Malachi 4:1).

But he opens the door of the New Testament with the promise of a new day that's about to dawn. God promises: "But for you who fear my name, the Sun of Righteousness will rise with healing in his wings" (Malachi 4:2). Wings can speak of God's sure and swift approach, of his shelter and solace, or of healing. The two beautiful metaphors in this text—the sunrise of righteousness and the wings of help and healing—paint the portrait of the mending of people's minds. Bethlehem saw the sunrise at Christmas, when Christ was born to dissipate the darkness of the human soul. Jesus came to save us from corruption, the heartache of divorce, and all manner of miserly ambitions. He came to lift us up on the wings of his healing atonement above all our selfishness.

From Bethlehem flies healing, swiftly down the troubled tunnels of time to those who fear his name. Because of that marvelous sunrise, we need not fear the sunset of our life. The Son of God has risen—with healing in his wings!

The Truth about the Truth

Jesus told him, "I am the way, the truth."
JOHN 14:6

What did Jesus mean when he said that? Did he claim to have a corner on all truth? Was he suggesting that other religions are false?

The Bible tells us that God does not *have* truth, he *is* truth; he is equal to his attributes. This means we can have tremendous assurance that what he has told us stands. "God is not a man, that he should lie" (Numbers 23:19).

Pilate asked Jesus, "What is truth?" (John 18:38). He should have asked, "*Who* is truth?" Then Jesus would have answered, "You are staring him right in the face!" Truth includes the idea of faithfulness. We can depend upon God's being the truth, telling the truth, and explaining the truth to us.

Jesus Christ, God incarnate, is the true Truth about the truth! First of all, he is the Truth about God. "No one has ever seen God. But his only Son, who is himself God, is near to the Father's heart; he has told us about him" (John 1:18). Second, he is the Truth about humanity. He told us that people are basically evil (see Mark 7:21-22) and that we love darkness rather than light (see John 3:19). Third, he is the Truth about salvation. There is a way sinful people can live with a holy God. It's very simple, really. The holy God must forgive their sins.

Since Jesus claimed to be the true and holy God, we can believe him when he tells us that "everyone who believes in him will not perish but have eternal life" (John 3:16). You can't trust the word of many people anymore. But I have news for you—you *can* trust Jesus!

Sitting on the Fence

Agrippa interrupted him. "Do you think you can make me a Christian so quickly?"

ACTS 26:28

It's not enough to be almost persuaded. You can be almost persuaded but lost! You can take your time and sit on the fence—but that will assure you a place with the devil and all his angels!

Sitting on the fence is easy. You can sit on the fence every Sunday at church. Thousands of respectable people do it every week. It's not very comfortable, but it certainly can be done.

Perhaps you don't want to bother God by asking him to pick up his pen and write down your name in his book. Or maybe you want to wait a while and live a little first. "Lord, make me holy—but not just yet," you pray! After all, you've heard that God can be such a spoilsport!

Maybe you are waiting for your best friend to make a decision—you've never been the first to make a move.

If you want to go to hell, simply do nothing. So what do you need to do to make absolutely sure you *don't* go to hell and *do* go to heaven? If you want to get off the fence, then all you have to do is jump. It will be a leap that lands you safely in the arms of Jesus! It will be the best thing you ever did in your whole life.

God Is a Perfect Gentleman

Look! Here I stand at the door and knock.

REVELATION 3:20

"But how do I take a leap of faith into the arms of Jesus?" you ask. "I want to go to heaven; I want to get down off my fence, but I need help. Show me how."

First of all, you have to understand four basic things. The first is the fact of sin. Believing you are a sinner means acknowledging that you are not perfect. Having said yes to that, the second thing you need to do is believe that your sin has separated you from a holy God. The third question is: Do you believe God loves you so much that he sent Jesus to save you from the consequences of your sin? If you can say yes to that question, then the last thing you need is to ask God to forgive your sin, come into your life, and write your name in his book in heaven. If you do not know how to ask him, make this prayer your own. "Dear Jesus, I believe you are a holy God, and I realize I am sinful. Forgive me. I want to go to heaven. Thank you for dying to make that possible. Come into my life, Lord Jesus, by your Holy Spirit."

Did you say it? Did you mean it? Then it is done! You are saved! He said so, and God is a perfect gentleman, so you can trust his word! He said, "If you hear me calling and open the door [of your heart], I will come in, and we will share a meal as friends" (Revelation 3:20). Thank him—right now!

What Next?

How can I know that Christ has come into my life? Will I feel different? Not necessarily. You may in a week, a month, or a year.

After all, if you make a business transaction and someone enters your name in a ledger in some bank a thousand miles away, you may not feel anything about it at all, especially if money transactions are new to you. But as you learn, you begin to get excited about living in the good of your investment. You will discover verses like "those the Father has given me will come to me, and I will never reject them"(John 6:37).

Therefore, go and make disciples of all the nations, baptizing them in the name of the Father and the Son and the Holy Spirit. Teach these new disciples to obey all the commands I have given you. And be sure of this: I am with you always, even to the end of the age.

MATTHEW 28:19-20

You can trust his Word. He has promised to keep you to the end—and beyond. He will help you now, and he will help you then. He will pray for you now, and he will present you before his Father and his angels with exceeding joy. He will introduce you to God in the courts of heaven as one who has trusted him to save you.

Why don't you tell someone what you have done? "For if you confess with your mouth that Jesus is Lord and believe in your heart that God raised him from the dead, you will be saved" (Romans 10:9). Confession is not only good for your soul, it is good for other souls, too! They may hear and believe as you have.

It's a good idea to join a church that teaches the Bible as the inspired Word of God. Get involved. Serve Jesus—then you will really feel at home when you get to heaven!